A Personal Journey

Ancient Buddhism, modern science, and working out how to make the most of life

by

William Woollard

Grosvenor House
Publishing Limited

The right of William Woollard to be identified as the author of this
work has been asserted in accordance with Section 78
of the Copyright, Designs and Patents Act 1988

The book cover picture is copyright to Sarah Lam Photography

This book is published by
Grosvenor House Publishing Ltd
Link House
140 The Broadway, Tolworth, Surrey, KT6 7HT.
www.grosvenorhousepublishing.co.uk

A CIP record for this book
is available from the British Library

ISBN 978-1-78623-097-3

Dedicated to the SGI for its constant
flow of encouragement and support,
year after year, and to my beloved wife Sarah
for being there for me every day.

Acknowledgments

Writing is a very solitary business but inevitably many people have played a part in the writing of this book. Questions and ideas that are thrown up at discussion meetings and seminars plant seeds that later emerge as themes in the writing. So my sincere thanks to all my Buddhist colleagues particularly in West London. I owe a great deal to them. And my sincere gratitude to people from many countries who have found something of value in my previous books and asked me to go on writing.

And I am particularly grateful to Mr Makiguchi, the great visionary who founded the lay Buddhist organisation, the Soka Gakkai, which has played such a major role in the spread of Buddhism to the West, for planting an idea in my head which has been an inspiration ever since, when he wrote,' *I could find no contradiction between science, philosophy, which is the basis of modern society, and the teaching of the Lotus Sutra.* '

A Note on the Author

Producer, director, writer, presenter, creator of several hundred hours of television, William's career has embraced the entire spectrum of programme production. But he has experienced several other careers in an eventful life. Oxford graduate. A fighter pilot with the RAF. A trouble shooter for an oil company in the jungles of Borneo and the deserts of Oman. A social scientist working on corporate social responsibility with major international organisations in Europe and the USA. Finally an award-winning television producer working on documentary programmes for several of the world's foremost networks in Europe and the USA.

Much travelled. Twice married. Four wonderful children. A life-time interest in comparative religion among many other things. He writes;' *I came to Buddhism with the deepest scepticism about its appropriateness or relevance in a modern western environment. I am now wholly convinced of its profound value to any life, anywhere, in any circumstances. I see that initial scepticism as perhaps my primary qualification for* writing *this book.'*

Contents

So what's this book about?

In my experience prefaces don't often get read. People tend to dash pell mell to the first chapter. I certainly do. But for those readers who happen to pause long enough to read this one, as its title suggests, this book is very much a personal project. Essentially it explores this relationship that I find both fascinating, and immensely valuable in terms of how I live my life, between two very different perspectives. One the Buddhist insights about human motivation and behaviour that have come to us from many centuries of meditation and reflection upon the human condition. And two, the wide-ranging new learning in this same area that has become part of our rich modern inheritance from many years of essentially science based observation and exploration.

Thus it's based very much on my own spiritual journey into Buddhism over the past 25 years or so, and my work as a science journalist for a rather longer period than that. From that dual perspective it embraces a range of themes and issues in Buddhist writings of course, but also from sociology and psychology and neuroscience for example that I have been reading about and researching over several years. Issues that are in no way remote or inaccessible, on the contrary they are directly relevant to how we all live our lives every single day, and provide the ways in which we seek to achieve a greater measure of well-being. And I have to say that it's the closeness of the relationship between these two ostensibly quite divergent sources of understanding that never ceases to amaze, and yes...to please me!

If I'm asked the direct question, who do I think might read it, I am sorely tempted to borrow the answer from the American author who said, no doubt somewhat tongue in cheek, that he would like to see his latest book... alongside all those copies of the Gideon Bible in countless hotel bedrooms around the world! Every author's wish indeed. But like him I like to think that there is something in this book that might interest and hopefully please many people. Because ultimately it is about some of the most basic and universal of human wishes, such as the fundamental desire for a stronger and more consistent sense of well-being at the core of our lives. About the crucial importance of a sense of connectedness and of genuine engagement with other people. About the life-transforming power of purpose, and of gratitude. And the intimate relationship between a sense of hope and optimism, and good health. And much more besides.

But Gideon-style distribution apart, within that very broad spectrum I would say that as I was writing the book I had two rather more specific audiences in mind.

One is made up of those people who are already Buddhist practitioners and who might perhaps be helped by this sort of discussion, to see their practice more clearly in a wider and undoubtedly more modern context. To see for example how many fundamental Buddhist perceptions are so closely aligned with the new knowledge and understanding about human behaviour and well-being that are emerging from wholly modern studies. As I discuss at some length as the book goes on, Buddhism clearly has a great deal to offer us in terms of its profound understanding of the roots of human pain and suffering, and how we might set about building more resilient and more fulfilling lives. In coming to terms with those teachings and seeking to grasp their true intent it is I believe, important to remember that we are not being asked to set aside the vast amount of new knowledge and understanding that comes to us today as part of our modern inheritance. Indeed the reverse is true.

Buddhism expressly asks us to examine and question any spiritual teachings we encounter on the basis of our own knowledge of the way the world works. Do they make sense in terms of our common experience, and what we learn from the studies that are taking place around us? We are not asked to accept Buddhist teachings as if they existed in a Buddhist bubble so to speak, set apart from all the knowledge and understanding that is part of this immensely rich modern inheritance; undoubtedly the richest inheritance of any generation the world has ever known. The hugely increased understanding we now have for example about our evolution...everything about us is the product of that complex evolutionary journey we have travelled. And how the human brain functions. And more, vastly more, whole libraries more about human motivation and behaviour, which was of course no part of anyone's understanding when Shakyamuni Buddha walked and taught in Northern India.

So I would argue, those of us who practice today have in a sense, an additional and considerable responsibility, in seeking to understand and explain to those around us the continued relevance and application of Shakyamuni's teachings, in this *modern context* that we all inhabit. That is to say, expressly in the light of our new understandings.

That thought leads on directly to the second audience I have in mind which is somewhat more diffuse. It encompasses those who might know something about Buddhism, might indeed know someone who practices regularly, but who find it difficult perhaps to move closer because they see it as a remote, abstract, inaccessible, and possibly a wholly impractical philosophy in today's hard-bitten, hard-driving, highly competitive culture. The plain fact is that for most of us in the West, when we hear the word Buddhism we don't have any familiar markers to hang onto. With Christianity, even for complete non-Christians, there are plenty. Whereas the mention of Buddhism summons up not much more than a series of National Geographic-type images, ornate temples in South East Asia, filled with immense god-like statues of the Buddha, prayer wheels in mountain-top monasteries, throngs of saffron-robed priests dodging the traffic in downtown Bangkok. Above all perhaps the stereotype of a vast nebulous, mystical philosophy with no clear boundaries.

What this book seeks to do among other things is to examine several of those stereotypes. But above all it is a purely personal attempt to set Buddhist teachings in a modern context, and to demonstrate not only their continuing relevance for anyone seeking a strong and value-creating spiritual dimension in their lives, but how closely those teachings are aligned with the findings from modern sociological studies. In this way, hopefully, it might attract readers who have a latent curiosity, but who might never otherwise pick up a book about Buddhism.

Put simply, this personal journey is about well-being in this life. About learning in a wholly practical way, how to build that resilient sense of well-being for oneself and others, no matter what the circumstances you might find yourself in. You certainly don't have to be especially knowledgeable or dedicated or indeed religious, in any way.

Buddhism teaches the extraordinary truth that well-being is not a matter of chance or accident, but essentially a matter of *choice*, and that we can all learn how to make that choice.

CHAPTER ONE

A Personal Journey

His name was Mr. Harris. It seems extraordinary to me as I sit down to write this book which is essentially about self-realisation, about making the very most of our lives, that for me the trail should start so far back in my experience. Evidence perhaps of the essential wisdom locked up in the old adage, the son is father to the man! Who was he? He was the senior science master at my grammar school in North London. He was a scientist and a humanist, but above all he was a genuinely inspirational teacher about life. When you first met him you might wonder why all your fellow students sang his praises and always wanted to be in his classes. He was a slight unassuming figure, mid 40's, with lightly greying hair, very undemonstrative but always with a ready smile for everyone. Invariably dressed in a battered brownish suit, or an equally battered brown tweed jacket, under his old and very faded academic gown. The original black cloth was so worn that it took on a greenish tinge as the sunlight shone through it when it flared out behind him as he strode down the corridor.

But as soon as he began to talk about this or that theory, or take you through the steps of an experiment on the bench, then it was as if he had suddenly entered his natural environment. It wasn't just that he knew what he was talking about, so that he automatically had the authority that a good teacher needs, but he clearly had a deeply innate enthusiasm for the very process of teaching, of drawing people in, of taking them on a journey. It just flowed out of him, so that you were drawn to engage with him and what he was talking about. Science lessons were always double periods, and yet the bell always came too soon.

And when it came, that bell, I still have this clear image of him looking up over his glasses, almost as if he had been in a different place in his head, and saying, *'Oh is that the bell? Oh well. Off you go then. See you on Thursday.'*

Why have thoughts of Mr. Harris come into my head after all this time? Well, if I think about the roots of this book, they do in some way seem to go all the way back to the time when this very ordinary but undoubtedly very gifted man, over the five or six years I was in contact with him, managed to plant in my head this enduring interest in digging deeper, in trying, even when it's a real struggle, to go on exploring until you understand the underlying basis of much of the stuff we encounter in daily life. His primary thesis was that it isn't so much the knowledge you acquire that is important, as the way in which you train your brain so to speak, the process of thinking your way towards that knowledge, the personal journey of exploration and examination that you take.

And that is perhaps the key life-lesson that came out of that five years of association. It wasn't so much the specific subject matter, although I thought it was pretty interesting stuff, it was that he taught us how to think and how to build an argument. *'Don't just give me the answer,'* he used to say, fixing the hapless student with his gaze, *'take me through how you got there'*

2

Take me through how you got there. That in many ways is the journey I take in this book.

My argument basically is that there is a huge amount of new knowledge and new understanding coming out of modern studies about how we function as human beings, and it opens up for us all sorts of interesting, new, and I firmly believe, really valuable perspectives on how we live and handle our lives. And so much of it simply doesn't get into the public domain. It's not grabby headline stuff so it doesn't make the newspapers. But it is I argue, the sort of stuff that most of us would dearly love to know about, and I'm not talking about anything particularly esoteric or inaccessible to the average reader once it's put in front of them. Just good, hard, _evidence-based_ information about so many aspects of our daily life.

And when I look back, there's no doubt that Mr Harris's direct, utterly down-to-earth approach to learning has turned out to be well…not just useful but absolutely invaluable… in every endeavour I have taken up. Including, strange as that may seem, embracing Buddhism as a guiding philosophy of my life.

And although when I eventually left school and went up to Oxford it wasn't to study anything to do with his subjects, with science that is, the approach to the _way_ we examine knowledge, and the _way_ we reach a deeper understanding of an issue, any issue in any field, never went away. And there's absolutely no doubt that it has been and still is an immensely enriching and rewarding strand in my life. In fact I think I could go the whole hog and say that it has profoundly changed the course of my life. My life would have been very different without that early and immensely beneficial influence.

Getting to grips with the world

So when I went in to the RAF for example and started my training as a fighter pilot, I found somewhat to my surprise, that I wasn't just completely at home diving into the details of the technical and the aeronautical programmes that were an essential element of the training. The method worked. Indeed to my complete surprise I flew away so to speak with the honours (I'm sure I've still got the honours scrolls in the back of a cupboard somewhere!) And when, several years later, I was invited to join the BBC's Science Department as a producer and presenter, it was in many ways like a coming home. Not being trained academically as a scientist was, I found not a handicap at all, in fact it was a great asset because once again it threw me back into that basic 'Harris' approach; it's not just the answer you want but the route to that answer, so that you get to understand the very bones of the issue. It meant that I posed questions and broke down the more esoteric technical stuff into explanations and images that made them far more accessible to a lay audience, like myself in fact.

In fact perhaps it's worth expanding very briefly on what I still look back on as one of the most creative and undoubtedly most satisfying and enjoyable periods of my life, not simply to reminisce about how immensely stimulating and yes, exciting it was, to be writing and producing television programmes every week of the year…I'm not a great believer in looking back…but because it does still play a significant role in how I write and what I write about.

So, very briefly, there were two flagship BBC science programmes at the time. One was the full-length, hour-long documentary known as *Horizon* which had a global reputation for what might be called the academic rigour of its programmes. It was said that it was the closest the BBC came to having its own science research department. It explored all the leading scientific issues of the time in some depth.

Then there was the weekly science magazine programme known enthusiastically as *Tomorrow's World*, and I use the word enthusiastically there deliberately, because that was undoubtedly one of its key characteristics; enthusiasm buoyed the programme up and flowed out of it in all directions. It was aimed at an altogether broader, more general, non-academically inclined audience. So with TW as we called it, the overriding demand was to take these often very complex and somewhat intractable scientific and technological issues, from all the fields of science, from particle physics to bridge building and everything in between, and make them entertaining and wholly accessible for this wider general audience. It was a great training period in good, down-to-earth communication. Hours were spent, often burning the midnight oil, to get this intractable science into an attractive and accessible story. I'm not sure I could have done that so successfully, if I hadn't served that apprenticeship with Mr Harris.

It was part of the genius of the BBC to house the production teams for both programmes on the same floor of the same building, to stimulate the generation of imaginative production ideas. And it was simply a great place to be, a genuine powerhouse of inquiry and debate and discussion.

So it wasn't just a very productive and very stimulating environment to work in, it was I believe a truly mind-shaping experience spread over 15 years or so. And the methods and disciplines that were laid down then, of digging deeper into the research material, and turning it over to examine the many sides of any argument, and above all, constantly striving…not so much to simplify…but to *clarify* the expression of difficult and complex ideas, have stayed with me through many more years of fascinating science journalism.

So here I am, sitting at my desk many years later, and yet I have no doubt that elements of those tough disciplines have shaped both the approach to the research and the way I write. And I'm pleased about that. I want it very much to be both a kind of exploration and a genuine conversation with the reader.

Getting more out of life

So what's this book really about? Well the basic thesis I set out to explore is I believe quite straightforward; it is that the more we know and understand about how we function, both as individuals and as social animals, then the better job we can make of living our lives. We may never actually put that thought into words, or even express it to ourselves in any explicit way, but I'm a fully paid up optimist, and I believe strongly that making the very most of our lives is *the* primary motivator. And the central argument of this book is that we can move a long way towards that objective, simply by *becoming aware* of the extraordinary flood of new understanding that has come out of recent research studies. This is not in any way daunting or inaccessible academic stuff. Not at all. When you get close to it is absolutely about the down-to-earth daily-ness of your life and mine.

So I see this book as a series of conversations, essays if you like, on subjects that I've long been interested in, and which I have spent some time researching, all of which seem to me to have a strong connection with this overarching theme of achieving greater resilience and optimism and well-being in our lives. I have no doubt that there isn't any single, dominant route to achieving that. But I do believe we all seek it in our various ways, and above all else, that greater *awareness* is the key to unlocking some of those ways.

And in fact we turn out to be in very good company. The resoundingly positive psychologist Professor Martin Seligman from Pennsylvania State University is one among many sociologists who have expressed a similar view;

> '...*we can now teach the skills of well-being...*' he writes, '*of how to have more positive emotion, more meaning, better relationships, and more positive accomplishments. Schools at every level should teach these skills...*'[1]

That's a hugely positive declaration isn't it? We can learn how to be more positive. And there's this from another prominent researcher working in the same field, arguing that when we are *actively seeking*, that is to say, putting genuine effort into making the most of our capabilities, that effort brings with it a whole slew of desirable benefits, increasing, as she puts it...

> '... *our energy levels, our immune system, our engagement with work and with other people, and our physical and mental health. In becoming happier we also bolster our feelings of self-confidence and self-esteem, ...A final and perhaps least appreciated plus, is that if we become happier, we benefit not only ourselves, but also our partners, families, communities, and even society at large.*'[2]

Would we not all want to build those effects into our lives, if only we knew where to look and how to go about getting hold of them?

A quiet revolution

We live in privileged times I suggest, in that we have been travelling through a kind of revolution over the past twenty years or so. A quiet revolution many would say because the kinds of studies into the basic stuff of human life that I've been talking about, may take some time to yield up their findings, and they're rarely if ever the stuff of headlines. But over this incredibly short period of time, there has been an unprecedented leap forward in our understanding of human motivation and behaviour, and the way we function as thinking, feeling human beings. And that word 'feeling' has a surprisingly important role to play. Although we all like to think of ourselves as largely rational and logical beings rather than emotional ones…in fact whole economic models are constructed around this idea of the strictly *rational* human decision maker…contrary to the popular wisdom it is only now being realised just how crucial a role our emotional faculties play in all our decision making.[3]

But to pursue the main thread of this argument, social scientists and economists and psychologists and neuroscientists, from their very different perspectives, are well into the process of assembling this multi-layered, multi-faceted picture of…well…of who we really are. Because that in effect is what it is; the motivations and compulsions and the underlying physiological systems that drive modern human behaviour, and more importantly for our argument, their effects on our sense of self, and how we feel about our lives, both good and bad.

And this is truly universal stuff. As philosopher and neuroscientist Sam Harris points out in his book *The Moral Landscape*,

> '...the neurophysiology of happiness and suffering...
> are bound to transcend culture, just as facts about
> physical and mental health do. Cancer in the highlands
> of New Guinea is still cancer; cholera is still cholera;...
> and so too I will argue, compassion is still compassion
> and well-being is still well-being.'[4]

With immense patience and care, sometimes with research projects that as we will see, have continued to track the lives of groups of people over many years, from their childhood often until they are well into their adult careers and married lives, these scientists have begun to put together an understanding of human life and motivation, and the effects of behaviour, that go way beyond anything we might have envisaged just a decade or so ago. And the key point is, that *new* knowledge and that *new* understanding are available to us, to know about and to use in the struggle that all of us, without exception, are engaged in, of trying to make the most of our lives.

And where in all this lies the spiritual dimension in our lives?

It's a key question isn't it?

What about the spiritual dimension?

That word spirituality is not one that has an easy passage in today's profoundly technological and extravagantly materialistic society, and most of us might struggle for a ready definition. I am using it here very much in the spirit of the definition, or the definitions indeed, because there are several, attempted by a modern American philosopher I greatly admire, Robert Solomon in his book *Spirituality for the Skeptic*, where he talks of the spiritual dimension in our

The spiritual dimension :

lives as...' ...*the tremendous effort to discover or realise our better selves.*'[5] That phrase 'tremendous effort' rings so true with me. No real understanding of our spirituality without real effort. It doesn't come easily.

He describes the personal journey he himself travelled, from a position of the most profound scepticism and rejection, to a deep understanding of the powerful role an active spiritual dimension plays in human life. He writes with complete frankness at the outset for example,

> '... *let me begin with a confession of sorts. I have never understood spirituality. Or rather, I have never paid much attention to it. When the subject was introduced I made a convenient excuse to leave, perhaps expressing myself inwardly with a muted groan...*'[6]

I have no doubt that many people might respond in a similar way when the word comes up, because in a way it has the power, doesn't it, to shine a spotlight into the very heart of our lives? What sort of people are we, deep down? But scepticism is of course a great asker of searching questions, and Solomon asks many on his journey to a deeper understanding.

> '*How can we both respect ourselves and adopt a kind of humility that puts us in our proper place in the world? How can we learn to think of ourselves in terms of our relations with other people, in terms of compassion and shared spirit as opposed to our acquisitive individualism?....Those seem to me to be the questions that lead us to spirituality, and this seems to be the perennial task and responsibility of all of us.*'[7]

An absolutely fundamental phrase there that lies at the very heart of any quest for a more meaningful spiritual life… thinking of ourselves in terms of our relations with other people. Having the courage to take up that task and set out on that journey can, he argues, fundamentally transform who we are. Thus he writes;

> '*Spirituality is ultimately social and global, a sense of ourselves identified with others and the world. But ultimately spirituality must also be understood in terms of transformation of the self. It's not just a conclusion or a vision, or a philosophy that one can try on like a new pair of pants. How we think and how we feel about ourselves has an impact on who we actually are… They change us. Make us different kinds of people, different kinds of beings.*' [8]

It has an impact on who we actually are. That's a huge and potentially life-changing thought isn't it, that expending the energy and the time to nurture an active spiritual dimension in our lives has the power to *transform?* That's the word he deliberately chooses to use, transform who we are, how we think and feel and above all therefore, how we act in our relationships with others and with the world about us. Elsewhere in the book he adds several key insights. Let me restrict myself to just two which help us considerably I think in getting much closer to a word that in many ways we shy away from in everyday conversation. So he argues strongly,

> '*Spirituality is not just organised religion, nor is it anti-science…or supernatural.*[9]

Those are both crucial understandings. Spirituality is not necessarily about religion. Nor is it in conflict with science as is so often argued. And finally, in a passage which could well have been written I suggest, by a Buddhist mentor,

> '...*Spirituality is adopting a framework or a positive attitude in which all sorts of possibilities open up that may not have been evident before... The facts of the world remain pretty much as they were before. Nevertheless everything changes. The world is born anew.*'[10]

That is I suggest a remarkable perception, that the recognition of the power of the spiritual dimension in our lives can change absolutely everything. Our world can be born anew, he says, without exaggeration. But that small constellation of definitions gives some idea of just how difficult it is to pin down the range of meanings and implications parcelled up in this important word, and equally, just how valuable it is to try to tease them out. But let me recount very briefly a recent public example that captures I suggest, the very essence of what I believe Robert Solomon is talking about.

It involves a young man called Peter Kassig, just 26 years of age, a former US Army Ranger. When he had moved away from military service, he chose to dedicate his life to helping others in distress. And he chose to do that by travelling to Syria and helping families struggling in the terrible life-destroying cauldron of the brutal civil war going on there.

He was taken prisoner by ISIS in October 2013. And he was violently executed by them in November 2014.

He was obviously a hugely courageous young man, and a deeply spiritual one, and although he must have feared death as we all do, in the weeks running up to his terrible and brutal public execution he was clearly thinking not about himself and the terrifying pain he was about to face but about his parents and the equally terrible ordeal they were about to go through. As a result he was able to smuggle out a note to his parents, in an effort to use *his spirituality* directly, to protect them, to carry them through that ordeal.

The immensely beautiful and simple words he wrote don't come from any scientific knowledge we might have about ourselves, they come from the very depths of his human spirituality. He wrote,

> '*Just know I am with you.*
>
> *Every stream, every lake, every field and river. In the woods and in the hills, in all the places you showed me. I love you.*'[11]

Utterly simple words yet expressive of the very depths of this young man's being. I suggest that it is impossible to read them without having an immediate and instinctive sense of what this word spirituality really means, and how profoundly important a dimension it is to all of us, if we are to live our lives and realise our humanity to the fullest.

The Buddhist dimension

But going back to Robert Solomon, his words resonate strongly with me, mainly because over the past 25 years or so I have made a very similar journey, although in my case it has occurred through my taking up a Buddhist practice. I have no doubt that as soon as I mention that word Buddhism it is likely to trigger a whole range of stereotypes in most western minds, and many questions of course. I am acutely aware of this in meeting people. Whenever we get to talking casually about Buddhism, there is very often a spark of interest. People want to know more than can be conveyed in a brief conversation. And yet at the same time there is often a reluctance to get involved in something as seemingly alien and other-worldly as Buddhism. I can wholly empathise with that view. As I've written elsewhere, no one wants to seem weird to his friends. I didn't!

So let me spend just a few minutes in the next chapter, to peel away that alien and other-worldly perception, and let in a bit of light.

CHAPTER TWO

A brief excursion into Buddhist humanism

Buddhism seeks to explain the reality of daily life. It doesn't present in any way a sort of utopian ideal, or an abstract or mystical vision of what life might be. It is a rich and detailed analysis of the dynamics of human life, that has been built up on the basis of the observations and the perceptions, as well as the inspiration, of some quite exceptionally gifted and enlightened people, whom we happen to call Buddhas. It is obviously not scientific in the sense of the strict modern scientific method of hypotheses and experimentation, but there are many comparisons and relationships to be found with modern scientific observations. It is no accident for example that many modern psychologists are deeply interested in Buddhist views about the essential nature of human motivation and behaviour, and many have actually incorporated long-established Buddhist practices into their therapies.[1] As the late philosopher and historian Arnold Toynbee has written,

> 'The Buddhist analysis of the dynamics of life is more detailed and subtle than any modern Western analysis I know of.'[2]

It comes as a something of a surprise to many people to learn that Buddhism is essentially atheistic or humanistic. That is to say it doesn't have at its heart the all-seeing, all-powerful creator-god figure that is central to most of the world's major religions, particularly those with which we are most familiar in western societies, Christianity, Islam, Judaism and Hinduism. That is very easy to say, and very easy to comprehend as an intellectual concept, but rather more difficult to grasp I suggest, on a daily, practical, down-to-earth level because the implications are so profound. Thus there is no divine hierarchy in Buddhism, and it is this factor above all that gives Buddhism its wholly distinctive character. Instead of there being a set of beliefs or dogma, accepted as having been *handed down* to mankind in various ways by a divine hierarchy, Buddhism is rooted from first to last in the lives of ordinary human beings. One major impli-cation is that since it is not attached to any definition of divinity, it doesn't have the exclusive religious *boundaries* that have been the source of so much conflict down the ages, and that still powerfully threaten the stability of the 21st Century world. I'm talking about the boundaries that divide the Islamic definition of divinity for example, from the Judaic, or the Judaic from the Christian, or indeed the Christian from the Hindu. Buddhism is wholly inclusive. No one or indeed no thing is excluded.

Thus it is a colossal humanist vision that reaches out to embrace man's relationship with himself, man's relation-ship with his fellow human beings, and man with his universal environment. Buddhism in effect draws three concentric circles round our lives. Ourselves at the centre. Then other people or society as a whole, a truly global society. Then the outer ring of the universal environment. So Buddhism is immensely forward looking, immensely modern you might say, in that it has always argued that all three are intimately interconnected in every way, and for us to live a truly full and fulfilling life it argues, we need to learn how to be creatively connected to all three. That is to say, we have to know how to fully respect our *own* life, with all its qualities and all its imperfections…understanding and embracing our faults and imperfections as well as our qualities is crucial to our sense of well being. We need to respect and support the lives of *others* in every way that we can conceive. And we need to play a constructive part in protecting and preserving the natural environment that sustains us all.

A man made religion

There are few clearer ways of expressing this vision I feel than to say that Buddhism is, in every way, a man-made rather than a god-made religion, although I must say at once that you won't of course find that idea expressed *in that way*, in any Buddhist text. But the vast body of Buddhist teachings essentially represent the wisdom and the insights, initially of one man, Shakyamuni Buddha, who lived in Northern India around 500 BCE, immensely extended and developed down the succeeding centuries by some of the finest minds in human history. But all of them supremely and utterly human. That is the essential starting point. None of them claimed any sort of divinity or divine connection, which clearly distinguishes them from historic figures such as Jesus and Mohammed, who constantly declared that they were the primary channel dedicated to bringing God's wisdom and God's wishes down to mankind. Shakyamuni by contrast, constantly makes clear in his manifold teachings his ordinary humanity. There are many references that we might use to reinforce this point. One for example comes from one of the greatest modern authorities on Buddhism, Daisaku Ikeda. In his compelling account of Shakyamuni's life he writes;

> *'...he was a man who in almost astonishingly plain and unaffected language, employing anecdotes and analogies that could be comprehended by anyone, sought to awaken in each individual the spirit that dwells in the inner being of all people.*[3]

Or this from no less an authority than the Dalai Lama himself;

> *'In fact the Buddha himself, in a famous statement ... exhorts his followers not to accept the validity of his teachings simply on the basis of reverence for him... the Buddha advises that people should test the truth of what he said through reasoned examination and personal experiment.'*[4]

So clearly nothing resembling an expression of divine authority. The eminent Buddhist historian from Cambrdge, Edward Conze, makes a very similar point when he writes,

> *'The Buddha (Shakyamuni) always stressed that he was a guide, not an authority, and that all religious propositions must be tested, including his own.'*[5]

And finally, a very definitive statement of Shakyamuni's ordinary humanity from a renowned modern Buddhist teacher, Thich Nhat Hahn, who writes,

> *'Buddha was not a God. He was a human being like you and me, and he suffered just as we do.'*[6]

Thus if we strip away all the legends and the mythologies that have inevitably accumulated around so big a life lived so long ago, Shakyamuni, the first historically recorded Buddha, and indeed all historical Buddhas down the years, have been ordinary human beings. They were undoubtedly *extraordinary* in terms of their wisdom, and the clarity of their vision, and their profound grasp of the realities of human life. And no doubt extraordinary too in terms of their personal charisma, and their ability to convey their understanding to others. But apart from that they don't claim to have what might be called a hot line to God. Indeed they constantly stress their ordinary humanity.

The central message
And perhaps the central message we should take from this is that the fundamental quality at the centre of their lives, which happens to be described as their *Buddha Nature* was also an inherent part of their ordinary humanity. It was not a thing apart. And that simple message is the very basis of all Buddhist teachings.

Put simply this Buddha Nature is often described as a deep-seated courage and resilience to overcome challenges, a profound compassion for the lives and values of other people, and a thoughtfulness or a wisdom to enable us to seek to create value out of all the situations we encounter, however difficult or challenging they might be. All very human-scale qualities.

So from this perspective, Buddhism is essentially about *empowering* people. Enabling us to make use of *all* the resources we have, spiritual as well as intellectual, to build strong and meaningful lives for ourselves…and for others… since our lives are so strongly interlinked with all those around us. Those who are near, and equally those who are far off. It argues essentially that we all have within us the *potential* to achieve that same life-shaping inner strength and resilience and hope and optimism.

It is not about a particularly *religious* dimension in our lives, that is perhaps the biggest misconception. It is simply a *human* quality, an inner spiritual resource that, Buddhism teaches, we can all learn how to harness and make use of in dealing with the stuff of our ordinary everyday lives.

Dynamic humanism

You will sometimes hear a Buddhist practice described as *dynamic humanism,* because its primary purpose is to do with *change,* with moving people's whole lives towards the positive end of the spectrum. As we all know only too well, few things are more difficult to change than deeply ingrained patterns of thought and behaviour. It has taken a lifetime to learn them and groove them into our lives. You could say they represent nothing less than who we are. So clearly it takes real energy and determination to set out to change them. We need the self-honesty to recognise that we want to change. We need the courage to put the change in motion. Above all perhaps we need the *conviction* that we have the potential to achieve the change, that we *can* genuinely move our lives forward in this way.

And even then, for most of us anyway, we can't do it without help. Without some sort of discipline or structure around which we can reinforce the determination, when it slips away, as it is bound to do. A structure really helps us to persevere with the effort to change our lives. That in essence, is what a Buddhist practice offers us. It offers us a structure, an immensely *practical method*, that enables us to take hold of our lives in a rational and measured way, and move them in the direction we wish to travel.

Buddhism is daily life

Thus despite the many stereotypes that prevail in the West, a Buddhist practice is not in any way esoteric or other-worldly. It is immensely practical and down-to-earth. It is wholly about creating a greater sense of well-being amidst the often harsh realities of this life. If you strip it down to its barest essentials, you might view it as a sort of personal, daily, life-time training programme, aimed at shifting our whole lives towards that positive end of the spectrum. Towards value creation. Not all that different in a sense, from a personal, daily, life-time training programme at the gym, aimed at achieving a higher level of physical fitness. Only with the Buddhist practice we are course talking about *spiritual* muscle, and about developing a *mental* toughness and resilience, to enable us to stand up to life's challenges.

We all recognise only too frequently that we live in an immensely demanding and challenging world, a world in which a mental toughness and resilience, allied of course to empathy and compassion, are undoubtedly great assets in our efforts to build a sustainable sense of well-being. Buddhism was actually created out of the perception that life is indeed tough, and that how we choose to *respond* to that toughness, determines absolutely the nature of our life. It argues that although we cannot of course change the inherently challenging nature of human life, it is possible to change fundamentally our *attitude* or our response to those challenges. That might seem on the face of it to be a pretty obvious statement. Is that all you might ask? But the difference in attitude Buddhism argues is crucial to achieving a difference in *outcome*.

Put simply, right at the heart of Buddhism lies this extraordinary paradox, that suffering is inevitable in any human life, but at the same time it is the *essential platform* we need to build the strength and the resilience to experience happiness. When we are weak our problems seem huge and tower over us. When we are strong those same problems appear to shrink in size and become resolvable. The essential issue therefore is not how to eliminate problems from our life, which is a manifest delusion, but how to grow a stronger spirit. And there is really only one way to achieve that...by overcoming problems. There is no other way!

What does that mean in terms of the ups and downs of daily life? Basically it means that instead of finding ourselves responding negatively or positively, to good or bad situations as they arise in our life, now up now down, depending essentially on the nature of the circumstances we encounter, we seek to build *an inner core* of optimism and resilience and confidence, so that we can more often respond positively, *no matter what* circumstances we encounter.

The vision

Does that mean we banish anxiety from our lives? Of course not. We're only human. Doubts, anxieties, concerns, frustrations, all remain part of the daily mix, since they are all part of our essential humanity. But they don't take over, or not so often. They don't drive us towards panic. Instead we steadily strengthen that inner core of optimism and resilience. And strengthen also the ability to hang onto the *vision*, the goal that we are seeking to achieve.

We are trying to strengthen in our lives the ability to see all things, that's right, *all things*, from a positive constructive point of view. However grey or uninspiring or even despairing they might seem initially, we want to learn how to turn them round and create value out of them. Needless to say that's tough. In no way can it be a one-step operation, any more than we would expect a fitness programme to involve one visit to the gym! If we really seek greater fitness, we all know that it involves a genuine commitment to a sustained programme. In a similar way, if we really seek this durable optimism, it clearly involves commitment to the process of nurturing it. We summon up from within the determination to set out on this path of change, and the daily practice helps us to sustain it in our daily lives. And when we fail as we are bound to do, the practice provides the structure and the discipline that enables us to pick ourselves up and get on with it again. And again. And again.

And as we get on with it, Buddhism argues, it has very much the same effect as tossing a rock into a pond. As we change, and set about living our lives on the basis of a different set of principles, so the ripples of that change spread out in ever widening circles.

We create our own environment

A basic Buddhist argument is that as we change, so we are steadily, imperceptibly perhaps, changing the *environment* we inhabit. As we change, as we move away from persistent cynicism perhaps, or anger, or negativity, or a powerfully self-focused, self-centred approach to life, with its concentration on our own ego, towards a more compassionate and more responsive approach to others, we find those same qualities reflected back at us from our environment. And that's not in any way just wishful thinking. If we give it a moment's thought, we can accept the basic idea quite readily I think. We all know that there is a constant interplay between ourselves and the society or the environment immediately around us. If we cast around in our memories we can all recall some direct experience of that. We know for example that a profoundly negative or pessimistic view of life, even from just one individual, can drag down the spirit of an entire group. And if that person happens to be in a leadership role, it can have a powerful effect on the spirit of an entire organisation. Conversely, a determinedly positive and optimistic approach to life can be immensely influential and infectious to a whole team, even in the most challenging circumstances.

Some of the recent research of the sociologist Nicholas Christakis, professor of Medical Sociology at Harvard, [7] continues to reveal just how far that influence can spread. His work over the past few years has revealed the truly remarkable extent to which our general mindset of optimism or pessimism for example, and our core life values, *do* indeed spread and ripple out into the society around us. And surprisingly perhaps, not simply throughout our *own* network of friends and acquaintances, but as Christakis has revealed, out through our *friends' networks* as well, whether or not we personally have any *awareness* or understanding of that process going on. It is, as he describes it, a constant process of interaction with our extended social environment, far wider than we might ourselves perceive it to be.

Essentially Buddhism teaches no more, or indeed no less than that. What it adds so valuably for us, is the *method*, through which we can set out on the road to achieving that consistent sense of optimism in our daily lives, and the positive influence on our environment.

Wider social impact

So Buddhism argues, when we set out on what we tend to think of as this purely *personal journey* towards greater optimism and resilience, we are likely to be focused very much on our own concerns. And why not indeed? We rarely if ever have the ability to live our lives at the level of grand strategy. Rather we live in the fine detail of moment to moment; in the moment of this happiness or of that anxiety. But imperceptibly, with the compassionate discipline of the daily practice, it becomes a wider social impulse. It is you might say that stone that we mentioned earlier, that we personally are dropping into the global pool. And every stone, however small, however personal and seemingly insignificant it might be, creates ripples, and ripples create *change.* Our personal change may initially have an effect only upon a relatively close-knit group of family and friends and colleagues at work perhaps. But the effect is real, and as we carry on, as we sustain this movement towards a more positive, more resilient, more compassionate approach to all the circumstances we encounter, so, Buddhism suggests, the ripples extend slowly, gradually perhaps, but nevertheless they continue, out into the local society and beyond.

(Changes us, and changes society)

From individual growth comes social growth. Thus Buddhism is fundamentally about social change, about creating a society based essentially on respect for the dignity of all life. As the Buddhist thinker Daisaku Ikeda has expressed it;

> '...there can be no lasting solution to the problems facing society that does not involve our individual state of life. '[8]

Who has responsibility?
The key point I would ask you to hang onto at this stage of the discussion, is that Buddhism in its wisdom, weaves a very practical concern for our general health, and the pursuit

of a long and active life, into all that it has to say about the spiritual aspects of our daily lives. Indeed it argues that just as *we* carry the responsibility for all the causes that we make, so *we* are responsible for doing everything we can to develop our understanding of what is, and what is not, likely to lead to a longer healthier life. At the very core of the Buddhist view of healthy life for example, lies the idea that we don't simply hand over responsibility for our health into the hands of the medical professionals. We *own* our own health it argues, and consequently we need both, the best medical or scientific help we can obtain, but always aided and abetted by our own understanding, and the choices that we make for ourselves, every day of our lives.

Thus, despite the many stereotypes to the contrary, a central argument of this book is that spirituality and science are not fundamentally in conflict; they are rather two *complementary* ways we have available to us, for approaching the circumstances of our lives mentally, in order to cope with them and understand them more fully. I think there is no question but that we need all the help, or you might say all the illumination we can get… from both dimensions… and since it is such an important issue for the way we see our lives, and yet one that is so little discussed, that's where we go next…to dig a little deeper into the implications of what we might call this *dual perspective*.

CHAPTER THREE

So what is the value
of a dual perspective?

Buddhist teachings and science, mainly social science, form the two main themes that run like twin threads throughout this book, and in many ways hold it together and give it it's meaning. I'm seeking to explore the relationship between these two dimensions, and more importantly, the synergy between them. They are of course very different, no one would question that, and they bring very different kinds of value into our lives. But what you might ask is the value inherent in pursuing such an exploration? What's the point?

I think my immediate answer would have to be that whatever field of knowledge or understanding we might be discussing, we simply can't ignore or set aside the fact that we all inhabit a knowledge-based, science-based society these days. Science in its various manifestations absolutely underpins the way we understand our world and our own place in it. But above all it reaches out and affects in varying degrees just about every aspect of our daily reality. And why would that not include this universal quest for greater sense of purpose and fulfilment and happiness in our lives?

Happiness is of course a slippery and elusive sort of subject because it is so subjective, It may also be, I have come to believe, a somewhat lightweight word when it stands alone for the broad range of feelings and emotions it is being called upon to convey, and that we will undoubtedly encounter as we seek to unravel the arguments. But is it now quite as slippery as it once was? That in a sense has become a pivotal question since never before in human history has there been so focused and so prolonged an effort by the sociologists and the psychologists and the neuroscientists to understand and reveal to us much more clearly what kinds of qualities, what kinds of values and behaviours allow a greater sense of happiness and well-being to emerge in our lives.

In many ways it could be argued that we live in very unusual times, in which very considerable and genuinely scientific energy is focused on trying to gain a deeper understanding of the kinds of things people have in their minds when they profess to a sense of completeness or satisfaction with their lives, or having been able to establish a stable and resilient and deep-seated sense of well-being. The kinds of things you might say that are of the greatest value to all of us since they enable us both as individuals and as members of communities and societies to work more creatively and harmoniously.

Some knowledgeable observers even suggest that we might be looking at the beginnings of a whole new science. Possibly. But at the very least we are being offered a whole new series of immensely valuable insights, a whole new way of looking at so many things about our motivation and our behaviour that we have until now taken for granted.

But the key point I want to make is that this is also of course very much the territory on which Buddhism walks. As we've seen Buddhism is often described as *dynamic humanism*. That is to say it is essentially about human relationships at various levels of intimacy. About man and his relationship to himself, man and his relationship to all other human beings, and man and his relationship to the wider universal environment. As it happens that idea conforms directly to one of the several definitions that philosopher Robert Solomon offers to us to help us understand more completely, the complex nature of human spirituality. As he expresses it,

> *'Spirituality is a larger sense of life. It means that we see beyond ourselves, first to other people, and then to nature...'*[1]

A larger sense of *human* life. That is the absolute key. With its essential belief in the power of the human spirit, Buddhism is strongly focused on the attainment of happiness as *the* fundamental objective of human life. That is life in the here and now, rather than some heavenly hereafter, which is of course a key differentiator. In that sense it seeks to harness what is undoubtedly one of the most powerful motivators in human life as an engine of change, to enable us to learn how to live fuller and happier lives in the very midst of life's inevitable problems and challenges. It teaches that achieving happiness for ourselves and others...that is a primary qualification, it cannot be our happiness at the expense or disregard of others...is essentially what life is about. But as you would expect happiness doesn't fall into our laps. Wanting it isn't having it. We have to *learn* how to achieve it, or how to *create* it for ourselves. We have to take that is the lumpy and discordant and intractable material out of which all our daily lives are made, and learn how to *transform* it into the stuff of happiness. And much of this book is about that very learning.

So, to bring those two threads together, the continuing stream of new knowledge and new understanding that science in its various forms makes available to us, represents if you like, our vast and immensely rich modern *inheritance*. Yours and mine. We can't avoid that inheritance and the inevitable questions about ancient teachings that it gives rise to. It is in a very real sense a fundamental part of the context in which we all live out our daily lives. So the key question that arises is, how should we relate the two; what Buddhism, with its centuries of accumulated insight and observation has to tell us about human motivation and behaviour, and that vast modern scientific inheritance that we have all become heirs to?

And it's clear isn't it, that this is not in any way a marginal issue?

There's a great deal at stake here for all of us. If these dual perspectives help clarify for us the kinds of beliefs and behaviours that *do* bring a sense of completeness and confidence and hope and resilience into our lives and, just as important, the things that *do not*, then they clearly have the potential to be truly life changing.

Buddhism embraces our modern inheritance

Buddhism clearly has a great deal to offer us in terms of its profound understanding of the roots of human joy and suffering, and how each of us in our different ways might set about using that understanding to build more resilient and more fulfilling lives, for ourselves and others. That constant embracing of others and the building of relationships lies at the very core of Buddhist teachings. In coming to terms with these teachings, and trying to fold them into our lives it's important to remember I suggest, that we are not being asked to *set aside* the vast amount of new knowledge and understanding that comes to us today as part of that modern inheritance we've just discussed. Indeed the reverse is true. Buddhism *expressly* requires us to examine and to question the spiritual teachings that we encounter, whatever their source, on the basis of our knowledge and understanding of the way the world works. Do they make sense in terms of our common experience? We are not asked to accept them as if they were somehow set apart from all the understanding, the experience, the knowledge that is part of our modern inheritance. As no less an authority than the Dalai Lama makes clear;

> '*Although Buddhism has come to evolve as a religion with a characteristic body of scriptures and rituals, strictly speaking, in Buddhism scriptural authority cannot outweigh an understanding based on reason and experience. In fact the Buddha himself, in a famous statement...exhorts his followers not to accept the validity of his teachings simply on the basis of reverence to him.... the Buddha advises that people should test the truth of what he has said through reasoned examination and personal experience.*'[2]

Moreover, as the research for this book has gone on, and broadened and deepened, I've come across so many ways in which these two widely different perspectives are not only eminently reconcilable, but strange as it might seem, they present views that are remarkably in step, about what kinds of values, above all what kinds of behaviours, enable the human animal to fashion a longer and more active and more meaningful life for itself. The degree of that congruence still surprises me to some extent, but it's nonetheless true.

On the basis of that journey of exploration the key argument I would want to make is that if we wish to live lives that we can truly grasp and inhabit and understand the meaning of, then it would seem clear we benefit beyond measure from the illumination and the increased awareness that we get from *both* these dimensions of human understanding. The *external* illumination if I may put it that way that comes from science, that describes for us as no other sphere of human activity can, the nature of the reality in which we live out our lives. And the *internal* illumination that comes from our spiritual perception that speaks to us as no other sphere of human activity can, of our joys and hopes and fears and griefs. Joys and hopes and fears and griefs are of course as real as rocks. They're just made of different stuff!

Taken together these twin 'illuminations' can help us to make the very most of this increasingly complex and high-pressured life that we are living. The two are far stronger together than apart, and each, I now firmly believe, is very much *less* than both. When I first wrote that sentence I thought it might be seen as somewhat controversial. I now believe that it is a crucial starting point on the journey towards a better understanding of what well-being is all about. It governs so much that is fundamental to how we think about our ordinary everyday lives and how we relate to our society.

It is often said that Buddhism *is* daily life. Well…all I am really seeking to do is to take it out into *today's* immensely enriched and knowledgeable daily life, and reveal just how relevant it remains.

The nature of a dual perspective

Of course it's crucial to bear in mind all the time just how different these two approaches are. In a sense that is an essential part of the *value* that we derive from them, the perspectives they offer are so very different. Buddhism for example isn't in the least scientific in its approach, but then it doesn't need to be. It doesn't seek or need what you might call scientific *validation* for what it has learned over the years about how best we can build for ourselves a full and meaningful and value-creating life. Its insights have been proven over many lifetimes in the toughest laboratory of all, human life itself. And indeed, speaking purely personally, proven yet again in the past two decades or so of my *own* life.

What about Science? While it is true to say that as an institution it basically doesn't do religion, it simply isn't equipped to deal with the specific area of spiritual or religious *belief*, or indeed isn't really concerned to do so. However, that having been said, there is no question that over the past couple of decades or so, the social sciences in particular have been constantly adding to our understanding of what it is that drives human behaviour and helps us to create for ourselves a sense of well-being. So there is now an immensely interesting and illuminating overlap between them, and there is I suggest, a huge amount of value and understanding to be gained from exploring it.

The illuminating overlap

So basically I wander backwards and forwards across the boundaries between Science and Buddhism, in order to achieve what seems to me the greatest value on each issue. At the very least it's an approach that I hope will clear away many of the misleading stereotypes about the nature of Buddhist thought that are still widely held in the West.

At best it establishes the undoubted relevance of many profound Buddhist perceptions to modern life. As you might
expect on some issues the discussion is more scientific, and
less Buddhist philosophy. On others it's the reverse, more
Buddhism and less science. But I don't make any apologies
for that approach. I'm seeking as I've said, above all to create
value, to raise awareness and to clear away misconceptions.

And fortunately for my argument, we don't have to search
very hard in the worlds both of science and philosophy, to
find a strong body of support for that basic approach.

We benefit greatly from both

We can call on Einstein for example, with his famous dictum
uttered at about the same time that he was shaking the
world of science to its foundations with his radical theories
of space-time and gravity;

> 'Science without religion is lame,' he declared, 'Religion
> without science is blind.'[3]

That clear bold statement very neatly embraces the argument. Buddhism is quite widely described as a philosophy
rather than a religion, because as we've seen, it is wholly
atheistic; a system of beliefs created entirely out of the
enlightenment and perceptions of very wise but nonetheless very ordinary human beings, rather than from any form
of divine intervention. But I would argue that the word
'religion' in Einstein's statement is used in a broad enough
sense to include the wider reaches of religious philosophy,
such as we find with Buddhism, rather than just formalised
religion. And of course today there are countless scientists
who walk completely in step with Einstein on this issue.
That is to say they spend their working lives pursuing what
might be described as a strictly scientific understanding of

our reality, as revealed by rigorous analysis and experiment, whilst clearly finding benefit from the very different perspectives offered by various forms of religious belief.

Then there is no less a commentator than the Dalai Lama. As it happened I came upon his fascinating book *The Universe in a Single Atom* late in my research but there I learned to my great pleasure that he has spent much of his life exploring this same complex and fascinating relationship between Buddhist philosophy and modern scientific discovery. Indeed his book carries a sub-title which seems to me to come very close indeed to what I intend by a dual perspective; it reads, *How Science and Spirituality can Serve our World*. He has been instrumental in having the study of modern physics for example, introduced into today's curriculum in Tibetan monastic colleges, to broaden the world view of the students in those institutions beyond the reach of the classical Buddhist texts.[4] And his position is very clear on the immense value of this dual approach, '...*we need both*,' he argues;

> '*There is more to human existence and to reality itself than current science can ever give access to. By the same token, spirituality must be tempered by the insights and discoveries of science. If as spiritual practitioners we ignore the discoveries of science, our practice is also impoverished...This is one of the reasons why I encourage my Buddhist colleagues to undertake the study of science, so that its insights can be integrated into the Buddhist world view.*'[5]

Those are undoubtedly very strong, very encouraging words for this dual approach from a World Buddhist leader, and he adds a crucial footnote,

> '...I believe that spirituality and science are different but complementary investigative approaches with the same greater goal, of seeking the truth.[6]

A thought that is almost precisely echoed by the late great historian and philosopher, Arnold Toynbee,

> 'Science and religion need not and ought not to be in conflict. They are two complementary ways of approaching the universe mentally in order to cope with it.[7]

What is utterly brilliant I think about that statement, is that it introduces the two fundamental ideas that really help us to grasp the best of both worlds. One is this idea of *complementarity*, that science and religious philosophy bring obviously different but *equally valuable* stuff into the context of our daily lives. The second is the idea locked up in that word, *'cope.'* The universe of our lives is tough enough to understand as it is, he is saying, we need all the help we can get in order to grapple with it and cope with it most creatively, and of course we get quite different kinds of help from science and religious philosophy.

And then we have the modern American philosopher Robert Solomon, already mentioned on several occasions, who is overwhelmingly concerned about the fact that in today's world, the important word *spirituality* has basically been hijacked by religion. In his book *Spirituality for The Skeptic* he sets out to redress the widespread misconception that the word refers solely or even mainly to religious belief, as opposed to the entire breadth and depth of human spiritual life. He is very much in the same camp as Einstein and Toynbee. As he expresses the closeness of this dual relationship, first somewhat informally; '...*spirituality is not at odds with, but rather in cahoots with science.*'[8]

And then more formally…

> *'Spirituality is supported and informed by science.'* He writes,*' The more we know about the world, the more we can appreciate it.'*[9]

And just one more notable modern scientist who has made a huge contribution to the long-running debate on this issue. He is Alister McGrath, a professor in a faculty that has a foot very firmly in both camps, the faculty of Science and Religion at Oxford. He was once an admitted atheist. He's now an eminent scientist in biophysics as well as a practising theologian and historian. In his latest book he presents an immensely powerful argument in support of what he calls *mutual enrichment;* which again I would suggest, is very close indeed to what I am seeking to describe as *the dual perspective.* We benefit immensely from both he argues, and science and religion undoubtedly learn from each other.[10]

Just how far they go

It's important to notice just how far these thoughtful and knowledgeable scholars are prepared to go. To a man they are telling us that we not only *benefit* from both these two sources of illumination, that is to say they both bring great value into our lives, but they go much further. They are prepared to argue that we can *only* make the very most of the rich and complex and turbulent and stressful lives that we are living, if we seek understanding from *both*, the spiritual and the scientific. And that rings true doesn't it? It sounds like plain common sense.

May I repeat my underlying thesis, the two are very much stronger together than apart, and each is very much less than both.

And just to bring this passage to a close, there is one final quote, this time from a man called Tsunesaburo Makiguchi, a visionary educational reformer from Japan, who 85 or so years ago founded the lay Buddhist organisation that has since played a major role in the spread of Buddhist values and beliefs into the western world, known today as Soka Gakai International or value creating society.

> 'I could find no contradiction,' he writes,' *between science, philosophy, which is the basis of modern society, and the teachings of the Lotus Sutra.'*[11]

The Lotus Sutra in that passage refers to the fundamental teachings of Buddhism as expressed in one of its greatest sutras or teachings, known universally as the Lotus Sutra. Notice that the essential phrase Makiguchi uses also embraces this fundamental idea of *complementarity*. They may look at the world we inhabit from very different perspectives, but he finds no *'contradiction'* he says, between the prevailing scientific understanding of our reality and what he is able to learn from Buddhist philosophy.

The fact is of course that we live and practice in the *real world*, and that world is changing perhaps most rapidly in this very area, in the knowledge and understanding of human behaviour and motivation, and bodily and mental health, and what contributes to a stable sense of well-being; all the areas that lie so close to the mainstream of Buddhist teachings. Given that viewpoint, it makes sense I suggest, to spend a bit of time at the beginning of the journey to explore the nature of the relationship that might exist between these two dimensions. It remains the same old world, it's just that our perception of it is somewhat different, and the changed perception can change fundamentally the way we behave towards ourselves and towards others.

That sounds fine, but what does it actually mean in practice? Well let's take just one central Buddhist concept, and see if we can find out. And that's where we go next.

CHAPTER FOUR

Oneness of self and environment

One of the most important ideas that Buddhism brings to us, and one of the most difficult perhaps to get the head round, is that we play a major role in *creating* our own environment. As we move from place to place Buddhism argues, we create the environment in which we have to function. Or to put it slightly more formally, it teaches that there is really no distinction between ourselves and the world around us, so that we and our environment don't simply interact in various ways, but that we are deeply and profoundly interconnected, part indeed of the same whole. This perception, which was a fundamental part of Shakyamuni's original enlightenment, is simply described as the oneness of self and environment.

It is unquestionably a huge idea, but one that is quite difficult to get to grips with as a realistic down-to-earth proposition. What real difference, we might ask, does this idea make to the way we actually *see* our daily reality? Is it just an interesting, philosophical, but somewhat esoteric issue that we don't really have to give much attention to? Or is it central?

Well let's begin to peel away some of the layers of meaning and see where it takes us.

So we all accept of course that we have a considerable effect upon our natural environment in ways that can be both constructive and destructive, just by the business of living on the planet. We may create a beautiful garden for example and carefully choose shrubs that butterflies love, and hang various bird feeders in the trees to help them get through a harsh winter. But we also create vast amounts of waste, and atmospheric pollution as we heat our houses and drive a car or fly in an aeroplane. And we are only too well aware that the more of us there are, and the more we do these things, then the bigger is the impact we make on our natural environment. To the point that it is now widely accepted that we will have to radically modify our habits, to reduce the destructive impact of our existence on the environment.

Conversely we are also constantly aware that our environment clearly has an effect upon us, albeit in a somewhat more transient way. We all know that if we get up on a sun-kissed spring morning then we feel considerably lighter and brighter on our walk to the station, than if the rain is belting down under leaden grey skies. We can find it really depressing to walk down a neglected litter-filled city street, with graffiti scrawled across the walls. Just as we can find it uplifting to see a cherry tree in full blossom over a garden wall, or the bright smile on the face of the lollipop lady as she helps the morning school kids across the road. We fully accept don't we, that there is this more or less constant interaction between our environment and our *spirit or our life state*, in this sort of generalised way, all through the day?

The Buddhist principle of oneness of self and environment embraces all that, everything indeed that might be covered by that sort of generalised, somewhat superficial interaction with bits of what goes on around us. But then it goes way beyond that. It declares, as I outlined a moment ago, that although we are unable to perceive it, there is a constant and profound and enduring interconnection between our individual life, and everything but everything around us.

So what real difference does it make?

But what about the implications of this principle? Is it, as I've said, just an interesting philosophical idea, or can it make a real difference in practical, down-to-earth terms, to the way we see and live our lives? Well at one level it certainly can, I suggest, make a very substantial impact on how we go about our daily lives. Why? Because it asks us to *examine* our own behaviour and be *aware*, be conscious of the effect our own life state and our behaviour has on those around us. Put simply Buddhism declares that at any particular time the environment in which we find ourselves is a reflection of our own inner, subjective life state at that time; not the physical environment of course but rather the social relations we are experiencing. It argues that if we are in an angry, belligerent, aggressive frame of mind for example, then that mood and that atmosphere, will be reflected back at us from the reactions of those around us, and from the friction and generally confrontational situations that are likely be generated. If on the other hand our life state is high and our approach is consistently optimistic and value-creating, then it declares, that optimistic life-enhancing energy will flow out into our environment, even in conflict-type situations, and have a profoundly positive influence on everyone we encounter and the way situations around us evolve.

I would argue that that claim, huge as it is, does fit in with most people's experience. We know that when our life state is high so that we are not so wrapped up in our own concerns, we are much more *sensitive* to what's going on around us. We are much more strongly alive to the fact that life states such as anger or generosity, pessimism or optimism are highly infectious; they can have a profound effect on the mood and the behaviour of a social group or a bunch of colleagues in an office. We all do better and feel better when we are surrounded by positive and optimistic people. We all find that our energies are blunted and sapped by being amongst colleagues or companions who are persistently pessimistic.

What is somewhat more difficult to come to terms with undoubtedly is this parallel idea that we and our environment don't simply interact in the ways we have described briefly above, but that we are somehow part of the same whole.

Part of the same whole

If you take it purely at face value it would seem to be a truly astounding idea, since it posits that the strict *dividing line* that we see so clearly between us and the various categories of matter that make up our environment is nothing more than an illusion, arising from our limited and partial vision. How can that be we say, we know we stop at our skin! The reality, Buddhism declares, is that humans, animals, plants, the earth indeed, are part and parcel of the same entity, or the same continuum. Not separate and distinct as we firmly believe, but intimately interconnected. And however strange that idea may seem when we first encounter it, it is an idea that has migrated well beyond Buddhism. Thus we find a modern English philosopher such as Anthony Grayling writing recently that our consciousness for example, perhaps the most *personalised* part of us, is constantly and intimately connected to our environment;

> 'The notion that thought is...essentially connected to the outside world is intended to illustrate the more

general idea that mind is not describable in terms of brain activity alone. Instead it must be understood as a relationship between that activity and the external social and physical environment.'[1]

The central thought there is wrapped up in that key word 'relationship.' He is describing an on-going relationship with the external social and physical environment. And what I find utterly extraordinary is that in reading a simple primer seeking to explain the basic teachings that Shakyamuni set out all those years ago you can encounter almost exactly the same pattern of thought then, as the philosopher and neuroscientist expound today. Don't ask me how that can be, but it is. You get precisely the same conclusion, that our consciousness cannot and does not exist solely *inside our heads* so to speak; its very existence is dependent upon a constant process of interaction and inter-relationship with our environment. Here is Grayling's thought almost precisely echoed in a passage for example from a brilliant book by a modern Buddhist teacher,

'..But how can we see our consciousness in a flower? The flower is our consciousness. It is the object of our perception. It is our perception. To perceive means to perceive something. Perception means the coming into existence of the perceiver and the perceived. The flower that we are looking at is part of our consciousness.'[2]

I'm not suggesting that this is an easy thought to take in over a cup of breakfast coffee! But I don't think we should be overly concerned that we find it a bit elusive. It is, as I've said a huge and unusual concept. The common tendency I suspect is to put it in the box marked 'mystical,' or even 'weird,' reserved for those things that Buddhism offers to us that lie beyond our everyday perception.

But we don't need to. Perhaps the most surprising thing is that if we cross the aisle so to speak to examine the other perspective that I have been attempting to describe, and turn to modern science for a bit of help, we find that it presents us with an explanation of the reality we all inhabit that is extraordinarily *similar* to this central Buddhist concept of the oneness of self and environment.

The fundamental connectivity

In fact just about wherever we turn in science we get a powerful confirmation of the profound *interconnectivity* that underlies everything we encounter. If we start with the biologists for example, they go to great lengths to describe the immense *diversity* of animal and plant and insect life on this planet. A superabundance of vitality. When I write those words I can't help but think of those years I spent travelling in the jungles of Borneo, the sheer overwhelming abundance of the plants and trees, and the diversity of the insects and the birds and the animal life in the canopy was simply astounding. You would expect that in a tropical jungle perhaps, but later on, when my life was spent travelling through the wide wastes of the Omani desert, even there, the ability of acacia trees and shrubs to push through the sand and assert their right to life in that immensely harsh environment was constantly surprising. We would stop and camp for the night behind a towering sand dune, and from nowhere the men would be able to rustle up enough wood for a fire in a few minutes.

But underlying that immense diversity of plant and animal life adapted to survive in such contrasting environments, the biologists point to a truly astounding and utterly fundamental *connectivity*; a singular *uniformity* you might say. As one scientific paper describes it;

> '...all the organisms you can see with the naked eye have
> one fundamental similarity. Like us they are constructed
> from the same kind of cell. Under the microscope the dif-
> ferences between plants, animals and fungi fall away to
> reveal a common internal structure.'[3]

'...one fundamental similarity' is a striking phrase isn't it, when we are talking about universal connectivity? What they are describing here is one of the most extraordinary and still little understood events in the evolution of life on earth, when *the fundamental complex cell* first came into being. It happens to be called a eukaryotic cell, but don't let an awkward sounding name get in the way of the central idea, which is that it was completely different from the sim-plicity of its immediate predecessors. As the paper goes on to describe,

> 'The biosphere would be unimaginably different had this
> 'eukaryotic' cell never evolved, making its origin one of
> the most critical events in the development of life on
> Earth.'[4]

And this complex eukaryotic cell, the cell with the awkward name if you like, became the *common building block* of all that immense superabundant diversity of life that exists around us...including ourselves. That is to say, there is undeniably an intimate and fundamental connectivity underlying all living things there have ever been on earth.

The distinguished American scientist and philosopher Daniel Dennett makes a similar point when he talks about the profound connectivity arising from the evolutionary family tree;

> *'There is,'* he writes, *' just one family tree, on which all
> living things that have ever lived on this planet can be
> found- not just animals but plants and algae and bacte-
> ria as well. You share a common ancestor with every
> chimpanzee, every worm, every blade of grass, every
> redwood tree.'[5]*

All living things that have ever lived on this planet. He
simply couldn't be more all-embracing could he? Thus the
interconnection is very profound indeed, and being aware
of it in this direct, full-frontal way cannot help but affect
how we think and feel about everything around us. As I
have written elsewhere,

> *'… just think of the implications. It means that the bunch
> of roses you give to your beloved partner on your anni-
> versary carries DNA that connects them closely to the
> hand that holds them. The family dog that takes you lov-
> ingly for a walk every morning, as mine does, hangs from
> the same family tree as yourself. There could be no clearer
> confirmation of Shakyamuni's perception all those years
> ago of a universal interconnectedness.'[6]*

And just to round this section off, the latest biological
research over the past ten years or so, into what we might
call perhaps the secret life of plants, would seem to bring
the plant world closer to us than has ever been thought
possible. Biologists and botanists have even begun to talk
about the existence of something that they choose to call
'plant neurobiology.' It is now being suggested that plants
have a much wider range of abilities than we have previously understood; that they can actively explore their
environment for example and are capable of *learning* and
modifying their behaviour to suit their purposes. The idea of

a plant *'learning,'* or having a purpose may sound extraordinary, but it is nonetheless becoming part of our understanding;

> *'In the past decade researchers have been making the case for taking plants more seriously. They are finding that plants have a sophisticated awareness of their environment and of each other and can communicate what they sense. ...Some botanists argue that they are intelligent beings, with a' neurobiology all of their own.'[6]*

So all those horticulturalists...not to mention royal princes... who have long argued that talking to plants makes them grow better may well have been on to something after all!

Made of the same goup

So that's Biology, with a whopping bundle of surprises, and if we turn to Physics, the science of the particles that make up all matter including ourselves, then the surprises are in many ways even greater. It is well proven for example, that however strange it may sound, all the heavier and more complex molecules that make up the various forms of matter on Earth, including our own flesh and blood and muscles and bones, not to mention our brains, the seat of our humanity, could *only* have been forged in one place, in the high temperatures and huge pressures that exist deep within the bodies of stars like our Sun. And then through the millennia, these molecules have been ejected out across the vast spaces of the universe when those stars eventually exploded as supernovae. As one paper describes it,

> *'The calcium in your bones like every other heavy atom in your body was forged in the fiery furnace of enormous*

stars, ten, one hundred, or even one thousand times the mass of the Sun.[8]

Christoff Koch, the brilliant researcher on the evolution of human consciousness, describes the sequence of extraordinary events that had to take place for human life to emerge on earth,

'A pioneering generation of stars had to die in spectacular supernovae to seed space with the heavier elements needed for the rise of self-replicating bags of chemicals, on a rocky planet orbiting a young star at just the right distance.'[9]

That's us, bags of self-replicating chemicals on a rocky planet called Earth! And the late Nobel-prize-winning American physicist Richard Feynman takes up the story, to describe for us the fine detail of the connectivity that links us so closely to our environment. We're made of the same stuff;

'First of all there is matter, and remarkably enough all matter is the same. The matter of which the stars are made is known to be the same as matter on earth...The same kinds of atoms appear to be in living creatures as in non-living creatures; frogs are made of the same 'goup' as rocks, only in different arrangements [10]

It's hard to think of any other scientist who would choose the word 'goup' to explain such a complicated idea, and get away with it. But here he is coolly bridging a gap that is extremely difficult for most of us to get our heads round, that gap that we see between the animate and the inanimate. Here he describes clearly for us the intimate interconnection that exists... at the level of the atom and the molecule... between frogs and dogs and cats and humans... and rocks!

Out of Africa

And one final reference I think just to point out the depth and breadth of the interconnection between all of us as modern human beings, whatever our superficial ethnic and cultural differences. And for that we go to a very distinguished lady from Kenya, the environmentalist and Nobel Peace Laureate, Wangerie Maathai. She reminds us with deep conviction and passion about something that again is well-proven, namely that all human beings who walk the planet are all descended from the same quite small group of people who lived long ago in a few valleys in East Africa;

> 'So far all the information that we have suggests that we come from somewhere within this part of the world, in East Africa, and that of course for many people must be surprising because I think we are used to being divided along ethnic lines, or along racial lines, and so we look all the time for reasons to be different from each other. So it must be surprising for some of us to realise that what differentiates us is usually very superficial, like the colour of our skins, or the colour of our eyes or the texture of our hair. But we are essentially all from the same stem, from the same origin. So I think that as we continue to understand ourselves and appreciate each other, and especially when we get to understand that we all come from the same origin, we will shed a lot of the prejudices that we have harboured in the past.'[11]

To underline just how extraordinary is the story locked up in that simple phrase, '...we all come from the same origin...'

here is philosopher and psychologist Sam Harris describing the same event,

> '...all human beings currently alive appear to have descended from a single population of hunter-gatherers that lived in Africa around 50,000BCE. These were the first members of our species to exhibit the technical and social innovations made possible by language. Genetic evidence indicates that a band of perhaps 150 of these people left Africa and gradually populated the rest of the earth.'[12]

A truly remarkable figure, a tribal band of just 150 or so people who walked out of Africa, and whose direct family descendants, that's us, went on to populate the rest of the Earth..

It is unquestionably difficult to conceive how Shakyamuni as a young man in Northern India all those years ago, and seeking desperately to understand the true nature of the reality in which we live out our lives on this planet, could possibly have perceived in his mind's eye so to speak, the depth and the breadth of the interconnection that binds us to everyone and everything that make up our environment. And how completely modern science bears out his vision, down to the level of the atom and the molecule...the undoubted oneness of self and environment.

The basis of compassion

We asked at the beginning of this chapter what difference does it make to the reality of our everyday lives, this understanding of the truly profound nature of the connection that binds us to all other people, all other living things? Buddhism suggests that perhaps the most overt effect is seen in the expression of compassion, the deep understanding of how we all in some sense share life and its struggles and difficulties. As the Buddhist writer Daisaku Ikeda expresses it so clearly;

'The misfortune of others is our misfortune. Our happiness is the happiness of others. To see ourselves in others and feel an inner oneness and unity with them represents a fundamental revolution in the way we view and live our lives.' [13]

This sense of 'inner oneness and unity' can amount he argues to a powerful revolution in the way we live our daily lives. Thus compassion is not in any way pity for those less fortunate than ourselves. It's much more about profound respect and understanding for ourselves and for everyone with whom we come in contact, so that we live through the ups and downs of each day with a much greater awareness of others people's needs. We all have this powerful instinctive need to place ourselves at the centre of our own universe, and we hear loud and clear the inner voice that shouts out our own needs and wants. We find it immensely difficult to see situations from the other person's point of view. It is compassion that gives us the willingness to understand that other point of view, even when it's opposed to our own, and the ability to embrace the difference.

One could certainly argue I suggest, that in today's truly global society, where nowhere is very far away any more, there has never been a greater need for the understanding and the compassion that binds us all together. I find it immensely illuminating that a modern philosopher such as Robert Solomon, should choose to bind together these two key words 'conjunction' and 'compassion' in echoing so closely Daisaku Ikeda's thought;

> '...*Buddhists identified compassion as the key to the conjunction of the individual self and all of the other selves with which it is conjoined, and for many Buddhists it also signalled the shift to spirituality. Very few Buddhists ever experience the nirvana described by the greatest sages, but every good Buddhist daily experiences the compassion for suffering that ties him or her to the world and to other people .*'[14]

The roots of behaviour

Human behaviour is of course the result of a complex and constantly changing dynamic. On a daily basis we are aware that we are pushed and pulled in so many directions by different forces, biological and cognitive and cultural. But everything about our relation to ourselves and to that environment, what it means to be a human being, what makes each of us who we are, *begins* with the brain...and that's where we go for the next couple of chapters, to dig a little deeper into a particular aspect of the human brain, namely how the long process of evolution reveals itself in our behaviour today. Professor Robert Winston, in his book *Human Instinct* takes up the theme introduced by Wangerei Maathai and Sam Harris, and repeatedly makes clear just how important this evolutionary dimension is to an understanding of how our brains function today.

> '*When we're thinking about the nature of human psychology,*' he writes, '*it helps to take into account the fact that, broadly speaking, we all have the same mental architecture. Our minds are those of our savannah ancestors, all of whom evolved into homo sapiens under the same*

environmental conditions and the same evolutionary pressures... The pressures to which we have been exposed over millennia, have left a mental and emotional legacy. Some of these emotions and reactions, derived from the species who were our ancestors, are unnecessary in a modern age, but these vestiges of a former existence are indelibly printed in our make-up.[14]

We have all inherited a mental and emotional *legacy* as he puts it that is *'indelibly printed.'* That is to say the brain that we take onto the District Line every morning to travel to work, or which we use to nurture our relationships with friends and colleagues, or to pursue this quest for a greater sense of well-being, has been shaped and formed by a long and complex evolutionary journey ... on the savannah's of East Africa long ago.

CHAPTER FIVE

The brain that evolution
has given us

The human brain has often been described as the most complex item in the entire universe.[1] The product of millions of years of extraordinary and subtle evolution. And yet for the most part we take it absolutely for granted, rarely giving a second thought as to how it actually functions. It is of course the seat of every thought and action, every experience we have, however slight and momentary and inconsequential, in some way derives from the brain; grabbing a piece of toast as you dive out of the door in the morning because you're a bit later than usual, choosing to run rather than stroll to the station perhaps, and going for an americano rather than your usual latte during the coffee break because you think you need a bigger lift. That constant flow of utterly minor thoughts and words and joys and anxieties that streams through our head as we go through the day, as well as all those huge philosophical questions that we rarely devote any time to, but which continue to demand more complete answers. Why are we here? What is consciousness? What is the basis of our morality? What do we really mean by intelligence? All are rooted in and derive from the brain.

And even if we do take it all for granted, as the philosopher Raymond Tallis reminds us in his book *The Kingdom of*

Infinite Space, the brain literally demands from us a quite different kind of relationship. What does he mean by that? Well most of the other main organs of the body show by their shape or structure or location, he argues, what they do and how they work. A joint is clearly a joint. The heart is clearly a pump. The lungs are clearly air sacs pumping air in and out. The brain however is set quite apart, encased within the thick protective skull, no moving parts, no joints, no valves. And if we ask ourselves which part of the body we most *identify* our sense of self with, the answer invariably is with somewhere just behind our foreheads. As one eminent neuroscientist has expressed it, in all the discussions about the nature of self, one of the key questions we have to answer is,

> '...*why you experience the world from a specific perspective, typically somewhere in the middle of the head?*'[2]

That is to say, *we have* a heart and a liver and arms and legs, whereas *we are* in some sense our brain. That is, as Raymond Tallis demonstrates, a fundamentally different emotional and psychological relationship. And it calls up of course the whole mind-separate-from-body debate triggered by the brilliant 17th Century French mathematician and philosopher Descartes, when he famously declared, '*Cogito ergo sum,' I think therefore I am.*' A debate which is to some extent still rumbling on all these decades later. Why? Because however repeatedly we are told, or understand intellectually, that the mind and the body are inextricably interlinked, in terms of our daily experience that is not quite how it feels. We are constantly aware of the vast, unlimited world of the imagination inside our heads, where we can travel anywhere and envision absolutely anything in a trice. The mind is literally a fully functioning time-travel machine. As opposed to the fixed and tangible space occupied by our physical bodies, permanently weighed down by the pull of the earth's gravity.

But once again, we live in times of the most extraordinary change in relation to our understanding of what the brain is all about. Of course much about its workings remains a mystery. Indeed, whether or not man has a big enough brain ever to *fully understand* the workings of his own brain is still a relevant question posed by many neuroscientists. No one is quite sure. But unquestionably over the past ten to fifteen years there has been a huge revolution. We have learned so much more about how the brain *actually functions* as we think and feel and imagine and respond. More perhaps in that short period than we have learned over all the previous centuries of exploration and examination. And clearly that new knowledge has given us a whole new series of insights into how we think about ourselves and understand ourselves, both acting as individuals and interacting in society with those around us.

The scanning revolution

The brain has been studied for centuries. We know for example that the ancient Egyptians carried out quite complex forms of brain surgery. It's not at all uncommon to find mummies with small holes cut into the skull through which it seems radical surgery was carried out. And they didn't of course have anaesthetics! But for many centuries learning about the brain has been very slow, hampered by the fact that it is so inaccessible, encased as it is within the protective box of the skull. So that our knowledge and understanding of the way the brain functions and in particular its relationship to our behaviour, which is the bit we're particularly interested in, have been based essentially on disability and serendipity.

Someone just happened to suffer an accident to the head, or a stroke for example, and the attempt has been made to correlate the damage to a particular part of the brain with particular changes in ability or behaviour, such as loss of speech, or an inability to make up properly constructed sentences, or loss of control over particular parts of the body. All those examples refer to actual case studies. Indeed open up virtually any standard text book on the brain and you will still come across descriptions of very much the same case studies of well documented accidents or brain operations, which led to particular advances in our knowledge of which bits of the brain are related to which kinds of behaviour. More recently, actual operations on the brain have of course led to an acceleration of mapping and learning. But it has been very much in that way, slowly and painstakingly, over many decades, that a patchwork profile has been built up of the various patterns of brain function.

Suddenly all that has changed. In just a handful of years the whole process has been transformed and accelerated immeasurably, by the widespread access to powerful new observational techniques such as magnetic resonance imaging machines, or functional MRI scanners as they are known, fMRI. Go into the Neuroscience Department of the famous Headington Hospital for example, just outside Oxford, and you find a whole floor of such powerful machines. They have completely revolutionised the way we learn about the brain, because they enable it to be studied for the very first time, in *real time*, as it is actually working, thinking thoughts and controlling actions. When you lie inside the narrow tunnel of one of these smooth, rounded, space-age machines, nothing much seems to be going on, but for the neuroscientist it's very much like having a brand new immensely accurate *microscope* that enables them to peer through the thick skull and watch the actual changes in the nature and patterns of brain activity. Which bits 'light up' for example, when you are thinking about love, or thinking about anger, and many more complex processes than those.

As science writer Rita Carter has described in her book, *Mapping The Mind,*

> *'Everyone should be enthralled by this venture because it is giving us greater understanding about one of the oldest and most fundamental of mysteries…the relationship between brain and mind. It is also providing fascinating insights into ourselves…it is now possible to locate and observe the mechanics of rage, violence, and misperception, and even to detect the physical signs of complex qualities of mind like kindness, humour, heartlessness, gregariousness, altruism, mother love and self-awareness.'*[3]

For everyone to be 'enthralled,' might I think be a bit of an ask, but I would ask you to note the key point that she makes, which is that we can now actually observe *'the physical signs of complex qualities of mind.'* We can begin to see, she is saying, what kind of activity kindness stimulates in the brain, and anger and altruism. That is a truly extraordinary leap forward. Of course there is much that remains unknown. The exploration and the understanding of the rich inner life that we all know as human consciousness for example is still known professionally as 'the hard problem,' because it has proved to be so impenetrable. Max Tegmark,

Professor of Physics at MIT, who has written extensively on the nature of consciousness as well as on the nature of physical reality frames for us what might be described perhaps as the ultimate question;

> *'Why are you conscious right now? Specifically why are you having a subjective experience of reading these words, seeing these colours and hearing these sounds, while the inanimate objects around you presumably aren't having any subjective experience at all?'*[4]

The staggering fact is that we simply can't answer that question…at least not yet. We don't know. We simply don't know at what point in our long evolution that this rich inner life began to emerge as a quality in the dense and complex bundle of atoms and molecules that happens to make up our brain.

But the fact remains that the remarkable new threshold that has been crossed in the last few years, has led to this period we are living through being labelled as *The Age of The Brain*. And just to put a measure on the scale of this revolution in neuroscience, Patricia Churchland from UCLA, eminent philosopher and writer about issues where philosophy and psychology and neuroscience overlap, has actually likened this development to the 17th century Copernican revelation in astronomy, that revealed that the Earth travels round the Sun, rather than the other way round. A revelation of course which totally transformed our view of man's place in the Universe. No longer was he at the very centre of it. He sat instead somewhere out on the margins of just one minor galaxy that swam in a vast universe of many billions of galaxies.[5] Essentially Churchland's startling comparison is saying that we are now living through a revolution on a

similar scale, about *how* our brain works, and, more importantly, the *implications* that new knowledge has, for our
understanding of the way we behave and respond to those
around us and to our environment.

And that's my main interest in this chapter. That is to say, it
is essentially practical rather than theoretical. What new
insights can we gain from this sort of research that help us
understand more about ourselves, and why we respond in
the ways that we do

Our brains are exceptionally large

For most of the animal kingdom brain size is closely related
to body size, for seemingly obvious reasons; the larger the
organism the more processing power is needed to control
and regulate it. Human beings are a remarkable exception
to that norm, our brains are fully three times larger than
would be expected for a primate of our size. Moreover they
are a very expensive organ to run. They make up only 2% of
our body weight, but they consume around 25% of all the
energy the body uses.[6] That is a crucial factor that has to
be taken into account, in trying to explain just how and
why we evolved such a large and expensive brain, when the
fact is that during that period we were living relatively
simple lives out on the savannahs of East Africa. What
combination of factors drove the evolution of so large and
so expensive a brain is still very much a mystery.

That big brain has around 100 billion neurons or nerve cells,
which are the primary cells of the brain and the nervous
system, along which the brain signals travel. And we have
over 100 trillion *connections*, or *synapses* as they are called,
where the neurons interconnect with one another in neural
networks. The neuroscientists tell us that it is in this dense

and intricate network of connections, the *wiring diagram* so to speak, that the power of the brain truly resides. Herein lies the key to whom we uniquely are. Neuroscientists have now built up a fairly detailed map of where different skills and abilities are located in everyone's brain, but the actual wiring diagram is vastly different for each one of us, since it reflects all that has happened to us as unique individuals in our lives; all our values, all our preferences, all our skills, all our multi-layered memories. So our genes provide crucial guidance on the way the brain is structured, but it is our personal on-going interactions with the world around us that creates the billions of connections that make us who we uniquely are, as we progress from infancy to adulthood.

Old dogs and new tricks

That insight ties in very closely with the radically new understanding of the brain's continuing flexibility or plasticity. For many decades the conventional wisdom has been that once we reach early adulthood our brains are pretty much fixed in terms of form and function. Yes they might change marginally, but the basic functioning wiring diagram so to speak was thought to be firmly established and fixed in place. That has long been the orthodox view. More recent research however has completely transformed that understanding, indeed it has turned it on its head. It is now known that the adult brain continues to retain very considerable powers of flexibility, or *neuro-plasticity*, as this quality is called by the neuroscientists, well on into our lives.

That is a valuable new insight, since it means that we retain tremendous possibilities in the extent to which we can *retrain* our brain throughout our lives. We now know if you like, that you *can* teach an old dog to learn new tricks. The old adage is plain wrong. Thus many older people may well have chosen not to take up new learning challenges, or explore new directions in their lives, not because they weren't capable, but because they were *conditioned* by the common stereotype that older brains simply can't hack it.

Another key implication that we would do well to take on board is that there would seem to be a genuine use-it-or-lose-it dimension to our brain's alertness and activity. Just as if we don't exercise muscles in particular parts of our body we know full well that they become flabby and weak, so we now know that if we don't exercise the immense flexibility of the brain, that flexibility, or particular bits of it, diminishes.

To quote a recent scientific article on learning ability for example, it declares, ' *The learning process carries on for life.*'[7] The article goes on to explain that one of the main reasons we have come to believe that there is a slowdown in later years is primarily because we simply tend to *challenge* ourselves less in later years, to spend less time learning new stuff. That is to say, we *don't use it* so much, so we think the loss is a natural consequence of ageing, and unfortunately that has become the commonly accepted wisdom.

Optimism can be learned

Moreover it has now become established that *how we think,* can fundamentally change the brain's wiring diagram, and therefore how it functions. At first hearing that may sound strange, since it is of course, the brain that's doing the thinking! One way this idea is often expressed by neuroscientists is to say that the *mind* can change the brain. Thus it has been shown conclusively that mental training and discipline, the *new* interests that we take up, the *new* choices that we learn to make, the *new* disciplines that we seek to master, can have a major influence on both the structure and the strength of the connections between crucial, life-shaping areas of the brain. It is that new understanding that enables psychologist and writer Daniel Goleman to claim in his seminal book, *Emotional Intelligence;'*

> *'Optimism and hope,'* he writes, *'like helplessness and despair can be learned… Developing a competency of any kind strengthens the sense of self-efficacy.'*[8]

And notice the powerfully supportive message carried in that final sentence, when we are talking as we are, about how we can improve and enhance our life-skills. He is arguing that new knowledge, new understanding, new skills in *any area* of our life, can directly affect our overall sense of self-efficacy, or as we might express it more commonly, our self-confidence, right across the spectrum of our lives.

Positive psychologist Professor Martin Seligman makes a very similar point in his book, *What You Can Change…and What You Can't,*

> *'Optimism,'* he declares, *'is a learned skill . Once learned it increases achievement at work and improves physical health.'*[9]

That again is an extraordinarily positive statement about the power of the human spirit that is, as it happens, completely in tune with a theme that lies at the very centre of Buddhist teachings. Namely that we can *train ourselves* to be more resilient and optimistic, and in doing so we can have a *direct influence* not only on our ability to achieve more in life, but, as Seligman points out, on our general physical well-being.

Is there anyone who wouldn't want increasing achievement at work and better health? I think not, and my central argument is that the *awareness* that we can achieve it, is the necessary first step along the path to doing so.

Emotions crucial to decision making

Elsewhere in the same book, Daniel Goleman takes us on a brief but immensely illuminating guided tour to illustrate just how crucial a role our emotions and feelings, or you might perhaps say our *life state* at any given moment, has to play in all our decision making processes. Whereas the common stereotype is that our emotions are somehow in conflict with our rational selves, and are more likely than not to disrupt rational decision making, research has shown something rather different. People who have suffered damage to the emotion-handling parts of their brain for example, struggle to make *any decisions* at all. They can flounder in a sort of indecisive limbo. It seems that we all need the *emotional areas* of the brain to play a crucial role in *evaluating* what we might call perhaps the underlying spiritual dimensions of a situation or a set of circumstances, and so enabling us to move to a decision, on all the kinds of issues large and small that we face every day of the week.[10]

Goleman's brilliant guided tour of the evolutionary architecture of our brain helps us to understand why that is the case. Let's take it!

The reptilian brain

It was Dr. Paul Maclean, the distinguished neuropsychologist from the National Institute of Mental Health in the USA, who first identified what he called *'the triune brain,'* that is the three main stages in the evolution of our brain that are in a sense replayed every time a human embryo develops in the womb.

Stage one or the earliest part of our brain to evolve is known as the brain stem, surrounding the top of the spinal chord. This is the most ancient part of the brain that evolved over 500 million years ago, so it's often called the 'reptilian brain,' which gives pause for thought doesn't it? This is how far we've travelled since our primitive beginnings. This bit of our brain isn't involved in our conscious processes at all, our thinking or learning for example. It is very much an *automatic regulator*, monitoring and regulating our fundamental life-support systems, such as breathing and heart rate, blood pressure and sleep rhythms. It also plays an important part in receiving and processing information about the actual movement and orientation of our body in space. [11]

The emotional brain

From that primitive 'reptilian' beginning, new structures grew up around the brain stem with the evolution of the first mammals. They're called the *limbic structures* because they're formed roughly in the shape of a ring. (limbus is the Latin for a ring). The limbic system is often called the *emotional brain* because these structures introduced a whole new range of emotional responses. Today when we are experiencing powerful emotions such as fear and love and hate and jealousy and anger, it is the limbic system that is involved. But a key point to note perhaps, is that when we look at our evolutionary journey, we human beings had an *emotional brain*, long before we had a rational, planning, thinking one, and that simple evolutionary fact still has powerful implications for our responses and our behaviours today.

As it evolved it seems that this limbic part of the brain introduced two crucial and closely interlinked capabilities. One was *memory*, the ability to remember and reconstruct past events, the other was *learning*, which is closely dependant on that ability to remember of course, the two are intimately interlinked. But a key point is that these utterly revolutionary developments gave our early mammalian ancestors a huge evolutionary advantage, since the ability to remember and learn from past experiences released them from a limited and largely automatic and instinctive range of responses. Learning brings with it the ability to adapt. So now they could constantly *adapt their responses* to the changes in events and circumstances and environments that they encountered as they went about their lives. It was a new ability that could radically transform their success rate in foraging and hunting for food for example, or in protecting themselves when they became the prey.

The rational, planning, imaginative brain

And finally, stage three, there was the immense leap forward in intellectual capability that came with the rapid growth, rapid that is of course in evolutionary terms, of the upper part of the brain, the neocortex as it's called. This is the great area of folded and convoluted tissue that grew out of the emotional centres to make up the expansive top layers of the brain. The brain basically tripled in size from around 500cc with the earliest human ancestors, the earliest hominids, to around 1400cc with us, *homo sapiens*. It is this enormous expansion of the upper and frontal areas of the brain over such a relatively short period in evolutionary terms that has pushed the front of the skull out to give us the high, straight-up forehead that is so significant a feature of our skull shape, compared with all our primate cousins.

It's as a result of that third and remarkable expansion in our brain's capacity …the 100 billion neurons that we've mentioned, and the 100 trillion connections or synapses, that can be constantly formed and reformed… that this evolved brain we've all inherited is almost infinitely malleable and flexible. And it has brought with it everything that makes us uniquely human. Because the neocortex is the thinking brain, the seat of thought. Here plans are made, words are formed, ideas are generated. It not only enables us to comprehend at lightning speed what the senses tell us about the physical world around us, but it has brought the ability to think about and communicate clearly and vividly about things that *don't exist* in that physical world. That is to say it brings all those higher *abstract* capacities for language and imagination and complex communication, and science and mathematics and philosophy, and all the extraordinary extensions of our intellectual capacity into art and culture.

As Yuval Harari expresses it in his book on human evolution, *Sapiens,*

> 'There are no gods in the universe, no nations, no money, no human rights, no laws, no justice, outside the common imagination of all human beings. '[12]

Above all perhaps it has brought this heightened capacity to learn and to *adapt* and so to surmount whatever difficulties and crises that have confronted the human species on its evolutionary journey. As one scientist has expressed it somewhat poetically, we have acquired a unique ability to respond to changes and challenges that occur in our environment;

> '...evolution put a kilogram of magic inside each human skull. The billions of neurons that make up the brain gave us the intellectual wherewithal to invent culture... that cumulative body of information we acquire through teaching, imitation and other transmissions. With

minor exceptions, humans are the only animals that have culture, and we are therefore unique in our ability to respond to environmental changes by evolving culturally...'[13]

The new social imperative

But as I mentioned briefly earlier, quite *why* our brains expanded at such an extraordinary rate, quite what changes in our direct ancestor's lives triggered this explosive growth in cognitive ability, is still very much a mystery that continues to puzzle anthropologists and evolutionary biologists and others. As Yuval Harari once again explains;

'For more than 2 million years human neural networks kept growing and growing, but apart from some flint knives and pointed sticks, humans had precious little to show for it. What then drove forward the evolution of the massive human brain during those 2 million years? Frankly we don't know.'[14]

That remains if you like a huge enigma; what could possibly have been the trigger? One leading modern hypothesis argues that this explosive growth of our brain was driven, not by the need to cope with any extreme climate or environmental changes, nor by the need to create radical new technologies in order to survive. Rather it argues, it was brought about as a direct result of our having to master the immense challenge and complexity of relating...*to other human beings*. During this period it seems that our ancestors began to live in larger tribal groups, and that created a completely different set of *social* pressures. How to live peacefully as a member of a larger group? How to hunt and cooperate with people you didn't know so well? How to communicate your intentions to partial strangers? Above all perhaps how to interpret and predict theirs? The *real* intentions of someone you scarcely knew, watching their facial expressions or the movement of their eyes, interpreting their unconscious body language. The ancient beginnings if you like, of the skills that we all need today to negotiate life successfully in the crowded shoulder-to-shoulder jungle of modern society.

This idea, which is sometimes called the new'social imperative' is one of the strongest theories put forward to explain this remarkable and rapid and above all, immensely empowering, expansion of the human brain. It seems most probable then that we owe the large brain that we all inherit at birth, this most extraordinary item in the entire universe, to this fundamental quality of cooperation and sociability. The very *essence* of being human if you like, is about mastering the skills of living successfully with, and forming cooperative relationships with… other people.

CHAPTER SIX

Let's not forget the emotional dimension

The psychologist Daniel Goleman is careful to remind us, at the end of his lightning tour of the evolutionary brain, that however powerful a device our rational, scheming, planning brain is, the fact is that our emotional brain came first, and it continues to play a hugely important role in the way we function today and every day. The neocortex, the rational, thinking, planning parts of the brain, the latest parts to evolve, actually grew out of the basic limbic structures. And we now know… almost entirely as a result of our ability to observe the brain while it is at work so to speak…that the two structures are powerfully interconnected through a huge number of neural pathways. The key point to note is that this enhanced connectivity gives the emotional centres immense power to influence the functioning of those rational, planning parts of the brain.

Thus one could argue, modern neuroscience has identified and clarified for us the importance of the fact that how we *feel* at any moment in time, what our *life state* is from moment to moment, plays a key role in the way that we actually perceive and evaluate situations and circumstances, and what decisions we arrive at, and thus, how we act, what *behaviour* we adopt.

That interplay between the emotional limbic system and the rational planning forebrain goes on all the time of course, even though we are not likely to be conscious of it. However much we may pride ourselves on being cool, calculating, rational human beings...as we so often do... human life is filled with events and occasions that are simply too *important*, as Daniel Goleman puts it, to be left to the intellect alone! We need the evaluating power of our emotions;

> '*Our emotions*' he writes '*...guide us in facing predica-ments and tasks too important to leave to the intellect alone...danger, painful loss, persisting towards a goal despite frustrations, bonding with a mate, building a family.*'[1]

Notice that he includes such key qualities as courage and resilience... persisting towards a goal despite frustrations... as crucially requiring the input of this emotional dimension. American neuroscientist Jill Bolte Taylor expresses a very similar point in her book *My Stroke of Insight*, in which she describes her own experience of living through the immensely challenging crisis of a major stroke and having to fight a long battle to regain her capabilities. She goes to the very heart of the matter when she writes;

> '... *although many of us may think of ourselves as thinking creatures that feel, biologically we are feeling creatures that think.*'[2]

Feeling creatures that think! That is I suggest, a brilliantly concise and immediately comprehendable way of describ-ing a surprising biological fact that has only been estab-lished in recent times; namely that there are far more connections carrying information *from* the limbic emotional centres of the brain up to the rational, controlling, planning cortex that lies just behind our forehead, than there are flowing the other way.[3] That is to say, the long process of human evolution has given the emotional centres the power to overwhelm the rational ones. Why might that be? The direct answer would seem to be that over the course of our complex history, our success and our survival have actually *depended* on the brain being wired in such a way as to ensure that our emotions, our evaluating centres you might say, have a strong influence in our decision making. Professor Joseph Le Doux is a neuroscientist at the Center for Neural Science in the US, and a prominent researcher in the field of the emotions, and he makes the point quite explicitly in his book *The Emotional Brain;*

> *'Emotions are things that happen to us, rather than things we make happen,'* He writes, *'Our conscious control over emotions is weak, and feelings often push out thinking...This is because the wiring of the brain favours emotion... connections from the emotional systems to the cognitive systems are stronger than the connections that run the other way.'*[4]

The wiring of the brain actually *favours* emotion he declares. So there if you like is the clear evolutionary explanation for something that we have all experienced many times, when we are all too keenly aware that we are making a decision that is strongly influenced by how we *feel* about an issue, rather than simply what our strictly rational brain is telling us. It is now clear that in those situations we're only being truly human! That is to say we're making use of the faculties that have served us so well down the ages.

Our emotional trip wire

As an illustration of this aspect of the way we sometimes think and behave, neuroscientists often point to a part of the ancient limbic structures that happens to be called the *amygdala*, which is made up of two small almond shaped bodies that nestle right in the centre of the brain. The *amygdala* is really about fear.[5] This is where fear is registered and generated. It has been described as a kind of emotional sentinel or trip wire that has had an absolutely crucial role to play in our ancestors' survival. As Robert Winston describes it;

> *'It's certainly a reflection of just how vital the fear reaction really was for the survival of our ancient ancestors that a special, dedicated brain system evolved to deal with it. The location of the amygdala gives us a clue to the precise nature of its role in processing fear. It has connections to the autonomic nervous system which controls physiological reflexes such as your heart and breathing rates...a special 'rapid response unit' if you like, primed to act quickly when presented with danger.'[6]*

So this specially designed rapid response unit sits there at the centre of our brain receiving signals directly from the senses, and if those signals contain anything that resembles a threat then the *amygdala* has the power to immediately *hijack* the brain so to speak, to take it over, to stimulate an *instant* decision to flee or to repulse the threat, instead of letting the high-powered rational thinking brain go through its slower, multi-layered process of trying to assess the situation and decide what to do. This instant amygdala-stimulated response may save only split seconds, but those split seconds have been precious in terms of saving the hunter's life say. That rustle in the undergrowth for example could just be the wind...but it might also be a sabre-toothed tiger.

And the plain mathematics of evolution determine that those ancestors who *were* able to respond instantly to that amygdala alarm, would have survived longer and had more offspring...leading directly to us. It has become an essential part of our modern inheritance, and it can only be helpful I suggest, in our being aware of its presence and how it works.

The modern dilemma

The key point of course is that although we are unlikely to encounter a sabre-toothed tiger on the daily commute to work these days, we still have the amygdala, ready to hijack the brain, and trigger that instant flight or fight response. Although it's likely to take a somewhat different form these days; the sudden outburst of reactionary anger, the bite-back response, the overwhelming surge of panic. It goes without saying that we have all experienced times when our emotion or our anger say, completely overwhelms our ability to function rationally and we just fly into a rage or have a melt down. We might well find ourselves asking afterwards, *'Where did all that come from!'* And it's a valid enough comment, because our modern brain has indeed been momentarily hijacked by an ancient deep-seated response system.

A fascinating corollary to that account is the fact that the nerve cells in this part of the brain become 'wired' together when we are very young, when we are infants in fact, even before we have sufficient language to put our thoughts or our emotions into words. And although this system continues of course to function throughout our lives, the evidence seems to be that it doesn't grow up so to speak, it doesn't mature. Its responses to the sensory stimuli it receives remain very much the same, even though the rest of us gets older. Which accounts for the fact that, as one neuroscientist has expressed it,

> 'When our emotional' buttons 'are pushed, we retain the ability to react to incoming stimulation as though we were a two year old, even when we are adults.'[7]

We retain the ability that is, however old we might be, to throw a completely spontaneous and unrehearsed two-year-old tantrum or fit of temper, as we all know to our cost!

Call in the emotional manager

However that having been said, it is precisely the experience we steadily build up in the outer layers of the cerebral cortex as we grow older, and the vastly greater awareness of how we function, that enables us to control, or to modulate, as some neuroscientists describe it, these automatic and instinctive emotional reactions to situations and events, to enable us to respond in a more measured and mature way. We all continue to have the occasional experience of completely losing our rag. Of course, we're only human! But most of the time, as adults, although we continue to *feel* the fear, or the anger, or the sudden rush of complete panic, we have learned how to seize control of the response at an earlier stage and moderate our response, to achieve a more constructive result.

Once again I think that simply knowing about this utterly basic and moment-to-moment connection between these two structures in the brain, the emotional limbic system and the rational prefrontal lobes, can give us a new and valuable insight. Hopefully we can see a little more clearly what's going on, to create just that fractional pause that enables us to handle those desperately fraught moments more effectively, and more creatively. It's interesting to say the least, that both modern psychologists and Buddhist teachings talk in very similar terms. Buddhism talks of greater clarity, of seeing more *clearly* the life state that we are in, as the key to our overcoming those angry outbursts that can have such a disturbing effect on our partners and families and friends. Modern psychology talks in terms of self-awareness.

> '*Self-awareness...recognising a feeling as it happens...is the key to emotional intelligence.* '[8]

Buddhism argues that it is only by increasing our awareness that we *are* actually in anger state for example, that we can learn how to create that fractional space between becoming aware of what we see as a trespass against us, and reacting angrily and possibly violently to it. It may only be the briefest gap of time, but that's all we need. It's enough for us to control the tongue, and to defuse that explosive, bite-back expression of anger.

Being advised to count to ten when we're in a potentially angry situation may be very old advice, but that doesn't stop it from being very wise advice. As psychologist Martin Seligman has paraphrased it, count to ten, count to twenty, sleep on it if you possibly can! Before you fire back an angry email. Or as one Buddhist teacher has expressed it to me somewhat more colloquially, we should learn to treat anger rather like cow pats...best handled when cold!

So how do we make good decisions?
The widespread stereotype is that when we're faced with making big decisions, or many small ones indeed, the last

thing we need is emotion of any kind. What we need above all, the common understanding has it, is cool, calculating rationality. Keep emotion out of it. That is the very basis of the concept of decision theory beloved of classical economists and many social scientists. According to this formulation, human beings are defined as strictly *'rational optimisers.'* That is to say, when these 'model' human beings are faced with difficult decisions they...or we... carefully define all the options, we then weigh up each option against all the others to arrive at a clear estimation of the *value* and the *implications* of each one, and then we choose the one that provides the greatest return or benefit.

Do we? Do we in fact go through anything approaching such a mechanistic process? Does that chime with your everyday experience? Very probably not. As one psychologist has written;

> *'There's the risible idea that humans are rational, and the dubious notion that we would be capable of on-the-hoof calculations of probability, even if we could access all the necessary information. Decision theory explains how we would make choices if we were logical computers or all knowing beings. But we're not. We are just rather clever apes with a brain shaped by natural selection to see us through this messy world.'*[9]

Indeed we are. And the key phrase in that passage undoubtedly is *'shaped by natural selection,'* since that is of course precisely how this moment-to-moment relationship between the emotional limbic system and the cool calculating prefrontal cortex has come about. It has evolved to enable us to make better choices and arrive at better decisions in a turbulent and messy and often dangerous world, not an economist's or anyone else's mathematically logical one.

An acknowledged expert on the function of the emotional limbic system is Dr. Antonio Damasio of the University of Iowa, who has spent many years studying the implications of *damage* to this limbic circuitry that is so crucial to our down-to-earth every day living. His research shows that where there is damage, although there may be no resultant deterioration whatsoever in qualities such as general intelligence or any other cognitive function, the business of decision-making *is* very seriously affected.

> *'Feelings are typically indispensable for rational decisions; they point us in the right direction, where dry logic can then be of best use...The emotional brain is as involved in reasoning as is the thinking brain.'*[10]

Feelings are 'indispensable' for good quality decision making he argues. That's a very big, all-encompassing word he chooses to us; not just useful, or helpful, but actually 'indispensable.'

And philosopher Robert Solomon sums up this immensely important modern understanding, *'rationality is not the defining structure of human experience.'*[11] as we have so commonly been led to believe.

> *'Rationality like spirituality, involves the heart as well as the mind....The emotions endow and bestow meaning to our experience.'*[12]

Such a powerful and persuasive phrase, emotions endow meaning to our experience. Thus we have an entirely new paradigm. The old one, the one that is still so deeply embedded in our culture, argues that we should seek in our lives an *ideal* of reason and rationality, freed from the influence, the pull, if I may put it that way, of emotional input. The psychologist Daniel Goleman argues that in the light of this new understanding we owe it to ourselves to adopt a new paradigm, an altogether different and more accurate perception of the balance between our emotional and our rational faculties;

> '*How we do in life is determined by both…it is not just IQ, but emotional intelligence that matters. Indeed intellect cannot work at its best without emotional intelligence…When these partners interact well, emotional intelligence rises…as does intellectual ability.*'[13]

That happens to be a relatively modern piece of knowledge. What is immensely interesting I would argue is that it is also an idea that is strongly reflected in classical Buddhist teachings. Buddhism has placed a great deal of emphasis on increasing our self awareness in this very area; on defining clearly for us for example what might be called the key emotions or life states that we all experience as we travel through each day, and how intimately they affect the way we deal with events. They happen to be described in Nichiren Buddhism as the Ten Worlds.[14] But the point I really want to make is that there is an immensely *practical* purpose underlying these teachings. It's about far more than simply increasing our knowledge or our understanding. The fundamental argument is that it is *only* with such increased self-awareness that we are really empowered to navigate our way more effectively, and above all more positively, through the shoals and quick sands and multiple relationships we all encounter in the course of every day's life.

CHAPTER SEVEN

Changing the wiring diagram

Some years ago the Professor of Neurology at Harvard University in Boston, Alvaro Pascual Leone,[1] carried out a series of extremely innovative experiments that have since become regarded as a landmark in studies of just how malleable and flexible our brain is. Whereas we tend to see the brain as a relatively fixed and unchanging entity, Leone's studies revealed, virtually for the first time, just how rapidly what we do and, just as important, how we think can radically *change* the neural networks and connections within the brain, the wiring diagram so to speak, and therefore the way it functions, and the way we behave.

So what did he do? He recruited a group of volunteer students who weren't musically trained in any way, and persuaded them to have a go at learning a simple five-finger piano exercise. So every day for a week they all trooped into his laboratory and sat down at the piano, and went through the basic discipline of practising the exercise.

It must have seemed a rather bizarre situation to many of them, and no doubt it was to some extent, science often moves in mysterious ways. But for everyone who volunteered for this experiment, there was clearly a considerable amount of concentration and effort involved in simply trying to wrap their brains around the task in hand; to get their fingers to move in a particular sequence and in a particular rhythm, which they had never been called upon to master before. Each day, after they had carried out the exercise there was more, they all had to undergo a form of brain scan to examine the effects on the area of the brain that controls finger movements. It happens to be called the motor cortex.

What is extraordinary is that at the end of just 5 days, the density of the grey matter... the number of neurons and synapses... in the part of the cortex allocated to controlling these fingers that had struggled to master an unfamiliar task, had significantly increased. That is to say, the process of training these musically untrained fingers, had *physically* changed the structure and the effectiveness of that particular bit of the brain. And the change had taken place in so short a period of time.

That in itself was already a surprising result. The Harvard studies, along with several others that were carried out at around the same time, revealed a wholly new insight. Namely that the developed or adult brain seemed to be infinitely more *malleable and flexible* than had hitherto been believed. Completely contrary to the received wisdom that had held sway for many decades, the studies suggested that we could re-train, and re-shape the adult brain by the new choices that we make and the new skills that we learn. And most importantly, we could *go on re-training* the brain similar to the way we can re-train and modify the shape and the effective functioning of muscles in the body, with discipline and exercise.

So it was as I've said, a landmark result that opened up a wholly new, and powerfully optimistic understanding of how we can retain this ability to re-mould and re-shape the brain, well on into our adult years.

The sheer power of thought

As if to further demonstrate this new understanding, Alvaro Leone went on to modify even further our understanding of the brain's malleability. He arranged for a second group of research volunteers to go through a very similar research-training programme. This time however the crucial modification was that he took away the piano! That is to say he got them to attempt exactly the same five-finger exercise, but *in thought only.* He gave them the same musical briefing, the same piece of music, and asked them to *think* their way through it on the same daily basis, for five days. So these volunteers were asked to sit there, hands still, fingers still, but brains no doubt working intensely, as they concentrated deeply on reading the music, and imagining just how they *would* move their hands and fingers in order to play the piano keys and create the sound…if only it were there! It must have seemed utterly weird.

But if the experiment was weird, the result was astounding. When this second research group was put through the brain scanner it was found that the same region of the brain had been modified in almost exactly the same way, as the brains of those who had actually touched the keys and made the music. That is to say, simply *thinking* about, or *imagining* the movement of the fingers, had re-shaped or re-organised if you will, that area of the brain, in the same way as if the piano had actually been played.

The results of these experiments have since received confirmation in many different ways, most notably perhaps in studies using fMRI scanners, where it has been shown that exactly the same areas of the brain 'light up' when we are contemplating or thinking about an action or a movement, as when we actually make the movement.

But back to the idea of change, or *neural plasticity* as it is commonly called in neuroscience, because that has been the main point in recounting this research. It was as I've said, a landmark result that opened up a wholly new understanding of the extent to which the brain can be reshaped or rewired so to speak. But perhaps most importantly it showed how we can *actively* work to extend and retain this mental agility well on into our adult and even advanced years.[2] It goes without saying that we all want an active and nimble brain, for as long as we can hang onto it, and this research shows that we can actually do something to achieve that goal, by the *challenges* that we continue to present to the brain, the new activities that we take up and new skills that we seek to learn, at all the stages of our life.

There is now absolutely no doubt about the validity of that idea. Moreover we have many examples of course of artists and musicians and engineers and scientists overcoming new intellectual challenges and producing radically new work even into their 60's and 70's and beyond. We can think of many famous examples from Matisse and Beethoven to Brunel and Faraday and Hawking, and many others. And we all possess basically the same brain as them!

The myelin surprise

There is an interesting and illuminating modern footnote to those Harvard studies, which underlines that very point. It has emerged from various bits of research that have taken place only over the past handful of years, so it's brand new knowledge, and in a sense it adds to our understanding of the great value we can derive from taking up new things and constantly presenting the brain with new challenges and tasks. The established view has always been that this flexibility and plasticity has been dependent upon the 'grey matter' as it's called, in the brain; that is to say the darker coloured parts of the brain that are densely packed with the neurons or brain cells, and their connections or synapses. It's on this 'grey matter' that the vast majority of brain studies over the years have been focused. By contrast the so-called 'white matter,' the myelin insulation that acts as a sheath of insulation around the neurons, has been relatively neglected. Only now is its crucial role in the flexibility of the brain becoming fully realised

That all sounds pretty esoteric stuff you might say, why is it so important? Well, put simply, it adds a whole new layer of meaning to the oft quoted phrase that the brain is to some extent a 'use it or lose it' organ.[3] To retain this remarkable level of adaptability and flexibility that is so valuable to us in our daily lives, it's now very clear that we have to make use of it, or we run the risk of losing it.

So what is this myelin stuff?

It's called 'white matter' because it is the whitish, fatty insulation that forms around the long nerve cell projections along which the brain's electrical signals travel. The myelin essentially stops that signal from leaking out into surrounding tissue and so maintains the signal's strength and speed of travel, and therefore, the brain's speed of response and the body's activation. The myelin actually begins to appear in the brain while the foetus is still developing in the womb, to enable some activity in the developing foetal brain. When the baby is born there is a rapid increase in the rate of myelin production which enables the rapid development of the baby's capabilities in those early years, enabling the child to learn to crawl and walk and talk for example, all before the age of four. After that it seems that there is a levelling off in myelin creation as the child's brain develops more slowly.

When we're passing through our turbulent teenage years it is significant that the crucial prefrontal cortex has not yet been coated with myelin. That's the part of the brain just behind the forehead that is responsible for all our planning and judgement and thinking ahead, and understanding the consequences of our actions. This absence of myelin is often presented as at least a partial explanation for the fact that teenagers can so often be wayward and unpredictable and dangerously impulsive in their behaviour!

This progressive myelin insulation process carries on into our 20's and 30's throughout the finer circuitry of the brain, and is thought to be complete by about the time we reach our 40's, which might be considered perhaps as our years of mature and reflective judgment. And then from the 60's onwards the insulation is commonly seen to fray and degenerate to some extent.[4] This degeneration coincides of course with the period of our life when, conventionally speaking, people might tend to wind down somewhat, and take up fewer *new activities* and so present the brain with fewer new challenges.

And that has been the widely accepted life-story of myelin, until very recently that is, when an enterprising neuroscientist from Oxford, decided to set up an experiment involving of all things… juggling. The result has been that myelin has at last come in out of the cold so to speak. As one neuroscientist has expressed it;

'It turns out that a most vital part of our cognitive potential has been hiding in plain sight.'5

It was widely believed that this neural insulation was very similar to the sort of plastic insulation we see wrapped around electrical cables. That is to say essentially passive, pretty much of a uniform thickness and once installed absolutely static. This new research has revealed the extraordinary fact that the myelin insulation is constantly changing to match the *demands* we choose to impose on the brain.

Bring on the jugglers

What on earth has juggling got to do with brain studies you might ask? Well it's precisely because of what we've been talking about, the' use it or lose it' principle. The vast majority of people don't happen to include juggling on their list of must-do activities, so it's a very *unusual* learning challenge to present to most people's brains. The purpose of the study was to bring together a group of ordinary people, of various ages and abilities, and quite simply, to get them to try to master this completely unusual challenge from scratch. And then to observe what changes if any were taking place in their brains, as they struggled with the pesky skittles.

The interesting point is that a few years earlier in 2004, a similar study had followed a very similar formula, only on that occasion the neuroscientists had looked at where they *expected* the changes in the wiring of the brain to take place, that is to say in the density of the 'grey matter,' the neurons and their synaptic connections. And their expectations were fulfilled. Just as in the five finger piano playing study at Harvard, getting people to learn a new skill changed the density of the neurons and synapses…the computing power if you like… in the area of the brain controlling motor skills.

What the Oxford neuroscientist did in this later series of juggling experiments was to look for changes where literally no one expected it, in the 'white matter,' in the myelin insulation. And she found it. After six weeks of juggling training there was a marked increase in the myelin insulation for the entire study group, which, the report concludes,

> '...would have enabled faster conduction along the circuits coordinating the juggling. What's more,' it goes on to say, 'the effect was seen in everyone who learned to juggle, regardless of how good they became, which means it is the learning process itself that is responsible.'[6]

And that is the essential point of the story for us. It is the fact of *trying* to master a new skill that stimulates the growth in brain flexibility and effectiveness, rather than the level of success. That is to say it is the *effort* we are prepared to put into taking up new activities or learning new skills, including it has since been discovered, extending ourselves a bit more than normal in our physical exercise, that enables us to retain this lively, agile, more effective brain.

This was the first research study to reveal that training, challenging ourselves to master new things of whatever kind, can alter the formation of 'white matter' in adults, and the findings have since been validated in a host of similar studies.[7]

The intelligence conundrum
While we're talking about mental ability and agility, I think it's worth looking briefly at the IQ issue to see if we can clarify some key questions that come up so frequently in conversation and in populist articles. The key word here I think is briefly, so that we don't disappear without trace into

the quicksands of the nature versus nurture debate! Intelligence or IQ has always been and remains a controversial subject. Partly because there is still active debate about what it *is* exactly that is being identified, and partly perhaps because there is a natural human resistance to reducing this infinitely diverse and multi-layered quality that we call our intellect or our intelligence, to a single number. We quite rightly resist being quantified in that way. On the other hand the claims that it is possible to create a variety of tests that give a pretty clear measure of an individual's intellectual capacity are now so deeply rooted in our culture that it's not going to go away any time soon. It's an established part of our environment and still part of many selection procedures of one kind or another.

On that basis, and bearing in mind the reservations, I think there are a number of points that are worth making just to broaden our *awareness* of the kinds of arguments that are being made, since that's what this book is essentially about, increasing our self-awareness. And if, as the psychologist Daniel Goleman among others has described it, self-awareness is '... *the keystone of emotional intelligence*,'[8] then it would definitely seem to be something worth having.

So let's start of with two or three significant *facts* on this issue, facts in the sense that they have been established by carefully controlled and repeated research studies and analyses, so that they give us at least something tangible to hang onto.

So what are these tests measuring?

It seems that when people do a range of quite different intelligence tests, they nevertheless achieve very similar results in all of them, no matter how different the format of the tests or their content. So much so that early in the 20th century the British psychologist Charles Spearman observed that what these tests were really measuring was an individual's *general factor of intelligence,* or 'g factor' as he called it for short. This 'g factor' is now widely accepted as a universal measure of an individual's ability to mentally handle and manipulate various kinds of information. What it describes is our general ability to reason and to learn and solve problems and handle complex information.

So we can definitely argue that whatever we choose to *call* what it is that is being recorded, intelligence, or basic intellectual ability, or common or garden nouse or whatever, it is a real 'something.' that is revealed across a range of tests. So a higher 'g factor' is clearly very useful during our academic years, when there is so much emphasis on learning and solving problems, and in our careers if our work involves a high intellectual dimension with complex problem solving.

But it's important to note as well that this 'g factor' is *not* particularly correlated with anything to do with what we might call emotional well-being or happiness in life, or indeed a disposition towards effort or application or hard work, which are clearly major factors affecting achievement or success in any field of activity.

The landmark twin studies.
So where do we get it from, this 'g factor?' Well there were some very famous landmark studies that were carried out in the 1990's that are often quoted in discussions, so they stand out as a sort of reference base that we can hang onto. These studies involved a large number of identical twins. Because they were *identical* they are considered as having the same genetic inheritance. However each pair of twins in

this big study had been separated for various reasons and brought up in quite different households. So for each individual child the genetic inheritance, or the *'nature'* part of the equation was the same, whereas the *nurture* factor, the *bringing-up* factor if you like, varied very considerably.

Despite being brought up in quite different domestic and educational environments in this way, each pair of identical twins nevertheless achieved very similar scores in a battery of IQ tests. Similar to a quite extraordinary degree. Indeed as one research paper expresses it,

> *'In fact, by adolescence, separated identical twins answer IQ tests almost as if they were the same person...'*[9]

That is such a remarkable result that I think that it's worth re-emphasising. Although each twin had been brought up in a completely different environment, when as teenagers, they sat down to do these tests they might well have been the same person! What does that mean? It's most frequently quoted to illustrate that the genetic inheritance factor, what they had both inherited, is far stronger than the bringing–up factor, in terms of this basic, general intellectual ability, this so-called 'g' factor.

And there's more, because a parallel study was carried out where this time they chose *non-identical twins.* That is to say they chose twins where there was a much greater divergence in the genetic inheritance of each individual child, but where they had been brought up together in the *same household*. So for this study, there was greater difference in the *'nature'* factor, the individual genetic inheritance, but exactly the same 'bringing-up' or *nurture* factor.

When these non-identical twins undertook the same battery of IQ tests each individual child achieved very different scores.

So these landmark twin studies have been widely taken to show that what we inherit from our parents and grandparents is clearly *the* dominant factor in determining this 'g factor,' or IQ dimension, or intellectual element, or whatever name we choose to give it, in our make-up.[10]

To bring this discussion right up to date, there has been a major, long running study carried out over the past 20 years or so, led by Robert Plomin of the Institute of Psychiatry at King's College in London, focusing on this same issue of how genes on the one hand, and the environment on the other, act in shaping our intellectual capacities as we develop from early childhood through to adulthood. The huge study has involved over 11,000 twins[11] What was the result? Well this vast study came up with answers very similar to those we have been discussing. Thus its findings again indicate that differences in intellectual or academic performance owe very much more to the genes we've inherited from our parents, than to other environmental factors.

Only one factor among many

However it's obviously important in responding to these major studies, to get the balance right. Thus they are *not* saying that such crucial factors as differences in educational environment for example, and other life influences we encounter as we develop, don't have a significant effect upon this intellectual dimension. Clearly they do, as we all know from our personal experience.

Moreover, positive psychologist Martin Seligman is one among many who work in this field, who goes much further, and suggests that the huge emphasis that is commonly placed on this intellectual dimension by society, as *the key* to achieving a creative and fulfilling life, define it how you will, material success, happiness, well-being, even academic success…is completely misplaced.

The key point to bear in mind, these sociologists argue, is that it is just *one* dimension among many. We don't live our lives within our intellectual capability so to speak. It's undoubtedly a very important factor of course, no one could possibly gainsay that. And it plays a key role during our educational years, and if what we have in mind is some form of academic career. But we live our lives as we all know, in the rough and tumble of events and circumstances and relationships and opportunities, and it scarcely needs saying that there are many other kinds of capability in the human make-up than purely intellectual ability. Listen for a brief moment for example to Howard Gardner, eminent psychologist at the Harvard School of Education;

> '*The single most important contribution education can make to a child's development is to help him (or her) towards a field where his talents best suit him, where he will be satisfied and competent. We've completely lost sight of that. Instead we subject everyone to an education where, if you succeed you will be best suited to be a college professor. And we evaluate everyone along the way according to whether they meet that narrow standard of success. We should spend less time ranking children and more time helping them to identify their natural competencies and gifts and cultivate those. There are hundreds and hundreds of ways to succeed, and many, many different abilities that will help you get there.*'[12]

Hundreds and hundreds of ways to succeed he argues, and that is I suggest, a brilliantly balanced argument against the widespread tendency to see the 'g factor' dimension, whatever we choose to call it, as *the* overriding measure of our ability to succeed, possibly because we don't have such clearly identifiable, *numerical* measures of these other abilities.

Over the past few years there has been a whole raft of research that in a sense develops the basic thesis expressed in Howard Gardner's statement. It serves to confirm what we all know from our personal experience in our relationships and our activities at home and at work and at play, that there are many other abilities and qualities of character, such as motivation and determination, and perseverance and resilience, and the ability to handle relationships, all of which are crucial in helping us to lead fulfilling and creative lives, and all of which we can cultivate and develop, through our own efforts and experience.

And as some of the recent research has confirmed, qualities that we might not readily think about putting on that list, far less quantifiable qualities such as *hope* and *optimism* for example, have been shown to have a *more* powerful influence than the IQ dimension, in helping us to achieve our goals in the hurly burly of everyday life.

The power of the hope dimension
What is most striking perhaps from these studies is that hope and optimism are revealed not just as…well…a kind of vague wish that things will turn out alright in the end. They are revealed as strong and primary *drivers* of resilience and determination and the will to push on. Thus we find the following kinds of conclusions being made;

> *'Hope, modern researchers are finding, does more than offer a bit of solace amid affliction; it plays a surprisingly potent role in life, offering an advantage in realms as diverse as school achievement, and bearing up in onerous jobs. Hope...is more than the sunny view that everything will turn out all right, it is believing you have both the will and the way to accomplish your goals, whatever they may be.'[13]*

So hope is a powerfully beneficial attribute, playing a surprisingly *potent* role across all the areas of our life. And optimism, which might be said to be hope's travelling companion, earns a similar evaluation.

> *'People who are optimistic see a failure as due to something that can be changed, so that they can succeed next time around, while pessimists take the blame for failure, ascribing it to some lasting characteristic that they are helpless to change.'[14]*

Let me quote just one among several studies, this one carried out by Martin Seligman at the University of Pennsylvania, which is particularly relevant to this discussion, since it was *specifically designed* to draw a comparison between this hope factor, as we might call it, and the intellectual dimension we've been talking about. Seligman persuaded 500 students at the beginning of their university life, to complete an optimism test that he had created for the purpose, so that he could give each student what might be called an *'optimism rating.'* A year later, at the end of their first year of studies, this 'optimism rating' proved to be a much better *predictor* of their exam results, than their IQ dimension. That is to say, the hope and optimism dimension in their make-up, had proved to be more influential in their

achievement, than their intelligence rating, even in the specifically academic environment. As Seligman commented
on these results,

> '*It is the combination of reasonable talent and the ability
> to keep going in the face of defeat that leads to success.
> What's missing in the tests of (academic) ability is moti-
> vation. What you need to know about someone is whether
> they will keep going when things get frustrating.*'[15]

That is unquestionably a striking phrase, the ability to keep
going in the face of setbacks. It's immensely interesting that
Buddhism emphasises an extraordinarily similar viewpoint;
resilience and perseverance it argues, are literally life
winning qualities.

So what might we take away from this?

Perhaps the most influential message that we might take
away from these studies, is that we can, if we are prepared
to make the effort, increase the influence of these positive
dimensions in opening up opportunities in our life. We can
that is, *train* ourselves to be hopeful and optimistic. You can
find that idea expressed again and again in these studies.
As we learned in an earlier chapter from Martin Seligman
for example;

> '*Optimism is a learned skill. Once learned it increases
> achievement at work and improves physical health.*' [16]

And that's an additional crucial point he is making isn't it?
It's not just about having a nice warm feeling within. The
confidence associated with optimism he is saying, is *life
giving*, it serves to enhance and improve the entire spectrum of our lives at work and at play.

So what this research is telling us is that so much depends upon the commitment and the *effort* we are prepared to put into the mix. If we are prepared to put the effort into mastering any competency, any skill, then the improved sense of self-worth and the confidence that follows, will not only generate a greater sense of hope and optimism about our own capabilities, but they will naturally flow into other areas of our life.

One of the things that stands out for me as I read these studies, is just how closely they mirror the essential purpose of a Buddhist practice. Buddhism, it could be argued, is all about generating an altogether greater dimension of hope and optimism and resilience in our lives, no matter what circumstances we encounter.

The Buddhist perspective

Buddhism presents us with an unusual paradox. Basically it teaches that the problems and the difficulties and the anxiety-making challenges that we all encounter as we go through life, and that we all spend so much time and energy and ingenuity in trying to avoid, are not only a valuable part of our life-training, they are *essential* to our overall well-being. The plain fact Buddhism argues, is that they provide the *only* available means for making the very most of ourselves; for becoming the strongest, most resilient and most optimistic individual we are capable of becoming. If that strikes you as being a somewhat eccentric, not to say perverse proposition, I can only say that that is precisely how it struck me when I first encountered it. Who needs problems you might say?

But of course needing them is not the issue. It's *dealing with them* effectively when they inevitably occur that is the key to our well-being. When everything is going well it goes without saying that we all prefer to focus on the sunshine in our lives. But as we all know only too well, sunshine is scarcely a permanent condition, reality has a nasty habit of clouding over. Love turns to heartbreak, wealth to hardship, harmony to conflict, health to sickness, and peace to war. The plain fact is that we are *conditioned* pretty much from our earliest childhood to respond to problems and difficulties *negatively*, to see them as the bane of our lives, to be avoided almost whatever the cost. But since they inevitably continue to occur in our lives, thick and fast, so does that negative response. The natural result is that problems and challenges become inextricably associated in our minds with anxiety and concern. We have if you like, *trained ourselves that way.*

The key to unlocking that situation, Buddhism teaches, is to stand back, and see the situation for what it really is. It's not so much the *problematic situation* that is causing the suffering, as our conditioned *response* to it. That may seem at first to be an unreal distinction, but in fact it is a fundamentally important one. So fundamental that once we grasp it, it can change our whole lives from the inside out. Buddhism argues that whether a problem is a cause of suffering or a source of personal growth depends essentially on the *attitude* we choose to adopt towards it. Nothing more nor less than that. It's our choice.

Taking up the personal challenge

In a way it takes us intriguingly back to that juggling we were talking about a moment ago. There we learned that simply being prepared to *tackle* the tricky problem of learning to juggle, and struggle to overcome it, was in itself an immensely beneficial process. And there are plenty of other physical parallels that help us to grasp that essential truth. Thus no weightlifter for example develops greater muscle strength, by lifting lighter and lighter weights. He has to tackle bigger challenges. No athlete can achieve peak fitness by avoiding the pain that comes from the toughest training. Indeed it is commonplace for athletes to talk of pushing themselves through the pain barrier. If the athlete chooses to adopt only soft and comfortable routines, then he or she can kiss goodbye to improving their personal best. And *personal best* in our daily lives is, in a way, what we are all seeking isn't it? Our best and most capable and most resilient selves.

The fact is, as we touched upon earlier, that Buddhism was created out of the perception that life itself is tough, and that how we choose to *respond* to that toughness determines the nature of the life we will lead. I don't think it's going too far to suggest that that is the *central perception* that Buddhism asks us to establish a relationship with.

The strange thing is that despite all the lessons that we get from our own lives, and from those around us, in a never-ending stream, we often choose to deny the reality. We like to see the problems and the challenges that we face as being somehow a deviation from the norm. *'This is not really how my life is,'* we say to ourselves, *' I just have to get through this difficult time, and then things will straighten out and I'll get back onto an even keel.'*

We know for sure that once we get over this little local difficulty we happen to be experiencing at the moment, this cash crisis, or the conflict we're having at work, or the stressful time we're going through with our partner, or whatever, then we'll be OK. Our life will return to its *normal* state of relative calm and equanimity. That's the life state we believe we want, the one completely without the problems and the stress.

It doesn't exist of course. The current crop of problems will be replaced by the next crop and so on. They are as natural a part of our life on this planet as gravity, and just as apples always fall downwards, so human life is always filled with complexity and challenge of one kind or another. And Buddhism, completely contrary to the widely-held stereotype in the West, isn't in any way about some form of *escapism*, or finding some refuge from the thrust and pace and troubling complexity of modern life, in some inner meditative sanctuary. Nor importantly, is it about *stoicism*, learning how to bear the burden or tough it out. Or about learning to remain immensely calm when all around you are losing theirs.

None of that. Or indeed anything like that. Above all perhaps Buddhism is about *challenge*. And if you think about it for just a moment, that takes us back in many ways to the research we've been discussing earlier in the chapter; the way in which taking up new activities and new challenges not only changes the wiring diagram so to speak, but is beneficial to the way the brain functions, and immensely beneficial to the way we live our lives.

A crucial change of attitude

So right at the heart of Buddhism lies the notion that although we cannot of course change the inherently complex and difficult nature of human life, it is possible to change fundamentally our *attitude* towards those difficulties. And the difference in attitude, Buddhism argues, is crucial to achieving a difference in outcome. Whether a problem that comes into our life simply causes anxiety and suffering, or is seen to be a challenge to overcome and therefore a source of personal growth, depends fundamentally on our attitude, both towards ourselves, how we *see* ourselves, as well as to the situation that we happen to be in.

A Buddhist practice is based essentially on achieving that attitude change. On training ourselves to be positive and optimistic and resilient in the face of the problems we all encounter, and will go on encountering. The process starts with being aware that such a change is possible, and the determination we make…determination rather than just a wish… that we intend to build that change into our lives. Remember psychologist Martin Seligman's immensely encouraging advice we heard a moment ago, that not only are we eminently capable of training ourselves to be more hopeful and optimistic and resilient, but when we do so, it has beneficial effects *right across the spectrum of our life and health.*[17]

Just as the athlete can train, to grow new muscle and to improve reflexes, to get the very best out of his or her body, so it seems abundantly clear, we can learn a new set of responses and ways of thinking. And Buddhism talks about it in terms of being a journey rather than a destination. A journey of continuous self-discovery, accepting responsibility for the bits of our life that are not working, and then developing on a step-by-step, day-by-day basis, the resilience and the courage and the compassion, so that we can face up to the challenge of changing them.

Chapter Eight

Effort and grit and the marshmallow test

Back in the late 1960's a series of somewhat unusual behavioural studies were carried out by an eminent psychologist at Stanford University in California, his name Walter Mischel. The studies themselves it has to be said, involved a group of young children, but what is totally surprising is the extent to which Mischel's observations arising from them, still have a profound influence today on any discussion we might have about establishing a stable and consistent sense of well-being in our lives. Why is that? Quite simply, because the studies opened up a new and wholly unexpected perspective on the extent to which certain qualities of character or personality, seemingly insignificant at such a young age, were yet shown to play a truly decisive role in the quality of these people's lives and their ability to achieve their goals well on into adulthood.

In that sense I suggest the studies clearly pose interesting questions for all of us.

They have since become known famously as the 'marshmallow test,' although that lightweight-sounding title scarcely gives an impression of the extraordinary influence they have had in subsequent years. So, very briefly, Mischel set up the studies working with a group of very young children who attended a pre-school kindergarten on the Stanford campus. Many of them in fact were the young children of faculty members and other employees. What he did quite simply was… on several occasions… to put before each of the children a highly desirable treat, a cookie or a marshmallow, which, he told them, they were perfectly entitled to eat straightaway. No problem. But he went on to explain, if they could just wait until he went on a small errand that would take him out of the room for 15 to 20 minutes or so, then they could double their pleasure, and have two treats instead of one! He then left the room, and the children's reactions were observed.

As you might expect, many of the children went straight ahead and gobbled up their tasty treat. But some had obviously made the swift calculation that two was twice as pleasurable as one. What's more, even at this very young age, and this is the key point, they were able to summon up sufficient self-control to wait until Mischel returned, when they were duly rewarded with their two treats. Mischel actually describes in his recent book, *The Marshmallow Test: Mastering self control*,[1] the various strategies the young children adopted to help themselves hang on for the 20 minutes; some turning their heads away from the cookie for example, so they didn't have to bear the pain of looking at it, others thinking up various games to distract themselves as the minutes ticked away!

So you might think, quite an intriguing, but otherwise totally inconsequential piece of research on childhood behaviour. But in fact the *implications* of that simple experiment, for the later adult lives of these young children, have proved to be far more profound and more enduring than anyone could possibly have predicted, Mischel included.

The astounding follow-up

Over the following years Mischel became interested in tracking whatever connection there might be between the restraint and self-control shown by some of those very young children, and the kinds of lives they were able to build for themselves as adults, compared with those who had chosen the instant gratification, grab-the-cookie route. The results were little short of astounding. During their high school years for example, he found that those who had displayed the restraint and the self-discipline were far more socially competent, they achieved significantly better academic results than their peer group, and they were better able to cope with the typical social and emotional challenges and difficulties they experienced in their teenage years. Even ten years after high school, when they had started their various careers, they were still outperforming their peer group in various key ways. As Mischel described in a recent interview;

> 'By the age of 25 to 30 we found these 'delayers,' as he calls those children who exercised the self-restraint, 'were more able to reach long-term goals, used risky drugs less, achieved higher educational levels, and had a significantly lower body mass index.'[2]

I have to say that last point is an extraordinary comment on the seriousness with which the obesity epidemic is viewed in the USA, namely that to be more or less normal in terms of body weight is now registered as a social achievement! But that aside, the point to hang onto is Mischel's central argument, that the considerable levels of self-discipline and determination that these people had shown at such a young age, had translated into measurably higher levels of achievement in adult life, not only in their working careers but in their married and social lives.

As recently as 2009, Mischel went further, he made use of the opportunity presented to him by the arrival of the new scanning technology to peer into the brains of these 'delayers.' He put them through an fMRI scanner, which simply didn't exist of course when he had first put the marshmallows and cookies in front of those children, or indeed when they had passed out of high school in the 80's. The scanning results really confirmed his earlier observations. He found consistently higher than average activity in the prefrontal cortex of these individuals. The prefrontal cortex is that bulge of the brain just behind the forehead which is involved in so many of our higher level activities, including problem solving and creative thinking and the control of impulsive behaviour.

Interestingly, in explaining the brain activity underlying this disciplined and goal-directed behaviour, he talks about something we discussed at some length in an earlier chapter, namely the constant, reciprocal interplay as we go about our daily lives, between the instant, emotional, limbic system at the heart of the brain, and the cool, slower, rational prefrontal cortex, which developed so much later in our evolutionary history. So he argues, it's the instant emotional limbic system which is instrumental in telling us to grab the cookie, or blow all our savings on whatever it is that excites our desires at any particular moment. It's the cooler, slower, prudent prefrontal cortex which advises us to hang on a minute, wouldn't it be wiser to wait until we get two, and shouldn't we put some of our savings away for a rainy day?

Walter Mischel offers us an utterly decisive conclusion.

> *'So learning to delay gratification early correlates with success as an adult, and,'* he goes on significantly,' *the techniques can be applied to everything from coping with heartbreak, to weight loss, retirement planning and giving up smoking.* '[3]

The key thing to notice here is that word 'learning' that he carefully slips into that first sentence. Because it makes a huge point. What he's saying is that it doesn't matter that we all have different personal starting points, and will therefore reach different levels of determination, because that of course is what it comes down to, fundamentally. But we *can* all learn. We can set about *developing* this fundamental quality, controlling impulse, exercising self discipline, summoning-up determination, and thereby move towards significantly greater personal level of achievement in just about *everything* that we encounter in everyday life, from our jobs to our social and family lives, to *'heartbreak, to weight loss, to retirement planning, to giving up smoking,'* as Mischel puts it. Little wonder that positive psychologist Martin Seligman describes this quality of self-disciplined restraint quite brilliantly as,

> *'the strength that enables the rest of the strengths.'*[4]

The link between self-discipline and achievement

The life-long implications of those research studies might still seem surprising, incredible even, to most of us, even though they were followed up over that extended period of three to four decades. But subsequent research of a similar kind has only served to underline and reinforce Mischel's findings. Angela Duckworth's research work is a very good example. She is from the University of Pennsylvania, a colleague indeed of Martin Seligman, and she has also worked with many groups of schoolchildren, although considerably later on in their school careers, teenagers in fact studying in the American eighth grade. Since there has been such a vast amount of research carried out on the relationship between IQ or general intelligence factor that we discussed earlier, and academic performance, Angela Duckworth moved sideways so to speak, and developed a way of examining the relationship between *self-discipline* and academic achievement.

Her results with her teenagers in many ways mirrored the Mischel findings. It was, she found, the students who scored the highest results on the self-discipline tests, who achieved significantly higher academic results. Why might that be? She suggests that being disciplined has a powerfully influential effect right across the spectrum of human behaviour. So these disciplined teenagers simply didn't fritter away so much time for example, they devoted more time to their homework, they spent much less time on screens, made sure they got to school on time, and so on.

But perhaps the most significant result that we should pick out from Duckworth's programme of research was that it shone a bright spotlight on the fact that the self-discipline ratings of the children were a *far better predictor* of their academic performance, than their IQ scores. What it showed in practice was that there was virtually no meaningful relationship between the IQ ratings of the students and their determination or self-discipline ratings. Many lower IQ children displayed considerable self-discipline for example, and many higher IQ children didn't.

But it was the self-determination ratings that won out. They revealed clearly who were the higher achievers in terms of academic results. So in that sense this research lays down a significant new marker in how we assess capability. It's the determined and self-disciplined people it would seem, who are likely to become the most capable people both academically and socially.[5]

The 'gritty' factor

Angela Duckworth has come up with the now much-quoted term 'grit,' or 'GRIT' as it's normally written, to describe the levels of self-determination that she has found correlate with the highest forms of personal achievement and success, both academic and social. And it's a good word isn't it, in the sense that it conveys an instantly clear message of what we are talking about? A deliberately tough-sounding term because it embraces a bunch of tough characteristics. Characteristics that clearly don't come without real effort. The ability for example to focus not just a fraction of our energies, but all of them, on the task in hand. The willingness to persevere despite setbacks, and stay committed to the objective. And not forgetting the will-power to push aside all those innumerable electronic distractions that hover around all our lives these days, however urgent they might seem at any particular time.

So they are tough and demanding characteristics, no question, but they aren't I suggest, beyond the ability of most of us to strive for. We might achieve them to different degrees of course, and in different time- scales, that's a given. We're all different. But the key point I think that comes out of the research is the sheer value of *awareness*. As psychologist Daniel Goleman keeps telling us, '*The first step is self-awareness*,'[6] Once we are aware of their significance, and the extraordinary contribution they can make to our ability to achieve our goals, we can all make the choice as to whether or not we wish to build that gritty stuff into our make up. If we can the rewards are considerable.

As Angela Duckworth has expressed it, *'grittier individuals are more successful than others, particularly in challenging situations.'*[7]

And it goes without saying doesn't it, that most of us want to be that 'grittier' person who can stand up to challenging situations and win through?

Just to round off this section, and to illustrate that it is a genuinely cross-cultural phenomenon, and not in any way restricted to a particular system or social environment, there has been a more recent and equally extraordinary study, this time from New Zealand. Extraordinary in the sense that it tracked a group of about a thousand children all the way from birth to their early thirties. That's right, fully three decades of life, and it took into account their social and economic environment right up to early adulthood. It's hard to imagine the kind of commitment it must take for a scientist to launch into a study such as this, that can come to dominate virtually a whole professional career? Anyway, this huge extended study came up with findings that profoundly confirm the work of Mischel and Duckworth. Namely that the children who exhibited higher levels of self-control and determination in their *primary* school years, showed up as higher achievers later on, not just in their careers, but as rounded individuals, with healthier and more emotionally stable social lives, and successful career paths.[8]

Can we train ourselves?

What this now very considerable body of research indicates is that those of us who are *naturally* determined and focused have an important and valuable gift, that, whether we realise it or not, has profoundly beneficial effects in just about every area of our lives. Being able to make determinations, and focus our intellectual and physical resources to achieve them, is an immensely life-enhancing characteristic. But once again I suggest, *becoming aware* of the research can in itself be life-changing, in the sense that it can become a powerful motivator for those of us who aren't quite so fortunate in the inheritance stakes. The obvious $64000 question is can we develop a greater amount of this GRIT factor in our own lives?

The research would seem to suggest that we can. It takes commitment and perseverance of course, but then that's no more than we would expect. GRIT doesn't fall into our laps so to speak. But given effort, there seems no doubt that we *can* train ourselves in this way. In fact several researchers, including psychologists like Roy Baumeister at Florida State University, (whom Martin Seligman describes as his favourite social psychologist no less)[9] goes so far as to liken our will-power and our ability to exercise self-control to a physical muscle. That's obviously encouraging, because we know for sure that our physical, bodily muscles *can* be trained and strengthened by regular work-outs at the gym, no matter how feeble they might be when we start out!

Of course, just as we take it for granted that the physical results in the gym are different for each one of us, so too are the results of the will-power training. But the key point is that we can all move forward from our basic starting point. Moreover there is a wider benefit. The studies show clearly that as people learn how to introduce a greater measure of self-discipline and determination into any particular area of their lives, so there are real and measurable spill-over benefits into other areas.

That really makes practical sense doesn't it? We can see that once we get started, there is a genuine virtuous circle set in motion which could lift our whole life-game onto a new level.[10] And as it happens this idea of stretching ourselves to achieve more of our potential is central to the Buddhist approach to life.

The Buddhist perspective

In my experience one of the most deeply-rooted and enduring western stereotypes about Buddhist philosophy would seem to be that it encourages an essentially *passive* approach to life. It's not difficult I think to see how that has arisen. Buddhism is famously *pacifist*, because it believes strongly that war and violence are not only powerfully destructive, but they rarely solve human problems. They serve rather to perpetuate and to create more violence and destruction. And many historians would I think argue that Buddhism has history...particularly the history of the last two centuries...on its side. But that basic *'pacifism'* is often taken to contain within it so to speak, the idea of *'passivism.'* Hence the widely held western belief that a Buddhist practice is essentially a form of *escapism*, and that Buddhists are likely to be quiet, withdrawn and somewhat diffident people, mainly intent upon seeking some kind of way out, some sort of refuge, from the sheer pace and challenge and general hurly burly of modern life.

Nothing could be further from the truth. Buddhism is of course a huge and all-inclusive philosophy so it certainly provides plenty to *think* about. But above all Buddhism is about behaviour, about the way people *live* their lives rather than simply the way they think about them. So it is constantly challenging people out of their comfort zone, encouraging and inspiring them to look for new ways of perceiving and realising their own potential, and new ways of creating value in their lives and the lives of those around them. So fundamentally it is about *challenge*, about self-belief, and about seeking to achieve a bigger life. Moreover Buddhism argues strongly, there is no set starting point, you can take up the challenge and benefit from it at any stage in your life's journey.

Developing a growth mindset

That powerfully progressive, optimistic approach to life is central to Buddhist philosophy and, surprising as it may seem, it is one that comes remarkably close to a growing movement in modern psychology that goes by the intriguing name of *'wise psychological interventions.'*[11] At the heart of this initiative is the idea of finding simple everyday ways of removing mental or psychological barriers that can keep people completely stuck in self-limiting and often damaging patterns of behaviour.

Some of the most influential work in this area, that is now having an effect in schools and colleges right across America, has been carried out by psychologist Carol Dweck, from Stanford University in California, who talks about the literally life-changing power of getting people to develop what she calls *'a growth mindset.'* Although of course there is no overt connection, as it happens her research over many years has focused on an area that comes very close indeed to one of the major objectives we are seeking through a daily Buddhist practice, namely a greater resilience; a greater

ability to face up to and overcome difficulties and challenges that continually confront us.

What she has learned from her studies is immensely accessible. It seems that the determining factor is whether or not
people have what she calls a 'fixed' or a 'growth mindset'
about their lives. That is to say, whether they tend to see
their abilities and their personality as largely fixed in place
and unchanging, or whether they believe that there is
always additional capacity for them to grow and develop.
Carol Dweck has demonstrated that simply getting people
to *believe* in themselves, to take on board this understanding that they *can* develop and extend their abilities through
the effort they are prepared to put in, and therefore rise
above the challenges they encounter, can be life-changing…at any stage of life.

> '*A growth mindset*' she argues,' *is advantageous at all
> stages of life. It allows you to take on more challenges
> and you don't get discouraged by setbacks or find effort
> undermining.*'[12]

A key phrase there of course is, '…*you don't get discouraged
by setbacks…*' It takes us back directly to Martin Seligman's
hope which he defined as '…*the ability to keep going in the
face of defeat.*' That is to say, as you develop this growth
mindset and a greater sense of self-belief, so you develop a
greater capability for coping with setbacks. We all experience set-backs of course. All of us. And we do so repeatedly.
And once again I return to my central argument, that simply
being aware of the potential to overcome them is itself a key
life-changing asset, because once we're aware of it, we can
begin to make more challenging choices for ourselves.

We can begin to develop this inner resilience and assurance that we *can* indeed, change and grow our lives.

As Buddhism tells us so often, *trying, actually making our best efforts, is itself succeeding.*

CHAPTER NINE

Get me to the gym in time

It might seem strange to find neuroscientists and psychologists breaking into the realm normally dominated by the physical education instructor, but that is what is happening. They are both now arguing that regular exercise could prove to be the surest way of maintaining and strengthening the brain's youthful activity.

Some twenty years ago, in the 1990's, a researcher at the prestigious Salk Institute at La Jolla in California, a geneticist called Fred Gage, carried out a seemingly routine experiment with mice. It will have become apparent to the reader by now that a great deal of what we might perhaps call *cutting edge* brain research is carried out on mice and rats. Partly because their brains bear remarkably similar characteristics to our own. Partly for the simple if saddening reason that... well their brains can be examined in detail after an experimental process has been completed. Enough said. Anyway, Fred Gage put these mice through a battery of exercise regimes in the lab to see how rapidly they could master them. The surprise came when the brains of the mice were examined not long afterwards. It was found that the exercise had stimulated the growth of entirely new neurons and connections in their brains. It seemed that a clear link had been established between physical activity in the body and beneficial growth activity in the brain.

That little-known experiment is now having far wider and undoubtedly surprising repercussions. It has long been accepted of course that regular physical exercise can play a very important role in reducing the risk we all carry of falling prey to various forms of bodily disease, heart disease in particular. More recent studies have considerably extended the list of serious, life-shortening illnesses for which regular physical exercise, even of a quite mild kind…a regular 30 minute stroll along the river bank for example or round the local park…can deliver a similar reduced risk, from several forms of cancer for example to the now widespread occurrence of type 2 diabetes, and obesity, both of which have become major issues challenging most western societies.

So as far as the body is concerned there is no doubt that getting out there, regularly, and getting the pulse rate up and the limbs working, is very good news indeed.

But what about the brain? Well psychiatrists and neuroscientists are now telling us that our overall physical fitness can have a profound and enduring effect on our minute-to-minute brain function and cognitive abilities. That is true they argue, throughout the crucial years of childhood development, when the brain is going through a constant series of radical changes as it grows into adulthood. But it is also true they claim, well on into the later years of life. Indeed it is apparently *never* too late to start. So we are being given a powerfully positive message at a time when all western societies are facing the problem of caring for an increasingly ageing population. In fact there is a growing school of thought that it is a decline in overall *physical fitness* that provides a possible explanation for why some people are more prone than others to developing various forms of dementia, a thesis supported by a whole range of studies in the USA and Europe over the past 20 years.[1]

Some interesting studies

One early study for example, carried out at the University of Illinois, and published in the highly respected scientific journal *Nature*, involved a group of elderly people who typically, had taken to living largely sedentary lives, with very little if any regular exercise. When they were encouraged to get up off the sofa and take part in a quite short but regular programme of exercise…and it was the regularity that was crucial rather than anything challenging about the nature of the exercise itself… there was an immediate beneficial effect. After only six months there was a marked improvement not just in their physical well-being as we would expect, but most importantly in their overall cognitive abilities, particularly in their ability with what is called *'executive function.'* Executive function has nothing to do with bossing other people around as you might assume, it's simply the ability to switch our attention from one mental task to another, without losing focus or making errors. Which is what we are constantly asking our brains to do of course, throughout the course of each day.[2]

Another more recent and much larger study, this time in Europe, was even more conclusive. Its great strength was that it followed 1500 people over no less than 20 years of their life, so a relatively large sample, monitored over a very long period of time. The findings were immensely encouraging for all of us. The study showed that when people in their 40's and 50's are prepared to exercise regularly…so there's that crucially important regularity again…although no more than twice a week, which is scarcely an onerous burden, the long-term benefits were literally life-changing. As a result of the exercise these people were…

> '…*much less likely to develop dementia by the time they reached their 60's and 70's, even when potentially confounding factors such as education, drinking and smoking were taken into account.'* And as the author goes on to comment,' *The result should serve as a warning to couch potatoes…*'[3]

So a relatively light but regular exercise regime helping to ward off the onset of such a quality-of-life-destroying illness as dementia.

More recent studies in the USA and across Europe have resulted in an even sharper focus. They have revealed that different forms of exercise can have markedly different cognitive effects. Thus it has been shown for example that aerobic and cardiovascular exercise, walking briskly or running or cycling can have hugely beneficial effects on the hippocampus which plays a crucial role in memory. While so-called strength training, with weights for example leads to better communication across the brain's neural networks, and promotes the growth of new neurons.[4]

So what are the explanations?
If we seek out what might be the underlying reasons for this marked improvement in brain activity with exercise, several theories have been put forward, all of which would seem to generally reinforce and support one another. So one explanation offered is that exercise radically improves blood flow to the brain. The brain is one of the most energy-hungry organs in the body, taking up as much as 25% of the body's

energy consumption, and as such it is highly dependent on a generous supply of oxygen and nutrients through the dense network of arteries and smaller blood vessels that supply it.[5] Regular physical exercise it seems, both extends this blood supply network, and keeps it in a healthy, functioning condition.

Another explanation is that exercise greatly reduces stress. Just the simple act of going for a walk in the park for example can bring about a marked lowering of our general stress levels. And that is crucially important to brain function, because the presence of high levels of stress hormones in the bloodstream can have a markedly inhibiting effect on our ability to think our way through problems clearly and logically. As we all know to our cost in the exam room! But we can all put the walk-in-the-park theory to the test any time. Try it. In fact I was aware of this research some time ago, so whenever I get stuck with my writing and can't seem to think my way round the blockage, I just grab Gatsby my dog, and off we go for a run in Richmond Park. He gets to chase the squirrels…always unsuccessfully I'm happy to say… and I get to breathe a bit faster and exercise the muscles and clear the brain. And time and time again it has done the trick. I sit back down at the keyboard and slice through the blockage. In fact when I think back to my days at Oxford, my tutor, the inspiring Neville Coghill, used to do pretty much the same thing. Half-way through a sticky tutorial he might well lever his long frame up out of his red armchair, and off we would go for a sharp turn around Merton Meadows to clear our brains. It rarely failed.

But back to these explanations, and one of the most intriguing and most persuasive is that physical exercise, even quite mild exercise in fact, increases the release of several key neurotransmitters, such as serotonin and noradrenaline and dopamine, all of which play a vital role in facilitating the passage of signals across the dense network of neural connections.[6] Moreover the exercise stimulates the release of fundamental growth factors that actually speed up neuronal development and the formation of *new connections* between brain cells.[7]

When you pull all those elements together it clearly adds up to a very powerful combination of beneficial effects arising *directly* from regular…regular rather than particularly strenuous notice…physical activity. And my central argument is that knowing about it enables us to make use of it, to fold it as a permanent and regular factor into the way we schedule our day's activities. Indeed it takes us back directly to a piece of Buddhist wisdom that we discussed in an earlier chapter. Buddhism weaves a very practical concern for our general health, and the pursuit of a long and active life, into all that it has to say about the spiritual aspects of our daily lives. It argues that just as *we* carry the responsibility for all the causes that we make, so *we* are responsible for developing our understanding of what is, and what is not, likely to lead to a longer healthier life. We don't simply hand over responsibility for our health into the hands of the medical professionals. We *own* our own health so to speak.

Activity is central to our evolutionary story

Interestingly several scientists, such as David Raichley for example, a biological anthropologist at the University of Arizona, go even further and argue that physical activity improves brain function because it always has so to speak. Activity they claim, has played a key role throughout our long process of evolution. Raichley writes for example;

'physical activity is a strong part of our evolutionary history...our whole physiological system is built on being athletic '[8]

It's a view that is strongly supported by many other scientists in this and related fields. Dr. Edward Archer for example is a physiologist involved in studies into the current obesity and diabetes epidemics. He argues,

'For most of human history, survival required huge amounts of physical exertion. Hunting, gathering, chopping wood, and carrying water provided a dose of physical activity that made deliberate exercise unnecessary. Yet over the past century socio-environmental changes slowly eliminated physical labour.'[9]

That is to say, we are not couch potatoes by nature, even if we may have become one by habit, or as a result of strong cultural influences such as television. Since we have evolved as physically active animals, the argument goes, we absolutely *need* this continuing physical activity to maintain our physiological and our intellectual well-being, rather than regarding it as a sort of take-it-or-leave-it optional extra. It is if you like, a fundamental part of the human package if we want to make the most of our lives.

As evidence in support of this evolutionary argument David Raichley points to the fact that although we are clearly not as physically strong or as fast as our primate cousins and many other animals, we do have far greater *athletic endurance*. We may not have been able to catch an antelope for example, or some other similar prey, leaping so swiftly away from us. But we were able to *run them down*, simply by persevering in our pursuit, mile after mile until they were exhausted. And of course that ability is seen today in our ability to run marathons. No other primate has anything like the human capacity to run for 26 miles! And as our ancestors loped over long distances to run down their prey in this way, so they too would have benefited from an increased flow of these same vital growth factors that we've been talking about, to stimulate neuronal development and increased connectivity in the brain.

Thus although it must be said that there is no conclusive evidence of the causal link, Raichley puts it forward as an interesting and plausible possibility, that it was the constant physical and athletic activity in our ancestors' daily lives, essential to finding food and killing prey and staying alive, that, at the very least contributed, to the significant leap forward in human intelligence.

Exercise as part of everyday

But whatever role this substantial physical activity played in our evolution, there is clearly a growing understanding of the beneficial role that it can play in modern lives, at all ages. In schools both in the US and in the UK for example, there is increasing awareness of the benefits of children having regular bouts of physical activity every single day. John Ratey, Professor of Clinical Psychology at Harvard Medical School is one among many passionate advocates of greater activity as an integral part of the school curriculum at all ages.

> *'We need to have kids moving every day,'* He declares,*'*
> *not just because it makes sense health-wise, but because*
> *it raises test scores.'*[11]

It benefits that is, both the student's body and his or her mind. And the same argument is seen to hold good for older people, in their 50's and 60's and beyond. Much has been made in recent years of the benefits for older people who wish to keep their brains sharp, of spending regular time on various kinds of purely cognitive or brain activity, such as doing crosswords for example or playing various mind games, or playing card games such as bridge. We are reminded however that a key aspect of those kinds of activity is that most often they are carried out while the individual is *physically inactive*, sitting in an armchair. That is to say, those very pastimes that are intended to stimulate the brain, encourage yet more physical inactivity.

Professor Arthur Kramer, a cognitive psychologist who has been working in this field for three decades, is one among many who makes the point that, by playing bridge, you might get much better at playing bridge, but the jury is still out as to whether those kinds of mind games help sustain *broader* cognitive ability. Whereas there is no doubt that increased *physical activity* and regular exercise programmes, can lead, within a matter of just a few months, to really significant improvements. Improvements in mental agility for example, and memory, and the ability to maintain focus on a task, which are beneficial right across the spectrum of the individual's daily life.

And the proof if you like is in the pudding. Professor Kramer who is now 62, very much puts his own advice into practice. He reads the daily paper while spinning along on an exercise bike. At work he goes to the lengths of using a stand-up desk, so he walks for as much as 60 minutes a day on the treadmill underneath. His guidance is uncompromising;

'It's never too late to begin getting these benefits. I'm often asked if I'm 70 will it help me? The answer is: absolutely yes.'[12]

'Absolutely yes' is a good point on which to end this discussion, but just to reinforce the point, I might add my personal experience to Professor Kramer's comments. Just about every day of the year, rain or shine, my beloved golden retriever Gatsby takes me for a 45 minute run in the park, and then several times a week I spend an hour or so working out in a nearby gym. Do I believe that this level of physical activity helps to keep my brain sharp? I have no doubt, absolutely yes!

CHAPTER TEN

The universal pursuit of happiness

It could well be argued I think, that Thomas Jefferson set in motion a revolution that still has a profound influence on the lives of many millions of Americans and others today, when he sat down in that little room in Philadelphia, in the long hot summer of 1776, to struggle with the writing of what was then known prosaically, as the report of the subcommittee of the Second Continental Congress. It subsequently became the great document we all know today as the American Declaration of Independence. The strange fact is that as he was writing and crossing out, and scribbling his revisions in his somewhat spidery hand, revisions that can still be seen today in the margins of the original document, he too was concerned profoundly with the well-being of individual people, set within the framework of the great new society they were in the process of creating. And the words that he wrote in seeking to express that complex idea have since become deeply embedded, not simply in the American psyche, but I suggest, in much of the world's consciousness, as a kind of ideal to be pursued, a spiritual Everest to be climbed.

'We hold these truths to be self evident,' he wrote,*' that all men are created equal, that they are endowed by their*

creator with certain unalienable(sic) Rights, that
among these are Life, Liberty and the pursuit of
Happiness.'[1]

Those lines are so direct and so extraordinarily bold that
they still have a powerful resonance when we read them
today, despite their instant familiarity. But the key point I
want to make is that in formulating this ideal, these fine
words didn't spring unaided into Jefferson's head. Not at all.
He was consciously walking in the footsteps and embracing
the ideas of a whole string of great philosophers who had
thought deeply about the human condition and, above all,
about how it might be made better. As Jefferson himself
acknowledged, he was going back to the thoughts of earlier
philosophers from Aristotle and Cicero in classical times, to
the great eighteenth century English philosophers, Locke
and Stuart Mill. So when he wrote about the pursuit of
happiness he wasn't talking about what we might call, for
the sake of shorthand, good cheer, laughter and general
light-heartedness. No, he was talking about something far
broader and deeper and more enduring. As the American
historian Garry Mills has attempted to describe it in his
insightful book, *Inventing America*,

'When Jefferson spoke of pursuing happiness he had
nothing vague or private in mind. He meant public
happiness, which is measurable; which is indeed the test
and justification of government.'

Incidentally, Abraham Lincoln, just about a century later,
was walking directly in Jefferson's footsteps when, in his
inaugural address he spoke of the power of altruism and
compassion,' *appealing to the better angels of our nature,'* as
he put it. Then, a further 100 years on, we have John

Kennedy, treading much the same path, challenging people to think not about what society can do for *them*, but what they can *contribute* to our society.

And as we move around this somewhat elusive and slippery word happiness, to get a better grip on what it means in our daily lives, I think it helps to bear in mind the words of Robert Solomon I quoted earlier, because they give us I think, a stable and steady starting point.

> *'How we think and feel about ourselves has an impact on who we actually are.'* These kinds of thoughts, he goes on, *'…don't just move us and inform us, or supplement our busy day to day existence. They change us, make us different kinds of people, different kinds of beings.'*[3]

Thus he is saying, striving to understand what we really mean when we talk about pursuing happiness, can have a transforming effect on our lives,*' make us different kinds of people.'*

So what are we talking about?

Whether we have an active spiritual life or not there is I suggest, a strong underlying sense in the West that happiness is very much a matter of…well chance or accident… rather than as a result of any particular approach or attitude to life. If you happen to have a generous helping of happiness then you can thank your lucky stars for it. With the unspoken implication that that is pretty much where it came from! There is a strong cultural tradition in the West that you can build *material* success from a lowly starting point and there are of course many frequently recounted examples of just that. Rags to riches and all that. However we don't it seems have a similar cultural tradition that applies to this area of happiness; that you can *build for your-self* a happy life whatever your starting-out circumstances happen to be. It just doesn't exist.

Buddhism however, with its essential humanism and its belief in the power of the human spirit does present us with just such a promise. It is essentially focused on the attainment of happiness, for oneself and others, as the fundamental objective of human life. In this life that is, in the here and now, rather than in some heavenly hereafter. Even as I write that, after many years of Buddhist practice, I am aware of just how bold and uncompromising a vision of life that is. All the more remarkable perhaps in that it is a view of life that was evolved all those centuries ago, and yet it accords very strongly with the views of today's evolutionary biologists and positive psychologists, who also define the pursuit of happiness as the ultimate motivational force in life. Ultimate in the sense that it doesn't require any further definition. It speaks for itself.

Moreover Buddhism argues that essentially it is a matter of *choice*, that whether we realise it or not, whether we understand it or not, we have within us all the resources we need to *choose* happiness in this life. Essentially it argues, it is a matter of self determination. And it goes much further, it proposes that we can learn how to achieve that goal not just in the good and the golden times, but anytime, even when things are resoundingly challenging and down-casting.

That is of course a huge and life-changing idea, and one that is so unusual, so counter-intuitive, that it is extremely difficult for most of us to accept when we first encounter it.

There must be some sort of catch we say to ourselves. It takes time to learn that there isn't. That the catch is primarily our own lack of conviction in ourselves.

A deeper understanding

Since it plays such a key and universal role in human motivation it would undoubtedly help, I suggest, before we go any further, if we try to establish a common understanding of what kinds of things we mean when we use this much-over-used word happiness, rather than just assuming that we are describing the same thing. Because undoubtedly vagueness is an issue. It is often said for example that happiness is such a *subjective* feeling that no adequate definition is possible. It's very much like the taste of the strawberry, we know what it is when we actually *experience* it, but we would be hard-pushed to attempt to define it! But that doesn't really get us much further does it, in terms of a deeper understanding?

Harvard psychologist and international happiness researcher Daniel Gilbert for example, argues that the toughest thing about studying happiness is that researchers measure quite different things, and then talk about them as if they were interchangeable. The modern French philosopher Pascal Bruckner goes much further. '*Happiness*,' he declares,' *is the vaguest word on earth, it's hopeless.*'[4]

And he would seem to have the full support of someone as experienced in the field of positive psychology as Martin Seligman, who is driven to exclaim in his book *Flourish*, that the word happiness itself;

> '…is so overused that it has become almost meaningless. It is an unworkable term for science, or for any practical

goals such as education, therapy, public policy or just changing your personal life.'[5]

And since that's precisely what we have in mind, changing our personal lives for the better, we should perhaps take serious note of his comments. Not only do we have the words *'overused,'* and *'almost meaningless'* squeezed into the same sentence, but we can all hear the frustration in his voice, as we were meant to of course. And that's my main argument. It's precisely because it *is* such an elusive and slippery word, and yet at the same time, such an important issue for every one of us, that we can only gain from picking the word up so to speak, and looking at it from all directions to see what emerges.

And there is a further point that arises perhaps because of it's overuse; the word happiness in the modern idiom, or to the modern ear conveys I suggest, a somewhat lightweight and transient emotion. The philosopher and neuroscientist Sam Harris touches upon this issue in *The Moral Landscape*, when he writes,

'Much of the scepticism I encounter when speaking about these issues comes from people who think' happiness' is a superficial state of mind and that there are far more important things in life than' being happy.'[6]

That is the very heart of the matter isn't it? If he is correct, and the happiness word summons up for most people a somewhat superficial state of mind, images of merriment and laughter and smiley faces and good cheer; things that are being experienced at a *particular moment* in time, essentially transient, then clearly there *are indeed* many more important things in life than that kind of happiness.

We need all the good cheer and merriment we can get into our lives. No question. But those images are undoubtedly *not* what is meant by happiness in the studies centred for example around positive psychology. Nor I might add, what is meant by the word happiness when it appears, as it does so frequently in Buddhist teachings, describing it as *the* central motivation in human life.

Moreover it can't mean can it, what we so often take for granted that it means, namely the *absence* of difficulties or anxieties in our life? If that were the case it would very rarely occur for anyone, given that for all of us, difficulties and problems of one kind or another are an absolutely staple part of our lives. Day in day out, we all face problems, whatever our status or our position or circumstances in life.

Thus happiness in Buddhism is unquestionably *not* defined as it is so often in the dreams we create for ourselves, as arriving at some place or some space in our lives where everything is sunshine and blue skies. That clearly is the stuff of dreams. Whereas Buddhism is daily life. Happiness in Buddhism is defined very much in terms of learning the kinds of *attitudes and values* we need to master to enable us to build this sense of stability and confidence and optimism that is strong enough and resilient enough not to be dismantled by all the tough stuff we encounter, the problems and the setbacks and the sorrows that we all struggle with on a daily basis.

What about well-being?

Perhaps the closest we come to an appropriate word or phrase, in both those contexts, and certainly one that seems to me to capture more fully what we are talking about in this particular discussion, is well-being. Why? Because it clearly expresses a much broader and deeper and more solidly based, and altogether less transient emotion. As expressed in a recent article on happiness research for example;

> *'Happiness in it's everyday sense is akin to pleasure or joy, something we experience in the moment...When psychologists talk about happiness, however, they usually use the term to mean our overall and long-term subjective well-being and life satisfaction.'[7]*

That is the absolute key to what we are talking about isn't it, the crucial experience of 'overall and long-term subjective well-being?'

A brief example from my own experience that helps perhaps to make the point occurred recently when I was invited to talk to an audience of businessmen about Buddhist values. When I happened to use the phrase, *'happiness in the work place ,'* there was I thought a noticeably cool reception. As soon as I switched to talking about *'well-being in the work place,'* there was an immediate understanding and appreciation of what we were really discussing, an altogether more substantial, more stable, more deeply-based state of life.

And once again that distinction finds support among the social scientists. As Daniel Goleman explains in some detail in his book *Working with Emotional Intelligence.* When comparisons are made between the effectiveness or the productivity of people at work, the difference is often found to lie not so much in the purely *technical* know-how or skills of different people, but much more broadly in their overall sense of stability and well-being, that becomes manifest in their greater capacity for handling relationships, or dealing in a calm and focused way with difficulties that arise.[8] We all want a stable and solidly-based boss don't we, in resolving crises at work, rather than an irritable and tetchy one?

Embracing sadness and loss

But perhaps most important of all, this phrase well-being has so much greater depth and capacity, that it can embrace within its compass without difficulty, the ideas of mischance and misfortune, and even of sadness and loss. That capacity, which again is certainly embodied in the Buddhist concept of happiness or well-being, finds multiple echoes in the work of modern sociologists such as professor Tal Ben-Shahar for example, who for many years taught in the positive psychology programme at Harvard. He talks directly about the need for us to *get real* when we are considering the concept of happiness. Optimism and happiness he argues cannot be about being eternally cheerful. That would be hopelessly unreal. Rather it has to be about getting up close to and getting to grips with the pains and problems we encounter every day, so that we truly understand them, and learn how to *work through them* to a better place.

Working through problems to a better place is, it seems to me, the very nature of well-being. So he talks of the immense value that we can generate in our lives by, as he puts it, learning to look for the *seeds of the positive*, in things that go wrong, rather than expending our energies hanging onto the sense of loss or damage or despair.[9]

The plain fact is that for as long as we continue to regard problems and difficulties as a direct challenge to our equanimity and peace of mind, then by definition, that equanimity and peace of mind will continue to be challenged! In a sense we are locking ourselves into what you might call a self-conditioning process. And since the problems inevitably continue to occur in our lives so does the negative response. In a way it becomes very much like Pavlov's dogs, we carefully forge this more or less unbreakable link in our minds between the occurrence of problems and the anxiety and stress with which we have always associated them. It becomes so much the way of the world for ourselves and all those around us that we never challenge it. We accept it as the only reality.

Is it conceivable that there might be a quite different reality?

Basically it's a matter of choice

Well once again Buddhism presents us with an unusual paradox. In fact it stands the usual response on its head. It argues that instead of responding to any kind of problem that we encounter negatively, and with the associated anxiety, it is eminently possible to *train ourselves* to see them quite differently. We have persistently trained ourselves to see them negatively. We can just as well Buddhism argues, train ourselves to see them positively.

The way Buddhism expresses that idea is to say that we need to grasp the immense power that resides in our *freedom of choice*. We can choose how we respond. It's as simple and as life-changing as that. No more, no less.

We have the intellectual and spiritual ability Buddhism argues, to make the *determination* to see problems and challenges not as an inevitably painful and anxiety-making factor in our lives, but positively , as an opportunity. Indeed you could argue, as the *only* opportunity we have to grow and develop our resilience and self-confidence and optimism and general all-round life capability.

Before you throw the book across the room with frustration, just stay with the argument for a bit because it still has some way to go. If you think about it, the common response to such a radical idea is bound to be deeply sceptical because it underlines just how deeply conditioned we all are to the negativity and anxiety that we allow problems to generate. We all of course prefer to concentrate on the sunshine and happiness in our lives but as we all know so well, harsh reality has this nasty and persistent habit of intruding. Indeed Buddhism was created out of that harsh reality, out of the perception that life is tough, and that making our happiness out of that toughness is so to speak, our deal. We just have to get on with it. So at the very heart of Buddhism we have this fundamental understanding, that how we *choose to respond* to that toughness, governs completely, indeed determines, the kind of life we can build for ourselves.

How we *choose* to respond determines our outcomes. And the more we learn to respond *positively*, the greater and more stable the sense of well-being we can create in our lives.

Moreover this age old Buddhist principle has become the driving force behind one of the most successful modern methods adopted by psychologists for the treatment of anxiety and depression, As one leading exponent of this method has expressed it, they have learned that they can transform a persons experience, by changing the way that person *views* or pays attention to that experience.[10] That is to say we can change fundamentally the actual nature of our experience by *choosing* to view it positively rather than negatively. Another major practitioner in this field, Dr. Steven Southwick from the Yale School of Medicine, expresses a very similar view. We should view the invaluable quality of resilience, he argues, the ability to rise above the problems and challenges all of us inevitably encounter as we go through the stuff of everyday, as a set of skills that can be *learned*, rather than as we normally tend to view it, as a characteristic or a disposition that some of us just happen to have been lucky enough to inherit. He writes;

> 'Much of the new evidence suggests that with a little practice, anyone can develop resilience.'[11]

Notice he carefully chooses to say 'anyone.' So, to sum up, If we genuinely seek to establish a strong and resilient sense of well-being at the core of our lives then that can only be found, Buddhism argues, in the very midst of all the problems that life throws at us, since that is the *only place there is*. That is the only reality! Indeed the more challenging the problems we encounter and overcome, the greater the potential happiness they can release, since they draw out greater inner courage and resilience to challenge and overcome them. We grow to become you might say, our most *capable selves*, and capability we come to learn, is a very important ingredient indeed in nurturing this stuff we call well-being in our lives.

The power of altruism

In the book I've quoted from a moment ago, *Flourish*, Martin Seligman recounts for us a brief but immensely illuminating anecdote about a colleague, Stephen Post;

> 'My friend Stephen Post,' he writes, 'Professor of Medical Humanities at Stony Brook, tells a story about his mother. When he was a young boy, and his mother saw that he was in a bad mood, she would say, 'Stephen, why don't you go out and help someone?' Empirically

Ma Post's maxim has been put to rigorous test, and we scientists have found that doing a kindness produces the single most reliable momentary increase in well-being of any exercise we have tested.'[12]

That has to be one of the most valuable life-lessons, packaged into just half-a-dozen lines. And what is extraordinary is that he's able to tell us that Ma Post's homespun wisdom has been put to *'rigorous'* scientific test, to confirm that simply doing something for other people, showing compassion or altruism, produces the single most reliable increase in our own well-being. This simple human story illustrates I suggest, a couple of other qualities that are fundamental to our understanding of what well-being is about.

One is that this experience, well-being, deeply-based happiness if you will, doesn't exist just in our own heads, although we commonly believe that to be the case. It is very much a *social* experience. We are in our deepest nature gregarious animals.

We have evolved to flourish within a network of social relationships. Our inner sense of well-being is generated essentially through the nature of the relationships we establish with the world around us, from the basic pleasure we take in our natural environment, through to the experience of human relationships at all levels in our lives. When we experience them, they strengthen and reinforce all our creative energies. When those relationships break down for whatever reason, the effects can be devastating in all areas of our life. We are not only less happy, we operate as individuals under stress, and our performance is greatly reduced. Psychologist Barbara Fredrickson for example, from the University of North Carolina, is one among many who describes social connectedness as a powerful *'wellness behaviour.'*[13]

Not in someone else's gift

The second understanding that we might take from the Ma Post anecdote is that our personal well-being is not so to say, in someone else's gift, we have to learn to *make it for ourselves.* That is undeniably a hard lesson to learn because we do commonly believe that our personal happiness is indeed dependent upon someone or something else; upon our partner for example, or our child, or our friends, or our job. Or on earning a million pounds. The plain fact is that we have to go out and make our long-term well-being for ourselves, out of our own determination and action, just as Stephen Post was asked by his perceptive mother to *take some action,* to go out and help someone else in order to lift himself out of his own negativity.

And that phrase, 'take some action,' is well worth taking to heart, because it carries a profound truth of its own. As one utterly practical Buddhist teacher put it to me once, if we think in terms of *pursuing* happiness in some way, then we are really on the wrong track, because none of us knows how to achieve that. Where do we start? In which direction do we run? We come much closer to it he argued, if we think of happiness as a sort of by-product, a quality that *emerges* into our lives when we take action to create value in some way, particularly in ways that have beneficial effects in *other people's* lives. That certainly chimes with what Martin Seligman told us a moment ago, about the results of his studies into altruism, and it's fascinating to find that Buddhist teacher's view, echoed directly, even down to the choice of words, by another prominent psychologist who works in this field, Sonja Lyubomirski from the University of California, when she writes,

> *'…even the familiar phrase' pursuit of happiness,'*
> *implies that happiness is an object that one has to chase*
> *or discover…I prefer to think of the 'creation' or the' con-*
> *struction' of happiness because research shows that it's*
> *in our power to fashion it for ourselves.'[14]*

We seem to have travelled a long way from Thomas Jefferson's timeless phrase, but we are I think getting a closer fix on what we mean when we use the happiness word aren't we? It's certainly not forcing ourselves to be cheerful regardless of what is going on in our lives. It doesn't help to look to others to deliver it for us. And it doesn't just happen to us as a result of good fortune. The kind of durable, deep-seated and above all resilient well-being that we are talking about can't simply be dependent upon the play of *external* events. This happens and we like it…and are happy. That happens and we don't like it…and are unhappy. Now up now down, a bit like a cork in a swell. It can only come, we now understand *from within.* We have to make it, through the values that we hold, and the choices that we make, and the kinds of altruistic and compassionate actions and responses that we fold into our lives.

The evolutionary question

There are two interesting and important lines of research that help us I think to bring this quest for greater under-standing bang up to date. One might be called the evolutionary question, this human hunger for happiness that modern psychology has identified as a universal quality. As one leading researcher expresses it;

> *'In almost every nation…from the United States to*
> *Greece and Slovenia, to South Korea and Argentina and*
> *Bahrain…when asked what they want most in life,*
> *people put happiness at the top of the list.'[15]*

Everything but everything that we are today is there because of some evolutionary advantage that it conferred at some time in the past. So we are compelled to ask, what part has the quest for well-being played in our evolutionary path? It turns out that it's a rather more complex and difficult question to answer than the evolutionary rationale for the prominent *negative* emotions that we all experience, such as fear and anger for example. Put at its simplest, it has been well established that fear clearly galvanises us to perceive and to avoid or run away from life-threatening dangers. Anger just as clearly strengthens and emboldens us to challenge and fight an aggressor. So these negative emotions it has been noted, equip us to deal effectively with immediate and short-term challenges.

But what might be the direct evolutionary benefits of well... pleasure, just feeling pretty good about life? One scientist who has taken it upon herself to find satisfying and above all practical answers to this question is psychologist Barbara Fredrickson whom I mentioned a moment ago. Over the course of a substantial series of studies Fredrickson has created what has now become widely known as the *'broaden and build'* explanation for positive emotions, that adds several new layers of meaning to the Buddhist perception that human happiness, human well-being, is the very purpose of our life.

So the *broaden* bit of Fredrickson's explanation basically describes the way in which all the positive emotions, hope, optimism, well-being in general, actually broaden and improve the *way our brains function* in a whole range of ways, and so enable us to be altogether more effective human beings, more creative, more imaginative, more compassionate, more courageous.

'Positive feelings,' she argues,' change the way our brains work, and expand the boundaries of our experience...'[16]

The *build* bit of the explanation essentially describes the way in which this day-to-day improved functioning arising from our positive and optimistic mind-set steadily builds up and strengthens our *longer-term ability* to face up to and overcome major challenges, which have occurred continually throughout the long path of our evolution. And of course, the capabilities our ancestors evolved as they made their way in jungle and savannah, have been passed on to us, as we make our way through our modern urban jungles.

We perform more effectively

From this series of really intriguing studies she cites several crucial ways in which this improvement in our overall functioning can be seen. So for example she has used brain-imaging studies to show that positive, optimistic, up-beat moods substantially increase the scope and the sharpness of our visual attention, so that we can gather in more information from our environment, and retain more. This has been buttressed by studies that show that students for example retain far more of their study material, when they are in a positive frame of mind, compared to their being stressed or depressed in some way. And this does ring true doesn't it, from our daily experience? We know that when we are in the best of moods and firing-on-all-cylinders as we put it, we are altogether more alert and more noticing and creative, altogether more efficient at handling the daily stuff of life.

A positive and optimistic mind-set also improves our spontaneous creativity. So crucially it increases our ability to get to grips with problems and come up with solutions. We've all had the experience of the office brain-storming session, when all the good ideas come pouring out of the refreshingly optimistic, up-beat colleague across the table.

And finally a positive mood vastly improves our social skills. We tend to like people more, and they like us. Again this may have come down to us from the small tribal groups in which our direct ancestors lived, but it is certainly part of our common everyday experience today.

According to Fredrickson's proposition, these emotional and social rewards, if I may put it that way, that come from this regular daily flow of positive experiences, gradually develop and reinforce a more resilient and positive state of mind, an altogether more solidly-based state of well-being.

'As positive emotions compound,' she claims,' people actually change for the better.'[17]

And changing for the better is essentially what this book is all about!

We are in effect training ourselves
Basically what Fredrickson is arguing I suggest, is that when we *consciously and deliberately* work at cultivating this up-beat, optimistic, positive outlook as we go about coping with the normal stuff of everyday, that makes us altogether more effective human beings. That's the reward we get, this pervasive sense of well-being. And as we repeat that day after day, we are in effect, *training ourselves*, even if we are not in any way aware of it in that sense. We are building for ourselves a tougher and more resilient spirit that will carry us more effectively through the rough times. Indeed you could say it's the stuff of all training. The violinist who

practices all day for weeks and months on end to be able to walk out onto the concert platform and overcome their nerves to deliver a stunning performance. The athletes who push themselves through the pain barrier every day on the practice track, so that they can walk out into the inferno of the Olympic arena and still deliver their personal best.

The extraordinary thing for me I have to say, is just how close Fredrickson's research findings come to the Buddhist understanding of a deep-seated sense of well-being, built upon our experience of facing up to and overcoming life's daily challenges.

The Buddhist perspective

Buddhism was born out of the perception that ordinary everyday human life contains a great deal of suffering, and the great desire to do something about it; to equip us if you like, to handle the tough stuff of life more effectively. Central to that is the idea of changing fundamentally the way in which we *view* all the problems and all that challenging stuff that comes at us as we go through life.

Put simply, Buddhism argues that we are all conditioned by our experience to see the problems and the difficulties we encounter as painful and unwelcome. Buddhism asks us to train ourselves to turn that view literally on its head. To see them not simply as an inevitably painful part of human life, but as *essential* to developing our inner strength and happiness. It doesn't take much reflection to see the life-transforming power of the idea. Take gravity for example. The ever-present pull of gravity on Earth, weighing down upon us, has forced our body to evolve a physique so strong and so muscular that we can not only bear that burden and walk upright, but we can run and jump and leap over obstacles and not even be aware of the burden.

The essential Buddhist proposition is that just as the burden of gravity is the essential environment that has enabled us to grow our muscular physique, so the burden of problems and difficulties is the environment that enables us to grow a strong and resilient and resourceful spirit. Indeed, if you think about it for a moment, they represent the *only* spiritual gym in town. The only way we can develop our ability to face up to challenges and to solve problems…is to face up to challenges and to solve problems. There is no other.

Nobody is saying that that is an easy lesson to learn or to apply. Of course it isn't. But we need to acquire the change in *perception* before we can start the learning process, and the plain fact is that if we look into our lives, we all have some experience of how it works. When we meet challenges head on, or overcome major problems we *do* feel a huge sense of personal achievement. We pass a big exam that was a real stretch. We overcome a serious illness. We help a friend overcome a disabling bout of anxiety, and the victory gives us a powerful sense of elation. And the bigger the problem overcome, the greater the sense of elation. For a while we feel strengthened and uplifted, and we experience a much greater confidence in our ability to handle life, not just in that particular area, but right across the spectrum of our lives. That's a key point. The effect is as broad and as far reaching as that. From the increased confidence comes the greatly increased sense of well-being.

Basically all that Buddhism is encouraging us to do is to hang onto that idea, to be aware of it, and to build on it and reinforce it with the energy and the inner confidence that comes from the daily practice. So that instead of it being a short-lived or a fleeting moment, it can become a daily one.

We are back if you like absolutely, with Fredrickson's proven concept of *broaden and build!*

I mentioned earlier that there were *two* interesting and important lines of research that we ought to follow up. One was Fredrickson's evolutionary studies, which we have just been discussing. The second is concerned with *how* we get there. What can we learn about the how and where of well-being, and that's where we go next.

CHAPTER ELEVEN

The how and the where of well-being

It is little short of remarkable just how much research there has been over the past decade or so, seeking to define more accurately what kinds of values and behaviour make people feel good about themselves and their lives and their relationships; what kinds of things people have uppermost in their minds when they talk about a sense of stability or fulfilment when they look across the totality of their lives. And that is of course an important point to emphasise, that we are talking about the *totality* of people's lives, the average sense of balance and well-being, rather than the inevitable short-term fluctuations from day to day, or week to week.

This sort of research has steadily grown from a trickle a decade or so ago, to a veritable avalanche. As Professor Layard from the London School of Economics has noted,

> *'Science used to be about the control of nature, but in recent decades, social science, psychology and neurology have given us a new ability to manage our inner selves and social structures so as to increase happiness.'*[1]

All I would add is that it's a great pity in my view, that so many, or even most of these studies rarely see the light of day outside publication in some relatively remote and inaccessible journal, such as *the Journal of Behaviour and Social Psychology*, or the *Review of General Psychology*, or the *Journal of Personality and Social Psychology*, which is where some of Barbara Fredrickson's rivetingly interesting evolutionary studies were published, that we discussed a moment ago. There they are read by professionals in the field, and often quoted in their equally fascinating papers, later to be published in similar equally inaccessible journals!

It's a great pity because the plain fact is that this research is about us. All of us ordinary people. And it's opening up for us a whole new world of insights into how we can set about making really beneficial changes in how we go about our daily lives. If we wish to of course, that is the key proviso, we alone have to generate the will. But in order to generate the will, we need of course to have the awareness.

Take for example something as seemingly simple as encouraging people who might be feeling a bit low, or deeply anxious, or even severely depressed, to keep a gratitude journal. What does that mean? It means setting up a routine so that on a daily basis the person actually writes down in a personal diary, just three or four things that have taken place during the day that they feel truly grateful for. Pretty simple yes? Not necessarily big things. A cheerful greeting from a neighbour. A warm and happy interchange with the check-out girl. A visit to a gallery. A brightly coloured chaffinch coming to the bird table. Very ordinary daily events But many studies have revealed overwhelmingly, that an action as simple and as easy to carry out, can give a powerful and above all an *enduring* boost to people's sense of well-being and their appreciation of the value of their lives. All that is actually happening is that people are actually taking the time and the trouble to *recognise* their gratitude, and then to *express* it, even if only to themselves.

What's more, this highly desirable result, an increased sense of connection and of well-being seems to hold true whatever their actual life-circumstances happen to be at the time, and that is such a key point and so counter-intuitive, that it's worth digging a little deeper.

It's not the circumstances that determine our life state

One of the most persistent comments that is made in these papers, and as it happens, in countless Buddhist commentaries as well, is one that most of us find very hard to grasp or believe in. Namely that we can create for ourselves a stable and enduring sense of well-being in our daily lives, almost regardless of the actual circumstances and events that we happen to be living through. That is as I've said, something that is very hard indeed for most of us to accept, and the sociologists clearly understand and acknowledge that enduring difficulty.[2]

But nevertheless, as they make clear, study after study reinforces the conclusion that the actual circumstances and events *in themselves*, have only a very small impact on our overall sense of well-being, either up or down, negative or positive. What I still find somewhat surprising is that the psychologists are so sure of their ground that they are actually prepared to put a figure on it, a surprisingly small figure at that! It seems clear that it is our underlying attitude to life, our *gratitude attitude* to life if you like, that has the dominant role to play in our on-going, day-to-day life state, rather than transient circumstances, even bad ones.

Here's a typical passage;

> '*As significant as our major life events are to each of us,*
> *studies suggest that they actually determine a tiny(sic)*
> *percentage of our happiness...many past investigations*
> *reveal that all life circumstances and events put together*
> *account for only about 10 percent of how happy different*
> *people are...although,'* the researcher adds in a slightly
> apologetic tone...' *you may find it hard to believe.'*[3]

Indeed we do. I ought to say at once that the figure itself is
not the crucial point. I quote that passage simply to underline the fact that there are grounds, from both long-
established Buddhist teachings, and now from numerous
objective, scientifically managed studies, to encourage us to
challenge and question our deeply-held convictions that
our current life circumstances play *the central and major role*
in our experience of well-being. They don't. As another
eminent sociologist puts it powerfully in just a dozen words,

> '*we are not simply victims of our situation, or indeed of*
> *our past.'*[4]

So what's the key implication? Well it seems that we could
do ourselves a really big favour simply by working harder to
take this new understanding on board. It has become clear
that the mindset that most of us continue to hang onto, that
our circumstances are *the dominant dimension* determining
our life state, is a major delusion or misperception on our
part. We are free to rise above our circumstances as soon as
we *choose* to do so.

And the sociologists and the psychologists now argue
strongly, that they have a much firmer grasp of the values

and the behaviours that will most readily enable us to make that life-changing choice. We have already talked at some length about the happiness-value of altruism, let's briefly look at three or four other life-enhancing behavioural strategies that we could immediately begin to build in to our lives. Nothing is stopping us! All we need is the awareness first of all. And then the *determination* to put that awareness to work.

Gratitude

Gratitude in so many ways runs in tandem with altruism. There is plenty of discussion in the research findings of the way in which a genuine spirit of gratitude can be literally life-transforming, unlocking a wealth of positive and beneficial effects for the giver as well as the receiver, and indeed for anyone within earshot, because it is such a warm and human interchange. Just going out of our way for example, to express our thanks to someone has been shown to have a positive effect on our sense of well-being for several days after the event itself. But that of course is just a beginning. They talk about gratitude as a much broader, *whole life* approach to the way we take each day, a wide-ranging gratitude attitude you might say. About having a keen and lively sense of appreciation for all the ordinary things in our life, not taking relationships for granted, recognising all that we have, as opposed to focusing on what we don't happen to have. They also talk interestingly of gratitude being *'incompatible with'* negative emotions such as anger and resentfulness. You simply can't be grateful and angry at the same time. And a deeply-held sense of gratitude can drive out negative thoughts. One psychologist actually describes it in that way. *'Gratitude,'* she writes, *'helps people cope with stress and trauma.'*[5]

So clearly gratitude, for small things as well as for big, can be a hugely powerful and beneficial quality to nurture if you like, as an essential element in the daily-ness of our lives.

Focusing on strengths rather than weaknesses

How many of us spend hours beating ourselves up over things we can't do, or that we got wrong? Hours of essentially wasted energy. The eminent psychologist Ruut Veenhoven from Erasmus University in Rotterdam, talks about the immense value to our sense of well-being in coming to know more clearly what our strengths are, and being completely honest to ourselves about our weaknesses or inabilities. And when you give it just a moment's thought, that is so obviously an essential step in developing an effective life strategy. Far better to focus our energies and our plans around our strengths, rather than being constantly anxious about our weaknesses, or beating ourselves up over them yet again. Or worse, trying to deny them and paper over them.

Veenhoven talks of the immense value of this kind of utterly practical, down-to-earth wisdom. He argues that one of the least talked-about secrets of a stable sense of well-being, is *'learning to love the life we have,'* learning that is to be comfortable with who we are, and what our qualities are. It's a view that ties in so closely with what we've just been talking about, in relation to building our gratitude and appreciation for what we *have*, as opposed to expending our energies yearning for what we simply *want*.

Living in the now

When we talk about grasping the value of the moment you might at first glance think that we are in a Buddhist seminar.

Buddhism often talks about the *'suchness'* of our immediate experience, as a way of describing the importance to the quality of our daily lives of raising the level of our awareness and our attention to the reality of *this* moment. Today's sociologists have come to a very similar view and they talk at some length and in great detail about the importance for the richness of our lives of learning to live in the now, making the most of *this* moment, *this* piece of work, *this* moment of relaxation in a summer garden, *this* conversation…the person who is with us now is *for this moment*, the most important person in our life. Rather than, as is so often the case, just *passing through* what we're doing at the moment, sometimes almost oblivious of it, because we're too busy or too anxious hurrying on the way to the next something. On so many occasions we find ourselves wrapped up in anxieties about something that has happened already, which we allow to go on spinning around inside our head, or devoting our attention to something that will happen later on or tomorrow. We all do it of course, all the time, without a moment's reflection.

When we do pause long enough to think about it, even momentarily, what we *choose* to notice, what we *choose* to pay attention to, *is* our experience, it *is* our life. So you can see the damaging effects of not paying attention to what we're doing now, because most of our attention is directed to what we're going to do next. As Eckhart Tolle, the writer on spiritual issues has expressed it,

> *'Do I want the present moment to be my friend or my enemy. The present moment is inseparable from life, so you are really deciding what kind of relationship you want to have with life.'*[6]

Remarkably, that thought takes us to a lesson that lies at the heart of a Buddhist practice, namely that the choice is always ours; the *cause* that we make in paying attention to the now of our lives, delivers the *effect* of an altogether richer life experience.

A sense of purpose

One of the things that struck me most forcibly when I first started to go to Buddhist discussion meetings and seminars, long before I myself took up the practice in any steady or meaningful way, was that people would very often say that they felt more focused somehow, even if they couldn't define precisely why. They no longer felt so blown off course by random events, or they felt able to make decisions more readily because they had a clearer sense of a *purpose or direction*. The extraordinary thing is that over the past few years there has been a veritable flood of social research on that very issue. The word purpose has become a sort of golden word because the research has highlighted the huge value inherent in our trying to establish a clear sense of direction or purpose in our lives, a stability you might say underlying the inevitable daily flux of events and incidents. It seems clear that it brings with it a whole slew of extraordinary benefits from living longer to sleeping better, less anxiety, greater resilience, more compassion, and a greater sense of all-round well-being. And this range of positive effects has been identified whether the individual is 20 or 70.[7]

So it's clearly something that we should consider nurturing, isn't it? This sense of being in some way attached to a purpose that is positive and value-creating, that derives of course from our core life-values, but is larger and broader than the daily detail of our own lives. For some people of course that higher purpose is found in religious belief, or by involvement in charitable or social work that enhances other people's lives. But by no means necessarily so. It might be expressed for example in a simple personal determination to create the most value in one's environment, whatever the circumstances.

Try slowing down

Try it! I'm an extremely active person, over active my wife Sarah says, always in too much of a hurry. But since getting to grips with Buddhist philosophy, not to mention all this sociology, I've really tried to *slow down*, in order to take in and experience whatever I'm doing from moment to moment. It's not easy. With our hugely active and restless minds, it's not a skill that comes easily to us. There is so much stuff coming at us from all directions, immersed as we are in our hyperactive, adrenaline-fuelled modern lifestyles, and with our constantly demanding 24/7 connectivity. We can experience so much guilt if we don't go on dealing with that list of uncompleted jobs, or the difficult email we haven't responded to yet, or the up-coming interview, or the errand we promised to run.

But then, lots of things of value are difficult to fold into our lives. Once we are *aware* of it however…awareness has become the mantra of this book…we can undoubtedly get better at it, and in my experience the reward is huge, and growing. It is a powerful life skill, learning to live in the now. In fact it's noteworthy that positive psychologist Martin Seligman extols what he calls '*the virtue of slowness.*' He writes,

> '*Mental speed comes at a cost. I found myself missing nuances and taking shortcuts when I should have taken the mental equivalent of a deep breath. I found myself skimming and scanning when I should have been*

reading every word. I found myself listening poorly to others. I would figure out where they were headed after their first few sentences and then interrupt. And I was anxious a lot of the time...speed and anxiety go together.'[8]

'Speed and anxiety go together'...I'm sure many of us can recognise ourselves in that. We've all taken those short cuts and given only half our attention to what we are seeing or what's being said to us. And having been there so often, I'm sure we can all see just how much we would gain from an increased awareness that where we are *right now*...is a pretty good place to be focusing our attention.

And finally...the connected life

This is undoubtedly one of the strongest themes that emerges from much of the research, the huge importance to our long-term well-being of *'the connected life'* as it's often called. A sense of connectedness or engagement, a real sense of involvement in the lives of family and friends and colleagues and communities, as a constant reminder of our wider humanity. Positive psychologist Sonja Lyubomirski puts it at the top of her list of fundamental constituents in a well-balanced and happy life.

'The centrality of social connections to our health and well-being cannot be overstressed.[9]

Psychologist Barbara Fredrickson describes connectedness as a *'potent wellness behaviour,'* and goes on to note that the reverse, a sense of isolation and separation, is comparable in it's potentially damaging effects on our health and well-being, to smoking, drinking too much alcohol, obesity and inactivity. The evolutionary biologists tell us that we are in our deepest nature, a cooperating animal; that we are at our most effective and most settled when we live and work and cooperate in family and social groups. As we mentioned earlier, psychologist and philosopher Sam Harris goes so far as to declare that there may be nothing more important to our sense of well-being, than our network of relationships,

> *'There may be nothing more important,'* he writes, *'than human cooperation…Cooperation is the stuff of which meaningful human lives and viable societies are made.'[10]*

What they are telling us so clearly is that when we do manage to build or experience these connected and cooperative relationships, they don't simply make us feel good about our lives, there is a profound multiplier effect. They reinforce all our creative energies so that we feel released or empowered to pursue many other fulfilling activities and objectives in our lives.

What are the implications of all that?

That is of course an all too brief exposition of just some of the findings that have come from a truly vast amount of social research over the past decade or so. So what are we to make of it? I would say that two things stand out for me above all. One is the extraordinary degree of confirmation that we get from different kinds of studies, carried out by quite different groups of sociologists, coming up with similar or supportive results. That's very important of course in terms of the confidence with which we can approach those results.

The second point is in my view even more significant. Namely that although the sociologists and psychologists involved make it clear that their work represents a substantial *addition* to our understanding of what it is that makes people feel good about their lives and their relationships, and what kind of values and behaviours help societies work effectively, when you examine it, so much of it sounds like plain common sense doesn't it? That is to say, these findings ring so true in our own experience. We *know for sure,* that we feel better, and work far more productively and effectively when we are generous and altruistic and cooperative, and wholly engaged with our family and friends and work colleagues and communities. That's what we all want for our lives, even though occasionally we can be diverted by circumstances from seeing that as our primary goal.

And let's not forget the scale of the benefit that can come from taking these lessons on board. An increase in our general sense of well-being is not in any way limited to our emotional or our mental activities, inside our heads so to speak. It is undoubtedly a *whole body* or *a whole life* experience. As one of the most prominent and respected researchers in the field has expressed it recently, when we manage to achieve a more consistent and stable sense of well-being in our lives,

> *'...we also improve other aspects of our lives...our energy levels, our immune system, our engagement with work, and with other people, and our physical and mental health. In becoming happier we also bolster our feelings of self-confidence and self-esteem, we come truly to believe that we are worthy human beings, worthy of respect. A final and perhaps least appreciated plus is that if we become happier we benefit not only ourselves but also our partners, families, communities and even society at large.'*[11]

Is there anybody out there who wouldn't want to achieve that sort of life state? And that's really my final point. These studies clearly are not dealing with inconsequential stuff that lies somewhere out on the margins of our life. They touch upon issues that lie right at the centre of all our lives from day to day. In raising our awareness, they enable us to make changes that can transform both our own ordinary daily lives, and have a profoundly beneficial effect on all those whose lives touch ours.

CHAPTER TWELVE

The oneness of mind and body

This phrase the oneness of mind and body undoubtedly falls a little awkwardly on the western ear. It seeks to transmit a principle that lies at the very heart of the Buddhist view of a healthy life. Put simply that view is that there is no fundamental distinction, or separation, to be made between the physical or bodily dimensions of our life, and the mental or the spiritual dimensions. Nichiren Buddhism often uses the beautiful clarity of the phrase, 'two but not two,' to express this idea. And if we dig a little deeper you can see how apt a phrase that is, because it embraces so neatly the idea that the mind and the body may well appear to work in fundamentally different ways, and to occupy different dimensions of what we perceive as our reality, but, Buddhism teaches, that is simply an incomplete and partial view of that reality. They are two different aspects of each individual life, as distinct and yet as intimately related as two sides of a sheet of paper, or as the body and its image in the mirror. Separate and yet inseparable. Move one and you move the other. Whatever affects one….and this is surely the key point…in some way affects the other.

It's important I think to balance the argument by recognising that in the western world in particular, there is a deeply embedded strand in our cultural and philosophical tradition that supports a somewhat contrary view. It was perhaps most famously expressed in the words of the 17th century French philosopher and mathematician Rene Descartes, when he made his declaration, *'cogito ergo sum,'*... *'I think therefore I am.'* which proposes a clear distinction between the *real me,* the 'I,' the Descartian thinking bit if you like, and the body, the doing bit. Both locked up in the same body of course, but essentially separate in the way they operate. Descartes' *dualism* as it is formally described, set in motion a debate that has rumbled on in one form or another just about ever since.

Admittedly, it's not the sort of issue that is likely to arise over a morning cup of coffee in the office; *'What do you think about old Descartes this morning then?'* But nonetheless, there is a question lurking here that is undoubtedly worth chewing over, not least because the profound implications of the mind/body relationship are still very much the subject of leading edge research projects in neuroscience and in medicine for example, and the more we learn about that relationship, the more important it is seen to be to our daily sense of well-being. Because of course our mind body relationship *is indeed* our daily life!

Moreover it's an issue around which there would seem to be very different and very interesting cultural traditions in the West and the East which can open up for us valuable new perspectives. As the late great historian and philosopher Arnold Toynbee was concerned to remind us, *'Westerners have much to learn in this field from Indian and East Asian experience.'*[1]

The dualist perspective

If we look briefly at the basis of the dualist view, it's not dif-ficult to lay out the basis for that sort of understanding. After all, we can see the body in all its aspects and in every detail of its relationship to the physical reality around us, whereas we can't see the mind in any shape or form. The body is above all tangible and always occupies a clearly defined space, whereas the mind, the psychic space inside our heads, is seemingly infinite and unbounded. Although we never describe it as such, it is truly a fully-functioning time-travel machine that can take us anywhere at any time, and summon up astounding and surprising structures of the imagination from absolutely nothing. You can be sitting in a bus on the way to High Holborn or to downtown Chicago for example, and your mind can be replaying an argument that you had in the office last week when you wished you had thought of a wittier response, or taking you once again on that holiday scuba dive where you saw those big reef sharks gliding beneath you.

That's on the purely personal level. On a wider cultural level, we can clearly see the evidence for this perception of *separateness* in the western cultural tradition. There is the idea for example that the mind and body are not simply fundamentally separate parts of the same being, but to some extent *in conflict* with each other, as having different objectives. That is particularly true of course in many reli-gious traditions, where the mind has long been represented as reflecting our more elevated spiritual aspirations, whereas the body is heavily bound to earth, the animal part of us, weighed down by its burden of animal instincts and desires.

The most obvious although by no means the only examples of this view are the well-documented acts of some religions when they have sought to intervene in this supposed conflict, always of course, on behalf of the mind/spirit. The infamous Inquisition for example, with its public executions, to illustrate that only the elimination of the corrupted bodies of its victims by burning them at the stake would release their troubled spirits to fly free. And Cromwell's Puritans, seeking to elevate the spirit by banning bodily pleasures such as maypole dancing and funfairs and rowdy football, in case they corrupted the dignity and the purity of the spirit. And the Victorians, with very strict rules about the way the body had to be dressed and presented and restricted from pleasures on Sundays. And although of course those measures seem to be way back in the past, cultural traditions typically have long roots. Even something as simple for example as giving up some physical pleasure for Lent, such as not drinking wine or eating chocolate, is a relic of that tradition; a purely symbolic physical punishment perhaps that is carried out to ease or lighten the path of the spirit in some subliminal way.

Two but not two

But what is surprising I think is just how strongly both our personal experience, and the gathering weight of medical and scientific evidence would seem to buttress and reinforce the 'two but not two' Buddhist interpretation of our reality. If we look at our personal experience for example, I suggest that without giving it a second thought, we instinctively make use of this moment-to-moment interaction and interplay between the mind and the body in the way we handle all our relationships. *Body language*, as we all know, often reveals more clearly than our actual words, what's really going on in our *minds*. In that sense it might be described as a perfect illustration of the 'two but not two' thesis. It's now widely recognised that body language plays a constant role in our interactions with other people, even between complete strangers.

And some leading evolutionary scientists argue that it always has. Indeed according to some theories it played a key role at a crucial evolutionary turning point. So when our direct ancestors, walked out of Africa across the middle-eastern land bridge, only some 100,000 or so years ago, they had already developed the huge brain that is about three times the size of the brains of our nearest non- human primates. The latest part of that brain to evolve was the outer undulating and convoluted layer of the brain, including the large prefrontal lobes, just behind the forehead, which is essentially the seat of thought; this is where all our distinctively human higher functions such as planning and strategising and language are carried out. It was this relatively late development that gave us a huge intellectual and evolutionary edge, and which, incidentally, pushed the human forehead forwards and upwards, to give us the high, straight forehead that is so distinctive of *homo sapiens*. As we mentioned briefly in Chapter Four, the question that still remains a subject of some controversy is why? Why this distinctive and crucial expansion of the human brain had occurred?

The fact is that life for our ancestors would seem to have been relatively straightforward. Obviously difficult and constantly challenging in terms of survival, but scarcely complex; hunting animals, gathering fruits and berries, making relatively simple stone tools, and coping with the periodic changes of climate. Indeed it is thought to have been a prolonged drying of the climate in East Africa that drove our ancestors to start the long trek northwards into Europe and eventually to encircle the entire world.[2]

So what was the trigger or the stimulus, the evolutionary pressure if you like, that led to this hugely significant, world-changing development of the human brain? Because these primitive ancestors of ours had evolved a brain that was capable of vastly more than would have been needed by their natural environment. It's the same as our brain remember, yours and mine, that has shown itself to be capable of almost endless innovation; splitting the atom and putting a man on the moon, and developing super computers and intelligent robots and writing Paradise Lost and the Brandenburg Concertos and creating the Mona Lisa, and on and on. So on the face of it, there would seem to be an amazing disjunction between the simple *needs* created by the environment they inhabited, and the immensely powerful and wide-ranging capabilities of the brain they evolved.

As we've touched upon briefly, the front-running theory argues that they needed this huge frontal brain development to cope, not with challenges from *without*, from their environment, but with challenges from *within*, dealing with the sheer complexities of human relationships. Dealing that is to say, with other human brains. Basically this hypothesis proposes that as family and tribal groups became larger and more diverse so the complexities of human relationships became ever more challenging, to the extent that successful living, and even survival, could be dependent upon the speed and the skill with which people could get inside other people's heads so to speak. Get a better fix on their real motives, or to detect their deception. So this bigger, swifter, immensely capable brain was needed to cope with the endless complexities of reading the *inner mental* motivations of others, from the *external* bodily signals they were transmitting, albeit subconsciously. The fundamental interconnection of mind and body. Were they really friendly or were they hostile? Were they true or were they false? Those who became most skilled at reading this mind/body connection clearly had the best chance of surviving in a dangerous world, and passing on their genes...to us, to you and me.

> *'...during human evolution the prime driver of our expanding brains was the growing size of our social groups, with the resulting need to keep track of all those relatives, rivals and allies.'*[3]

Robin Dunbar, renowned evolutionary psychologist from Oxford University goes so far as to claim that the size of the brain of any particular species, human beings included, is *directly related*, to the size and complexity of the social group in which it lives;

> *'It takes intelligence,'* he argues, *'to live in a bonded, layered social system...you need to know the structure of the whole social network of the group. This is important because when you threaten me you risk upsetting my friends too, and they may come to my aid. In other words, you must be aware of the wider social consequences of your actions. The cognitive demands of this are reflected in the link between the size of a species' social group, and the size of its brain...or more specifically...the size of the frontal lobes, since this is where calculations about social relationships seem to be made.'*[4]

As I understand it, the jury is still out on whether or not this neat and plausible hypothesis is an adequate explanation for the great growth spurt that occurred in the frontal lobes of our direct ancestors. But whether it is or not, there is widespread agreement that as members of the human tribe we have become immensely skilled at reading all the subtle, *external* symbols of the face and body, to get a better grip on what is going on in another person's *mind*; seeing, that is to say, the profound and constant link between mind and body, the Buddhist 'two but not two.' It's an ability that has been given a proper scientific name, it's called 'theory of mind,' and it is clearly an ability that is fundamental to human relationships. As Robin Dunbar describes it, '*it has enormous cultural implications.*'[5]

The Sally-Anne test.

Just how important perhaps can be judged from the fact that this crucial faculty has been shown to develop remarkably early on in our childhood. Presumably because in evolutionary terms, that would give us many years to refine and develop our abilities, so that by the time we become adult and really need it, we have become pretty expert at it. In fact there's a little scientific test, or a game almost, that is apparently used with groups of young children to establish the arrival in their development of this theory of mind. It's called the Sally-Anne test because it involves a couple of little doll puppets called…that's right… Sally and Anne…and a child's toy such as a little ball or something similar. So with both the Sally and Anne puppets present in the room, the ball is put into basket A and the lid is closed. Then the Sally puppet is taken out of the room. The Anne puppet then takes the ball out of basket A and puts it into basket B, and again closes the lid so that it's hidden from view, after which the Sally puppet comes back into the room.

The audience of young children present are then asked where they think Sally will look for that ball.

Up until the age of three most children will respond loudly and confidently, that Sally will look in the second container, basket B. *They* know of course that's where the ball is, and they don't have the capability at that age to conceive or imagine that Sally would think differently from them. But around the age of four there is apparently a complete change of perception. Most four or five year olds have acquired a theory of mind. That is to say they realise full well that other people can have quite *different thoughts* from their own. Thus they would respond...just as loudly...that Sally would look in the basket A, that is to say, where the ball *had been* when she left the room.

So, already at that very young age, as members of the human tribe, it would seem we're beginning to learn how to read or interpret the external physical symbols we receive from the face and body and behaviour of other people, to try to get a grip on what is going on inside their heads. We don't always get it right of course. We're only human! But it's very much part of our ordinary daily life. We take it totally for granted, if we think even for a moment, not only about our circle of close friends and colleagues, but even about casual acquaintances and strangers. We are completely accustomed to making estimates about inner character and motivation, and even about subtle changes in mood and feeling, working solely from facial expressions and gestures and body posture, through to the movement of the eyes and level of voice and so on. Every hour of every day we exercise this skill. Today of course it is unlikely to be our survival that depends upon getting it right. It might just be that we recognise that it's a good time to leave our boss's office, or to move out of our partner's missile range! But whatever it may be, we are responding to the *conviction* deep within us, about the intimacy and continuity between the seen and the unseen, between the mind and body.

And fortunately we have today a growing body of scientific and medical evidence that serves not only to buttress that conviction, but to reveal to us one of the most important implications of this constant interaction, and indeed one of the main reasons for discussing this issue, the extent to which our *state of mind* plays a key role in terms for example, of resisting and overcoming bodily illness. It is a growing field of scientific research.

The placebo effect

Medical scientists and doctors have long known that the way we think and feel about medical treatments can radically influence how our bodies respond to them. That is to say, believing in our heads that a treatment works, may well trigger the desired effect in the body, even if the treatment is inert, a simple sugar pill say or a saline injection.[6] This is perhaps most clearly seen in what is called the placebo effect.

So very briefly, in carrying out studies on the effects of new drugs there is a so-called gold-standard test protocol, known as a 'double blind' trial. It has nothing to do with blindness of course, it simply describes the procedure whereby one group of test patients will be given the actual drug, while a second closely matched group, the control group as its called, will be given an equivalent and look-alike dose of some wholly inert substance such as a sugar pill or something similar. But in order for the 'double blind' to be effective, both groups have to be truly blind, that is to say none of the people involved in the trial knows whether they are getting the actual drug or the sugar pill.

The purpose of this approach is of course to enable the scientists to see clearly the difference in the effect on the two similar groups of people, between those who take the drug, and those who don't. Everybody recruited into the test is aware of the rules of the process.

However it is now well proven that some people who receive the dummy pill nevertheless demonstrate positive healing effects, often to a remarkable extent, as if in fact they had been receiving the actual drug. That is to say, the mere *belief* that they had been receiving the medicine has had the same, or a very similar effect on the body, as actually taking it. This is the so-called placebo effect, and it has often been shown to have a significant physiological effect upon the body.

> '...the placebo response is far from imaginary. Trials have shown measurable changes such as the release of natural painkillers, altered neuronal firing patterns, lowered blood pressure or heart rate and boosted immune response, all depending upon the beliefs of the patient.[7]*

The mind that is, profoundly affecting the body's response, two but not two indeed. Moreover, in a series of quite remarkable recent studies organised jointly by scientists from Harvard Medical School and from the University of Hull in the UK, patients have been shown to respond positively, even when *they were told* that the pill they were being given was made of an inert substance. As one of the scientists involved, Irving Kirsch, a psychologist from Hull University explained, *'Everybody thought it wouldn't happen...'[8]* Although, he goes on, they were very careful in setting up the experiment to explain to the participants the possibility of achieving significant improvement in symptoms through *'mind-body self-healing processes.'[9]*

Even raising the issue of mind-body healing processes is of course profoundly controversial, and I am very conscious of the need to do so only on the basis of proven research results. But there is no question that this is an issue that has steadily been gaining traction in the scientific and medical communities over the past few years. Let me just quote one further extremely interesting and influential statement from another scientist, Steven Cole, professor of medicine and psychiatry at the University of California at Los Angeles, who has been carrying out research exploring the complexities of the relationship between personality traits and the immune system. He would seem to have no doubts whatsoever when he declares,

> 'The biggest take-home message is that what happens in our health is connected to what happens in our heads and what happens in our lives.'[10]

The healing power of optimism

I feel I need to emphasise that Nichiren Buddhism does not in any way teach that we can somehow replace modern medicine by the application of strong belief. Buddhism makes it clear that we need both. The wisdom to get the very best analysis and treatment that modern medicine can provide, but also the wisdom to recognise the importance of our own continuing role. We don't achieve the best results by simply handing over responsibility for our health and well-being to the medical profession. We need the courage if you like to accept the *ultimate responsibility*, to recognise the crucial importance of our own life state, to our personal healing.

And that is amply borne out by the research. There is an increasing body of evidence to show that a strongly optimistic and positive approach to life helps us to recover from operations and boosts the immune system, and so can enhance our ability to resist and overcome illness. A high life state if you like is a very powerful medicine in its own right.

Unfortunately, the converse is also true. A persistently negative life state is now clearly associated with a deterioration in many of the body's crucial systems. Different researchers highlight different physiological effects but they include several life-threatening conditions, including a generally weakened immune response and therefore a susceptibility to illness. As one article sums it up for us, *'It is well accepted that negative thoughts and anxiety can make us ill.'*[11]

The Buddhist perspective

I started this discussion from a Buddhist standpoint and I go back to Buddhism for the summation. If we look at all those strands of medical and scientific observations on mind-body interaction, from a strictly Buddhist standpoint, it would seem clear that a daily Buddhist practice places in our hands an immensely powerful tool, since it offers us a practical and accessible method for challenging the negative aspects of our life, and manifesting the positive. Every day we can choose to challenge the negativity in our lives, which we now know can have such harmful effects upon our physiological health. Every day we can choose to shift our lives towards the positive end of the spectrum, which we now know brings so many healthful effects. Nobody says it is easy, but why should we expect it to be? It is a huge benefit. We have to work at it. The key point I wish to make is that Buddhism gives us the method with which to go to work.

As no less a body than the World Health Organisation defines it for us, good health should not be seen as merely the *absence* of sickness or anxiety at any particular point in time. It should be seen rather as the enjoyment of a strong and positive life state. From my personal experience I am arguing that a Buddhist practice enables us to work on this crucial mind-body interface every day, to strengthen our optimism every day, which in turn enables us to challenge the sickness and the anxiety that will inevitably come into our life, rather than be cast down by it.

CHAPTER THIRTEEN

Getting a handle on negativity

The psychologists tell us that we spend a lot of time talking to ourselves. In a sort of on-going dialogue of reasoning with ourselves, and rehearsing and working things over in our mind, we hold this more or less constant inner, ruminating conversation. I certainly recognise the truth of that in my own life. It's very much a part of the way I develop ideas, essentially talking them through with myself, accepting this aspect and then rejecting or modifying that one. This inner conversation is very much part of our thinking process. Although I would argue that in general it is so much a part of the background and texture of our lives, that we tend to take it utterly for granted. Somehow we scarcely notice that it's going on. However one of those voices is a *negative* one, a powerful and immensely knowledgeable advocate for *not* doing things, for *not* challenging our situation, for *not* making the effort, because...well, is it really worth it?

As it happens this modern psychological understanding is very much in keeping with the Buddhist perception of human nature, namely that we all have a negative aspect to our nature to some degree, even those of us who happen to be blessed with the sunniest and most positive of temperaments. Indeed both Buddhism and modern psychology are very much in tune when they teach that we will *always* have it as a fundamental strand in our humanity, however generally positive the spirit we learn to develop and maintain. And if we think even momentarily about our personal experience, we can clearly recognise that negativity *is* indeed one of our *potential* life states, lurking there you might say, always ready to take over if something goes even mildly wrong. We've all been there many times, even if we don't actually label it as negativity. We are much more likely perhaps to talk about being a bit *down*, or a bit *low*, or feeling less confident and capable when we're faced with a particularly tough and challenging moment; our normal level of confidence suddenly replaced by an underlying sense of self-doubt and a vague anxiety.

It is a common experience

Many people talk about this low-level background negativity getting up with them in the morning, because that is when it can so often make its presence felt. People often say for example that early mornings are a kind of low point for them, when they feel they have to dig themselves out of a hole. Hence perhaps the global addiction to the regular morning pick-me-up fix of caffeine. But it's not just the mornings is it? There are many times when it can stick around for much of the day. Indeed it seems that to feel generally *'a bit low,'* is quite a common experience for many of us these days. Psychologists talk for example about a general low-level, background anxiety as being one of the features of our time, in this busy, crowded, time-slicing, adrenaline-fuelled culture that most of us inhabit. The psychologist and writer Daniel Goleman for example has dubbed our time, *the age of melancholy*, because there seems to be more depression about than in previous generations. Elsewhere in his influential book *Emotional Intelligence* he goes so far as to say,

'Perhaps the most disturbing single piece of data in this book comes from a massive survey of parents and teachers and shows a worldwide trend for the present generation of children to be more troubled emotionally than the last, more lonely and depressed, more angry and unruly, more nervous and prone to worry, more impulsive and aggressive.'[1]

That is undoubtedly a disturbing passage to read. But even Martin Seligman, the boundlessly optimistic founding father of the positive psychology movement in the US, comments strongly on this particular aspect of modern society in the West. He writes,

'Why do anxiety, anger and sadness pervade so much of our lives...concurrent with so much success, wealth and the absence of biological need in the lives of privileged Americans?'[2]

For Americans in that passage we can of course include all of us who are fortunate enough to live in the ultra-privileged western-way-of-life parts of the world. He goes on to attempt an explanation.

'People by and large are astonishingly attracted to the catastrophic (that is to say negative) interpretation of things. Not just neurotics, not just depressives...but most of us, much of the time.'[3]

Those are indeed surprisingly inclusive phrases he chooses to use, *'People by and large,'* and *'... most of us much of the time,'* but when we start to research around this issue we encounter similar views from many different directions.

Psychologist Sally Winston, for example, co-director of an important institution in this field, the Anxiety and Stress Disorders Institute of Maryland USA, is one among many who makes a very similar point, when she declares,

> 'One of the problems of chronic worriers is that they tend to have predictions of catastrophic outcomes that crowd out their consciousness.'[4]

So it would seem that there is a substantial conjunction of views in the scientific community. Indeed we might argue that it adds up to a very significant perception that is being passed on to us, almost you might say, as a wake-up call. Because however prevalent it might be, we don't spend much time talking about the negative or the anxious side of our make up do we? It's something that we tend to push right out into the margins of our consciousness. But the effects of sustained, albeit low-level anxiety, negativity, worry, call it what you will, can be very considerable, and as you might expect, none of them are beneficial.

Some of the physiological effects

On a physiological level the main problem seems to arise from the sustained presence of the hormone cortisol in the bloodstream.[5] It's commonly called the stress hormone because higher than normal concentrations are found in the blood of people who feel themselves to be stressed out or deeply anxious, for real or imagined reasons. And it's the cortisol that is believed to cause most of the cellular damage when it stays in the body for prolonged periods.[6]

Some of the effects have been described as follows;

> 'Excess stress hormones wear on the body, nipping away at the DNA that keeps cells dividing and long lived,

constricting the blood vessels and causing blood pres-sure to rise. Even the immune system is affected, as white blood cells that normally patrol for bacteria and viruses aren't produced at normal, disease-fighting levels.'[7]

So not beneficial to say the least. But this book isn't of course a medical text book, and what I'm really interested in are the effects on individual and social *behaviour*, because those are the areas, it seems to me, where if we have a greater awareness of what is going on, or going *wrong* in this case, then we can take some action to reduce or even perhaps eliminate the damage.

On an individual level

If we dig a little deeper and ask ourselves why many of us have this tendency, as Martin Seligman and Nancy Winston both point out, to interpret events in a somewhat negative way, perhaps part of the explanation might lie in the fact that this negative voice that we've been talking about, knows us infinitely well. We have no hiding place you might say. It knows all our weaknesses and our vulnerabilities… because of course it *is* us. So it can frame the arguments it whispers into our ear to match precisely those weaknesses and vulnerabilities. And if we let it go on unchallenged, it can go on sniping and whittling away at our self-confidence and our courage for much of the day, constantly taking advantage of those half-formed inner stirrings of doubt and uncertainty that we scarcely admit to ourselves. So it knows precisely for example, why we *won't* succeed in this or that endeavour, why we *won't* get the job, or the praise, or the promotion or those exam grades we need to qualify for university, or whatever it happens to be that we are seeking to achieve.

The key point to hang onto is that when we are strong and confident with a high life state, or when we've just had a significant personal victory, we can often just brush this insidious negativity aside, and laugh at it, or simply ignore it into silence. It is when we are down, with a low life state, or we've just suffered a rejection of some kind, that this inner negative voice can be all that is needed to tip us into a powerfully anxious or defeatist frame of mind. Negativity or anxiety in that sense can disarm us, or render us immobile. And over time that can be truly life-changing in a negative way. Life can become, *'there's no point in even trying, I won't succeed,'* instead of as it should be, *'I really think I can make a go of this if I push myself.'*

So it can really be of value to learn effective ways of challenging this sort of negative, self-defeating anxiety. And there are several.

On a social level

I came across something in the research recently that really took me by surprise, because it was so... mechanical... is the word that comes to mind... for a social observation, and yet so effective. That something is called the Losada Ratio, named after the psychologist Marcial Losada, who led the research from which the concept has been derived. Losada's work has focused on developing ways in which teams of people can work most effectively together, and what this particular method does is to look at the ratio between the *positive* words and phrases and the *negative* ones, that occur in the regular communications between individuals or groups of people. When researchers went out into society and actually looked at the implications of this ratio, the results were wholly astounding.

One research group for example was allowed into business meetings across a wide range of 60 or so companies of different sizes. What they did was, on the face of it, quite mechanical. They transcribed everything that was said at a series of business meetings in each of those companies. Everything. Then they worked out the ration of positive words and phrases to the negative ones. The results were surprising even to the researchers, for they found that there seemed to be a very significant cut-off point. In those companies where there was a clear majority of positive comments to negative ones in communications between the managers...to be more precise at least *three* positive comments for every negative one, those companies were flourishing. At anything below that ratio, *less than three to one*, the companies were ailing in varying degrees. That startling finding has now been used at many management training courses.[8]

If that surprises you as much as it did me, it doesn't end there.

The psychologist John Gottman is one of America's leading researchers and consultants in the business of marriage and relationships, exploring and explaining what it is that makes for a successful partnerships, and the kinds of things that can lead to marriages or relationships breaking down. He is famous for, among other things, proposing the idea that it's not only how couples fight that matters in building a lasting relationship... all couples have their fights... but how they learn to *make up* after a fight has occurred![9] He too has applied the same Losada concept in studying how partners communicate with each other and, extraordinarily, he has come up with very similar findings. He has found that where there are less than about *three positive* communications for every *negative one*, then the relationship could be heading for trouble. In fact he argues that you need at least *five positives* to every negative to be confident of having a strong and enduring relationship.[10]

I suggested that you might find this piece of research surprising, and it surely is. But what it illustrates above all is just how unaware we can be of the effects of self-absorbed, anxious or negative elements in our behaviour and our conversations, and just how powerfully that in many ways *mindless* negativity, can affect our relationships. At work and at home.

So what can we do about it?

Most of us I'm sure won't have been aware of anything so specific as the Losada ratio, but if we think about it even casually, we can all recall some experience of how this kind of subliminal almost *unconscious* projection of negativity can have lasting effects in our everyday life. As I've already mentioned elsewhere, we can all immediately recognise for example, the huge difference between the positive, optimistic, generous colleague we all happen to know at work who is always there to help others, or to get things done, even in the most challenging and unlikely circumstances, and the reverse of that, the disheartening, even paralysing effect, that a single negatively-inclined or overly-anxious colleague can have in similar circumstances.

That is true also I suggest of our own negativity. When it's not recognised, and challenged, it can have a powerfully destructive effect, not just in our own lives, but in the lives of all those around us, all those whom our life touches. And the key word there is '*recognised*,' because it is the recognition above all else, our growing *awareness* if you like, of what is going on, that leads us to challenge the anxiety and the negativity and take positive action. It is only by being constantly vigilant and mindful of the reality of our negativity and its potential influence on our life state, that we are able to go into battle against it, and so begin the process of change. That idea, which, I must mention, is absolutely central to the Buddhist approach to tackling negativity, is now fully borne out by some of the latest psychological and neurological studies.

We can train ourselves

As a result of more advanced technologies such as the fMRI brain scanning machines we've touched upon in earlier chapters, which enable the brain to be observed in real time so to speak, while it is actually functioning, there is now a much more detailed, a much more sophisticated understanding of the different neural pathways involved when we experience strong negative emotions such as fear and panic on the one hand, and the *low-level* background anxiety and worry and general negativity that we have been discussing here. The neural circuits for these *lower level* emotional responses crucially take in the prefrontal cortex. That's the extensive frontal area of the brain just behind the forehead, that is responsible for all the higher level functions, such as planning and comprehending and organising and reasoning. As psychologist Daniel Goleman explains, the effect of this routing,

'…adds to a feeling what we think about it.'[11]

That turns out to be a crucial difference, because the addition of the *thinking*, means that we can *train* ourselves to overcome and surmount this form of negativity and low-level anxiety. Psychologists often use the term 'habituation,' to describe this form of self-training. That is to say, we don't *simply accept* the negativity or anxiety as inevitable. We learn that we can question its origin and challenge it, and in this way we learn steadily that we can overcome the negativity, and come out on the other side emotionally strengthened by the victory.

A crucial shift in attitude

If I may stay with the Buddhist teaching just for a moment, that is precisely the shift in approach or attitude that we are seeking to develop with the discipline of the daily Buddhist practice. The problems if you like remain the same, but our sense of being able to overcome them changes profoundly. And problems that we feel we can overcome change in character. They are no longer so threatening or so anxiety-creating. In fact we consciously change the words we use to describe them. We call them *challenges*, and the change is immensely significant. Problems are negative and can steal away our hope, whereas challenges are stimulating and can raise our spirits.

The remarkable thing is that almost exactly the same understanding emerges from modern psychology. For example we have psychologist Sally Winston, from whom we quoted earlier declaring that,

> *'Anxiety is neither helpful nor hurtful. It's your response to anxiety that is helpful or hurtful. '12*

That is to say, once we learn to *challenge* the source of the anxiety, we come to recognise that so often it is simply a waste of time and energy that is doing nothing to help us change the situation, or achieve our objectives. Once we've made that step, then we can modify our response to the situation, to be more positive about it. Harvard Medical School psychologist Diego Pizzagalli goes further along the same road,

> 'What is important is your appraisal of the situation and your assessment of your coping strategies. If you perceive you can cope, you will not feel as stressed.'[13]

It's important to emphasise that we are not talking here about *stoicism*; that is to say, simply putting up with our negativity or anxiety over some problem, and being broad-shouldered in bearing the burden. What we are seeking is the *transformation* of our attitude towards these situations, so that we achieve for ourselves, and those around us, a more consistent sense of well-being. It's not easy of course, nor ever wholly won. As I've mentioned, Buddhism often presents the battle against negativity as a *daily* encounter, one of the main reasons for the discipline of the daily practice. It equips us with a *proven method*, proven over many generations of practitioners, to help us summon up our positive and optimistic spirit to take out with us into the day we are about to live, and drive out the negativity.

And it's also important to be clear that being optimistic definitely does not mean being *unrealistic*. So it doesn't mean denying the existence of the negative or the anxious, or just pushing away any unfavourable information that comes at us. It doesn't mean constantly trying to control situations that simply lie outside our control. It does mean applying *effort*. Making a conscious effort to challenge the negativity as soon as it arises, and thus moving on to make that difficult positive choice, rather than that easier negative one. Our optimism that is, has to be broad enough and deep enough to embrace the sad and the painful and the suffering, as well as the joyful.

Does it work?

However hard it may be to achieve, there is absolutely no question from my personal experience *that it works*. In the past year I have emerged from a battle with cancer that has gone on for over four years. I can now, with the greatest pleasure imaginable, use the past tense because I've come through to the other side of the tunnel so to speak. I've been signed off by my consultant and from now on it's just a question of monitoring. So I can now say that it *was* a battle that involved me in a fair bit of physical and mental pain. I can still hear the hum of the radiotherapy machine that I lay in so often as part of my treatment. But the key point I want to make clear is that as soon as I became aware of the cancer's existence I made the determination to *embrace it* as part of my life. An unwelcome part, but nonetheless, part of me. I'm as scared as anybody about major illness, but by embracing it I felt enabled to fight it positively, rather than simply trying to push it away, which wouldn't have achieved anything. And that determination did have an extraordinary effect; I became aware that my stable optimism about life, my overall sense of well-being, was not dependant upon only *good* things happening to me. My Buddhist practice has it seems, enabled me to embrace the bad, and create value out of it.

CHAPTER FOURTEEN

So how do we achieve that change of attitude?

A profound and lasting change of attitude is undoubtedly one of the most difficult challenges we can take on. Understandably enough perhaps, since we've taken years building up the attitudes that we hold, so that in a very real sense they *are* us. We can change our *views* of course on various issues of the day that come and go without any problem, in the course of a single discussion indeed. We all like to pride ourselves on keeping a good flexible open mind on social and political stuff. But fundamental beliefs or attitudes about life the universe and everything? They go much deeper. We have to wrestle a fair bit with ourselves in order to shift them substantially.

That is the case I would suggest, certainly for most of us, in terms of our attitude to the problems and pains and difficulties that come at us in a more or less constant stream, in one area of our life or another. Man was born to troubles as the sparks fly upwards, Job famously tells us in the Old Testament. That's as true now as it was then. Perhaps the difference is that these days the problems are likely to be more complex, given the infinitely greater complexity of our daily lives. But no one wants pains or problems of any kind do they? Or the anxiety and the stress and tension that arise as they threaten to emerge in our lives. So the very natural human response is to argue that since we can't stand them, we have to do everything possible to avoid them. Or better still get rid of them! Eliminate them from our lives. And that would seem to be pretty much the universal attitude that has evolved. We spend huge amounts of time and money and ingenuity in trying to create a defensive system to keep the challenging and the anxiety-creating side of life at bay. And where we aren't completely successful in the defensive system building business, as we can't be of course, then we have evolved a whole series of secondary strategies to plug the gaps.

So we choose to *ignore* them for example, or *run away* from them, in the hope that they will eventually go away, or sort of evaporate. The reality, as most of us have experienced at one time or another, is that problems ignored have a very nasty habit of becoming problems magnified. So that what was once eminently resolvable, if only we'd had the courage to face up to it when it first appeared on the horizon, can become big enough to cause serious or even disastrous disruption to our lives. Or we very commonly push the problems sideways and claim it has nothing to do with us. That is to say we mentally *dump* the responsibility onto someone or some circumstance outside ourselves; pointing to anything so long as it's not ourselves as the cause of the problem and therefore the *owner* of it.

If there are problems within a relationship for example, then it's not our fault we are likely to say, it's clearly because the other half of the relationship has to change something about *themselves* to put things right. If there's trouble at work it's likely to be because the boss or colleagues are being totally unreasonable, or obstinate or simply unfair. Any reasonable person can see that can't they?

And what happens with these very commonly used strategies, is that we end up at a dead end. Nothing changes. So the friction or the frustration keeps on re-emerging, and it can lead eventually to the break-up of an otherwise sound relationship, or an enduring state of tension and unease at work. We've all been there at some stage in our lives, and several times more than likely, because we all tend to repeat patterns of behaviour. We are very much creatures of habit.

The fiction we've created for ourselves

Moreover although problems and crises of one kind or another, and the general worries and anxieties that they bring, continue to occupy a considerable portion of our time and energies, most weeks of the year in fact, we're quite happy to hang onto the idea that these problems are a completely *abnormal exception* to the normal flows and patterns of our life. It's a kind of fiction that we have spun for ourselves. In fact if you think about it, this particular fiction is very deeply rooted indeed. No matter how frequently they occur, or how disturbing they may be in blowing us off track, we persuade ourselves time and time again, that as soon as this particular accident or setback or hiccup or crisis has passed us by, our life will revert to its normal, routine, *untroubled state*. Why? Because that's the life state we've convinced ourselves we need if we're going to be really happy. You know, the one without any hassle!

You could say that is the idealised, unreal life state that we're all pretty much addicted to. Despite the fact that none of us knows anyone who lives such a life. Not a single person. Not even the wealthiest and most talented people, who you would think, could most easily buy the protection to ensure such a life, if it were available. Indeed as we know only too well from the gossip-filled 24/7 media machine, such people have a truckload of problems of their own, even if they are likely to seem from the outside, to be rather different from ours.

Let's be absolutely clear, several of those strategies that we've discussed have their rightful place in any life. Of course. We haven't evolved them for nothing. No one for example would question the prudence of arranging whatever insulation we can, since we live in troubled times. And although the fiction strategy may not keep any actual problems at bay, it probably helps to lessen our anxiety over those problems, and anxiety can be both damaging to our health and paralysing. But the key question that we might put to ourselves is… can this really be the best we can do?

I put it in that way because this is not some academic or theoretical question is it? It is absolutely close up and very personal for every one of us. We're talking about real life-time strategies here. This is how we actually *handle* the daily detail of our lives. And I think we could put forward a very strong case indeed, that devising or learning a more effective way of approaching and handling ordinary daily problems, has got to be one of the most important steps we could possibly take along the road to greater well-being in our lives. I mean, what could be more important?

So we share a deep and common interest I suggest, in posing this question as to whether the strategies that most of us employ are good enough. Are they anywhere close to the best strategies that we can come up with for our ordinary everyday lives?

So where might we turn?

I would like to turn to Buddhism at this point, for no other reason than that Buddhism is good at dealing with problems, since it was actually born out of the realisation that the nature of human life is always tough and challenging, and frequently involves considerable pain and suffering and anxiety and grief...for all of us. Suffering is part and parcel of our ordinary humanity. No one on the planet is immune. And that simple, utterly basic statement could, I firmly believe, be the starting point for a profound change of attitude. It could open up a whole new approach to way we perceive and deal with the problems big and small that come into all our lives.

So what Buddhism does is to establish the datum for us. It asks us to recognise that very toughness and challenge and suffering in setting our levels of *expectation*. That is the starting point if you like. And once we perceive that, it immediately begins to toughen us up mentally if I may put it that way. We can see that there's absolutely nothing to be gained from going on as we so often do, about, *'why is this happening to me?'* or *'what have I done to deserve this?* Or basing our hopes for happiness on some longed-for problem-free future. None of us will have a problem free future. Ever.

There are many Buddhist texts which make the simple point,

> *'Though worldly troubles may arise, never let them disturb you. No one can avoid problems.*[1]

Literally no one. The *'never '* in that text is a bit demanding of course, we're only human, and we're unlikely to achieve a state whereby we are *never* disturbed by problems that occur in their lives, even if the writer of the text did! But that doesn't alter the fundamental truth inherent in the philosophy; namely that once we truly comprehend the *nature of our reality*, that problems are very much the norm in our lives, rather than the exception, then our mind-set and hence our response, is bound to be radically different. Rather than being *derailed* by the problem, whatever it is, we are much more likely to just buckle down and set about *solving* it. Which is undoubtedly an altogether more positive and creative response isn't it?

Everything begins with us

Moreover Buddhism constantly reminds us that in *our lives*, everything begins with us. That may not sound on the face of it, to be a particularly revolutionary idea, but it is remarkable how often this apparently obvious principle is ignored or overlooked. It is *our life* in every sense. So if there is friction or frustration or challenge coming at us from various directions, then the place to look for the root cause Buddhism argues, is…guess where…within our own life. That may be difficult for us to accept. Often *very* difficult. We may have to go through a huge internal debate to reconcile ourselves to its truth. But if you think about it even for a minute or two, that is what we mean when we talk about being responsible for *our* lives. And we don't often argue do we, that someone else should be responsible for our lives? That's childhood rather than adulthood.

So, Buddhism asks us to reflect a little, what is it about *our* behaviour, *our* thoughts, *our* words and actions, that is giving rise to this difficulty or problem? How do *we* need to change in order to resolve this difficult issue? What subliminal signals are we giving off that trigger this response from our boss or

Life is problems. That's what life is.

our partner or our friend? That may initially, as I've said, be a very hard lesson to take on board. Sometimes we can manage it, sometimes we can't. Again we're only human. But when we *can* it carries with it an immeasurably huge benefit that occurs in no other way. When… and only when… we fully recognise that the *cause* comes from within our own life, then so too does the *remedy*. It lies within our control.

So the problem-solving equation in so many relationships becomes quite different. Instead of, '…*if only my partner would change we could be so much happier*…' which is a very tough call because it's outside our control, it becomes, '… *what things about myself do I need to change that will sweep this problem out of our lives*…' which is so much simpler because we do have control. There is nothing to stop us initiating the change, at any time of our own choosing, and so opening up the possibility of real progress.

The self-conditioning process

We are responsible for our own lives. That in a sense is the starting point for everything. And what we are seeking to learn, to train ourselves to grasp if you like, is that we should see all the various problems and difficulties that confront all of us on a daily basis, simply as facts of life. That's all. Nothing more nor nothing less than that. Once again that is clearly not a particularly earth-shattering idea is it? But it is remarkable how often we seem to overlook it, and just how difficult it is to achieve. And the fact is that for as long as we are not in that position; for as long as we take everyday problems and difficulties *personally*, that is to say as a direct challenge to our *personal* equanimity and happiness, and allow ourselves to be upset and feel anxiety and stress, then we are indeed training ourselves, *conditioning* ourselves, to always respond in that way.

We are in a sense locking ourselves into our own conditioning process, even if we are quite unaware of it. But once in, it is quite difficult to escape. Round and round we go like a hamster on a wheel. The problems inevitably continue to occur, we *choose* to see them as a disruption to our personal happiness and peace of mind, so inevitably we respond to them with powerful negativity. How could it be otherwise? And so over the years we forge this more or less unbreakable link in our minds between the occurrence of problems and the negative response, the anxiety and stress which we have always associated with them.

And although it's possible to read through those words with casual ease, we are of course talking about people's *real lives*, and the burden of anxiety and stress which so many people experience as an ordinary part of their daily life. It can become so deeply embedded that it is never challenged. It simply doesn't seem possible that there can be a quite different response.

One might almost argue that Buddhism was created to persuade us that there is.

A change of perception
And let me stay with that thought, because it opens up for us a clear way out of this stressful, and indeed harmful cycle of negative response. Buddhism is not of course the only philosophy to offer such a solution, but it is undoubtedly an effective one. Speaking personally, it has changed my life in so many ways. I've acquired a buoyancy and an optimism in the face of quite considerable problems of health and so on, that still surprises me. So briefly, Buddhism argues that the way we look at any situation or environment is of the greatest importance. That is to say, it is not so much the *external*

circumstances that govern how a given situation affects us, but the *internal* response, how we *choose to see it.* It's not so much the problem that occurs that causes us to suffer, so much as how we *respond* to that problem. That in itself is a huge life lesson isn't it? The recognition that we have the choice, that we can make the determination to respond to problems and difficulties *positively* and *optimistically*, rather than negatively. And that determination represents in a sense the turning of the corner, the beginning of a new approach. No one is saying that it's easy to make that determination. Of course not. But once we can, the benefits to our daily life are huge.

Getting real

It also takes us directly to an understanding that lies at the very heart of Buddhist teachings; you could say in fact that it is *the* essential perception we need to grasp, to break out of that cycle of self-conditioning. So Buddhism asks us to look again at the relationship between happiness or well-being on the one hand, and suffering on the other, and to challenge our deeply rooted view that they are entirely different and separate experiences, that lie really at opposite ends of the wide spectrum of human experience. That is simply a partial and incomplete view of our reality, Buddhism argues; we haven't thought it through deeply enough. On the contrary they are closely and intimately interconnected, almost like the two sides of a sheet of paper.

How can that be we might ask? We intensely dislike suffering and we run away from it whenever we can. And we run towards happiness because we love it so much. They must therefore lie in opposite directions. Stop running for a moment Buddhism argues, and look a bit harder at your reality. And if we do that we can come to see that our basic premise is at fault. For if we continue to hang onto the idea that our happiness in this life is dependent on our achieving a smooth, untroubled existence largely free from all those anxieties and pains and problems, then it doesn't take all that hard a look to recognise that it is a strategy doomed to failure. Why? Because there is *no such place!*

As I've said, none of us knows anybody who lives there. Not a single person.

So all Buddhism is saying to us, when it comes down to it, is *'get real!'* And it is by no means alone in saying that. Today's positive psychologists for example, make a very similar argument. That is to say, if we seek to establish a strong and resilient sense of well-being at the core of our lives, as we undoubtedly do, then that can only be found in the very midst of the problems and suffering that life throws at us, since that is *the only place there is*. That is the only reality. They lie therefore, our happiness and our problems, cheek by jowl, in precisely the same direction.

Our most capable self

And once that perception is put to us, we immediately see its reality. And we can go on to see the natural corollary, that the greater and more challenging the problems we are able to embrace in this way, the greater the potential happiness they can release since they demand so much more of us. They compel us to summon up so much more courage and resilience to overcome them; they make us *grow* you might say, to become our most capable selves. And personal capability is a hugely important ingredient in the making of this stuff that we call well-being. We all dearly want to be…and we want to be seen to be by our family and friends and colleagues…capable human beings.

The renowned positive psychologist Professor Martin Seligman writes decisively about the challenge of moving from essentially *'pessimistic habits of thinking,'* as he calls them, towards optimism, but he has no doubt that the change can be made; *'These habitual beliefs are just that, mere beliefs,'*[2] and the key therefore to establishing a more solid and optimistic base for our daily lives is to dispute with, or challenge, those habitually pessimistic beliefs within ourselves;

> *'The main skill of optimistic thinking,'* he writes, *'is disputing. This is a skill everyone has...Once you acquire the skills of optimism, they stay.'*[3]

Disputing, that is to say, challenging the negativity.

Does that chime with our experience?

That's a key question isn't it? Does it make sense in terms of our daily life? And although when we first bump into this idea it may well seem wholly counter-intuitive, if we think about it even briefly it makes complete sense. Basically by embracing or facing up to and resolving problems we can hugely increase our sense of self-worth and personal capability. How else? Think back to times when you have succeeded in surmounting a really difficult challenge in your life, something that you felt had the potential to knock you off balance, or radically change your life, something that could well have inspired a certain amount of fear or panic. When we overcome these potentially life-diminishing challenges we get a powerful boost to our sense of self-confidence and capability. We feel strengthened, and the bigger the threat to our stability we've overcome, the bigger the boost. For some considerable time afterwards we experience a much greater confidence in our ability to deal with things in general, not simply in that particular area, but right across the spectrum of our life and activities.

Thus all Buddhism is saying in a sense, is hang onto that perception, that understanding. Since we have some experience of this potential in our lives it argues, we can learn how to build upon it and extend it. If we can do it once, why not twice, why not many more times?

Clearly we can't achieve great victories every day, but then we don't need to. Life doesn't demand that of us, or rarely. But we can certainly achieve small victories all the time, and the inherent sense of capability and well-being can become an extended experience, constantly renewing the positive energy and the optimism.

Built to last

I think there are two things above all to hang onto to help us to make that determination I mentioned earlier. One is that this is a philosophy built to last. It's not fragile or ephemeral, because it is built out of the real circumstances of our lives, as they really are, often turbulent and disappointing and tough and challenging, rather than as we frequently wish them to be, soft and easy. Buddhism isn't a soft touch, because of course, life isn't a soft touch.

The second is that the sense of well-being that this strategy promises is constructed and put together piece by piece from *within* rather than from without. It comes only from the courage and the resilience and the renewed determination that we steadily learn how to draw out from within ourselves, every time a problem pops up. We are in effect on a journey. We are training ourselves to become ace problem solvers, because we've come to recognise, that's the quickest route to the self-confidence and sense of self-worth and capability and well-being, that we would all like to have in our lives.

What about other research?

Good question, because as has been mentioned so often in the course of this book, however well-established the teachings that come to us from Buddhism in this case, it simply doesn't make sense not to make use of all the sources of information that are available to us in the modern world. Buddhism itself would argue that, not least in the context of its central teaching that we are wholly responsible for what goes on in our lives.

And if we look at some of the social and psychological research over the past ten to fifteen years or so, on dealing with the kinds of problems that confront all of us in the normal daily progress of our lives, we find a quite extraordinary similarity of view with much of what we've just been discussing. The use of that word 'similarity' is important, because of course the scientists don't have anything remotely Buddhist in mind when they are setting up their research studies. They are simply seeking to understand more clearly the range and the nature of human response to troubles. And you may have to dig beneath the objective and scientific formality of phrases such as *'construing benefit in trauma.'* But once you do, to get down to the human detail of the studies, the reward in terms of the understanding that emerges from them is considerable. Moreover we find ourselves in very familiar territory.

So for example, where the problem is of an everyday nature, the sort of thing that we can all encounter any day of the week; having money problems over paying household bills for example, or a troubling and disturbing dispute with a partner that seems to run on, or a general dissatisfaction and frustration at work say, the psychologists talk about '*problem-focused coping*[4] That is to say, focusing our energies on the problem and its implications, rather than trying to suppress it or ignore it and letting it fester on, and above all, making a solid determination to do something about it. Drawing up a plan of action for example and then putting it into effect. Even if it only *partially* resolves the issues, it represents a positive movement forwards, as opposed to stasis. That whole approach would seem to come very close to what we were discussing earlier, about the huge benefits we experience from facing up to our problems, embracing them indeed, in order to achieve some resolution, rather than running away from them.

Where the problem is clearly not everyday, and not resolvable in that way, because it involves for example the death of a loved one, or the break-up of a long-term relationship, or a life-threatening illness such as cancer, where the emotional impact can be simply overwhelming and uncontrollable, the psychologists talk of '*emotion-focused coping*'.[5] That is to say, searching for ways to lessen the personal emotional burden by *sharing it* for example. Seeking support from close friends and colleagues, and particularly by getting involved in activities where you can play a role in helping *other people* get through their problems, so that you are drawn away from your own grief. Once again that sort of advice, based on psychological understanding, sits very close indeed to the Buddhist understanding of the powerful role in healing played by compassion and altruism, seeking to create value in other people's lives, rather than being focused upon our own immediate pain and problems.

Emerging on the other side

Moreover, both Buddhism and modern psychology[6] talk about the immense emotional benefit that can be created by encouraging people to try to reach beyond their immediate pain and grief; to grasp the learning, or the personal growth, or the deeper appreciation of each day of life, that can come from going through such a challenging experience, and emerging on the other side. And there are many examples of such a journey in the research studies, although of course it is never other than a huge personal challenge. As the American psychologist Sonja Lyubomirski expresses it;

> 'The higher you aim in terms of how you cope with trauma, the more you will achieve...But remember that post-traumatic growth, and happiness for that matter is not the same as always being joyful or carefree. Indeed most survivors experience a great deal of distress at the same time as reporting strengthening and progress. So the uphill road that leads to a more fulfilling and more meaningful life may be laid with stones and punctuated by troughs. There's absolutely nothing good about tragedy and loss, but something good can come from the struggle in their aftermath.[7]

Something good can come from the struggle. Indeed. The psychologist and writer Daniel Goleman expresses a very similar idea when he writes that, against all the odds, it is possible for us to become aware of a 'constructive contribution,' that suffering can make to our lives;

> 'There is much to be said for the constructive contribution of suffering to the creative and spiritual life; suffering can temper the soul.'[8]

So it is clearly possible for us to master this powerful lesson that suffering is by no means solely negative, that something immensely valuable and life-enhancing can come from our struggle against adversity. I started this chapter on a Buddhist note and I would like to end it on one. Daisaku Ikeda is one of the greatest thinkers and writers on the role of Buddhism in modern society. He ties together many of the ideas we have been discussing in this chapter when he writes,

'Buddhist optimism is not the escapist optimism of those who throw up their arms in the air and say,' Somehow or other things will work out.' Rather it means clearly recognising evil as evil, and suffering as suffering, and resolutely fighting to overcome it. It means believing in one's ability and strength to struggle against any evil or obstacle. It is to possess a fighting optimism.[9]

A personal training programme

So a Buddhist practice isn't in any way about a form of *escapism*. About seeking some inner meditative refuge away from the pace and clamour and constant challenge of modern life. Although that is of course one of the most widely held stereotypes in the western world of what Buddhism is about, namely getting away from it all, or most of it. Buddhism is above all about that *'fighting optimism,'* that Daisaku Ikeda describes, and the challenging of pessimistic thoughts that Martin Seligman writes about so strongly; about challenging those attitudes and behaviours that don't lead to positive outcomes.

That can be uncomfortable of course. We all know it's far easier *not* to challenge difficulties, to go on simply complaining about problems, or responding to them instinctively, which so often means negatively. As we mentioned at the very beginning of this chapter, few things in life are more difficult than challenging patterns of thought or behaviour that we have spent years embedding into our lives. It takes real self-knowledge and courage and great perseverance to try to change them.

But setting out to achieve that change in perspective, that change in attitude, is essentially the role that the daily Buddhist practice plays. It might perhaps be seen rather as a daily *personal training programme* in how to challenge the negative, because that's what it achieves. Indeed the real greatness of this practice in my experience is precisely that; it enables us to acquire that slight shift in understanding, that slight shift in perspective, and strange as it may seem, that is all that is needed. It may only be a slight change, but time and time again it enables us to be more flexible, to look at the problem or the difficulty with a completely different attitude that breaks the deadlock, that then leads on to meaningful, positive, sometimes even remarkable outcomes in people's lives. And every time it does so of course it reinforces the confidence and the determination to tackle the next issue that comes along in a similar way.

And in that way we find ourselves moving steadily from being generally anxious and negative about problems, to being focused and positive about resolving them. So the problems remain the same of course, but our sense of being able to resolve them without a troubling burden of anxiety has changed profoundly. And problems that we feel confident we can challenge actually change in character. They no longer seem so looming or so threatening. As soon as you say, '*I've got this challenge coming up next week,*' you feel differently about it, don't you? You feel immediately that you are preparing to stand against it…and win.

It would surely help to carry around with us the wisdom that psychologist Martin Seligman has offered to us,

'Once you acquire the skills of optimism, they stay.[10]

CHAPTER FIFTEEN

The attention imperative

How often have we all been told by our teachers and lecturers at various times in our education, about the crucial importance of focus; stop daydreaming out of the window they insist and buckle down. Concentrate on the lecture or the paper or the mathematical problem that is right in front of our noses. Neuroscientists go so far as to argue that controlling and focusing our attention is just about the *most important thing* that the brain can do, since it *determines* absolutely, what we are conscious of from moment to moment, and therefore in a sense what our life is; what we can *achieve* and what we can *learn*. It is if you like the ultimate expression of the importance of living in the now. The plain truth is that however great our innate abilities might be, if we can't focus on what we are seeking to achieve, then we are severely limiting our chances of achieving it. So it follows that if we *can* improve the quality of our attention, or the strength of our ability to focus, we are opening up the potential of improving our performance in every task we undertake, everything we do, every day of our lives.[1]

The way that it actually works in practice is that to enable us to navigate our way through the crowded clamour of every day, and to make sense of the world from moment to moment, the brain learns very quickly to filter out the vast majority of what goes on around us. It does that so efficiently that we are completely unaware of it happening. As neuroscientist and philosopher Sam Harris has described it,

'We are conscious of only a tiny fraction of the information that our brains process in each moment.'[2]

But the result of this automatic filtering is immensely important to everything we do. In fact we simply couldn't function effectively without it. It means we are freed off so to speak, to *concentrate*; to concentrate our attention on the tiny part of all that activity which is foremost in our consciousness at that time. Of course, as we know from our daily experience, some people are better at it than others. Some people have butterfly-like minds, easily distracted, and finding it relatively difficult or even impossible to focus down on the issue in front of them for more than a few minutes at a time. Others have been lucky enough to have inherited...or been determined enough to have developed...a razor-sharp eyes-down focus on the task in hand.

Two forms of attention

It seems that there is now a satisfying scientific or neuro-physiological explanation for that difference. It seems that in the long process of human evolution, we have developed not one but two forms of attention. One is dubbed the 'bottom-up attention system,' which automatically *grabs* our attention away from whatever else we are doing, when it is stimulated by an extraneous event, a sudden movement or an unexpected sound or touch. We're back to that rustle in the long grass moment again; is it a prowling leopard or is it just a breath of wind? This system is very fast and above all it's *always on* so to speak, that's the key to its power. And it doesn't take much imagination to see how utterly invaluable this grab-the-attention system must have been in saving our ancestors' lives many times over, when they were stalking their supper through the bush, or trekking at night across the savannahs. And today perhaps, when dashing across Piccadilly Circus in the rush hour!

The other system is dubbed the 'top-down attention system' and as its name implies, it is the result of conscious effort; the deliberate application of the will to focus our minds on this particular issue or event that is in front of us right now, and to maintain that attention until we've worked through to the end of whatever it is that has to be done.

Is there anything we can do practically?

So, can we improve this all-important ability to focus our attention? There is on-going research seeking to provide a definitive answer, but meanwhile the key proposition on offer is that in today's hectic, time-slicing, hyper-connected age, the mere *awareness* of these two attention systems of the brain and how they work, can in itself be an invaluable aid. if we want to achieve success in any field or endeavour; academic or creative, social or business.

Why? Because it means that when we *know* that we are in a truly eyes-down-and-focus time, then we can invest more *concentration energy* so to speak, in holding our focus, and not letting it just leak away into other areas. We also know that it makes sense to do whatever we can to *insulate ourselves* from the possibility of the 'bottom up' system grabbing our attention as a result of obvious distractions, by switching off the smart phone for example and the email alert, We all know how utterly frustrating it can be when you're in the middle of what you consider to be an important conversation with someone, focusing all your attention on what you are trying to convey, when their phone squawks and their attention is automatically grabbed away by their 'bottom-up' system...and you know you've lost them!

Neuroscientists have seriously begun to use the word 'addiction' to describe our new behaviours in relation to our digital companions. It seems in fact that obsessively checking our emails and our smartphones and postings on facebook and instagram and the rest, produces exactly the same response *in the brain* as other far more damaging addictions such as drugs. Namely the release of a rush of dopamine deep inside the brain and its uptake by receptors.... followed by a feeling of pleasure.[3] But do we really want to be 'addicted' in this way?

Attention is a finite resource

Because that phrase I used a moment ago, *'concentration energy,'* turns out to be very accurate; we are using energy. What's more the neuroscientists tell us that it's *scarce* energy. That is to say getting the brain to really concentrate to its fullest extent on an issue is not an infinite resource, but very much a *finite* one. Constantly turning away from the task in hand to check our emails and our I-phones can not only become a genuine modern addiction, as we all know only too well, but it can seriously *deplete* that finite concentration energy. As neuroscientist Daniel Levitin from McGill University in Montreal has expressed it;

'Attention is a limited resource...Each time we shift attention, there is a metabolic cost we pay in glucose. We don't actually do two or three or ten things at once, we

just switch from one to another to another. Some brain activities are more expensive than others, and switching attention is among the most expensive.'[4]

That's an interesting new insight isn't it, that rapidly switching attention from one thing to another is not clever multitasking as we fondly believe? It seems we are deluding ourselves. In fact we are not only using up our scarce focusing resource, we may indeed be *wasting it.* But perhaps by far the most valuable lesson we might take away from this is that the more we make the conscious determination that we *are* going to focus our whole attention on this particular task, the more we are in effect, *training the brain* to do just that. The advice we received earlier from psychologist Daniel Goleman is wholly relevant here,

'...the new watchword in brain science is' neuroplasticity,' the notion that the brain continually changes as a result of our experience....'[5]

That is to say, the more we direct our attention to a task, and keep it there, the more we become *capable* of directing our attention to a task and keeping it there. It becomes a learned behaviour. And of course the reverse is true, the more we allow our attention to wander and be distracted by the phone alert for example, the more difficult we find it to really concentrate our attention on any particular task. We learn so to speak, to seek the *pleasure* of distraction. Doesn't that ring so true!

How we learn

There seems to be no limit to the knowledge that can fit into the brain's memory systems. As one recent paper has expressed it,

'As far as we know no one has ever run out of storage space.[6]

That may seem extraordinary in the computer age, when we are very familiar with the idea of fixed limits to storage. And what makes it even more surprising is the fact that learning is something that the brain does *naturally* so to speak. That essentially is what it is, a learning machine, that we now know actually goes into action some time before we are born, acquiring the sound of the mother's heart beat for example, and other sounds that go on outside the womb, and it continues from then on, acquiring and storing information throughout our entire lives. Although only a fraction of the stuff that the brain squirrels away can be recovered, the strange paradox is that we find that we can't consciously *unlearn* useless material by commanding the brain to dump it, once it has been acquired. There isn't so to speak a conscious delete function.

In fact if we try to command the brain to forget something, the more it seems to become embedded. The psychologists talk about this situation in various ways. Some talk in terms of the mind having in a sense, a mind of it's own! Others that you can't *force* the mind. What they are alluding to is that if you are beset with thoughts, particularly negative thoughts or feelings about a particular situation, you can't just *tell the mind* to stop thinking about it, because it won't. In fact the reverse seems to happen. The more you tell your brain to let go of any particular anxiety, to drop it at once and not give it another thought, the more fiercely it hangs onto it and turns it over and examines it from every possible angle and insists on presenting it's findings to you. Try it.

In one famous mind-control study, Harvard psychologist Daniel Wegner, who has been described as the founding father of thought suppression research, involved volunteers in what has become widely known as the white bears experiment. Very briefly, he took two groups of volunteers. One was told that they could think about anything they wanted for a period of five minutes, including, if they wished, white polar bears! The second group was asked to focus solely on verbalising their on-going stream of consciousness for the same period of 5 minutes, but specifically *not* to let their thoughts wander onto the subject of white bears. The utterly perverse result was that the second group, the white-bears-forbidden group ended up thinking about them considerably more than the first anything-goes-including-white-bears group! That is to say, deliberately trying to force the mind away from a particular theme, seems to produce precisely the reverse effect.[7]

I mention this issue only because it serves to illustrate one of the most powerful effects of the central Buddhist practices of meditation or chanting. What these techniques do in effect is to help us create something that is immensely difficult to create, namely a clear *mental space*. They provide that is a gentle and immensely effective mechanism for getting 'ourselves' out-of-the-way, so to speak, and giving the endlessly restless mind space and time to settle *on its own*.

The net result is that we are left calmer and clearer, even if we happen to be faced by a challenging problem or a crisis. This is precisely how it is described by a group of modern psychologists who use these basic Buddhist practices very effectively indeed as a form of therapy in tackling persistent depression. As they describe the process;

'… attempts to steady, calm or control our mind often merely stir things up, and make everything less clear.

But we can get out of our own way, and stop contribut-
ing to the cloudiness of the mind by encouraging it to
alight and dwell on a single object of attention for a time.
When we intentionally let go of our urge to force things
in a particular way, the mind naturally settles all by
itself, leaving us both calmer and clearer.'[8]

Can we improve our ability to learn?

But what about the fundamental question that we're all
interested in, can we improve on the brain's natural rate of
acquisition, can we get better at learning? The answer seems
to be that we can to some extent, by understanding how the
learning process takes place, and then by being very disciplined about how we apply it. So as we process information
the brain is constantly making new connections between
networks of neurons, and breaking or trimming back old
and less used connections. When we are deeply focused on
learning, that is to say *challenging* the brain to acquire new
knowledge, the actual *making of new neural connections*
takes place surprisingly quickly, literally within a matter of
hours, the brain is that malleable. But once those new connections have been made, the key to whether or not the new
brain circuits, and therefore that new learning is *retained*,
seems to depend crucially upon the new networks being
re-used frequently. The more they are re-used the stronger
the learning is embedded. What happens in fact is that
because they're re-used again and again they become an
easier and more efficient pathway for nerve signals.

So the key to improving the learning process would seem to
be not a million miles away from what experienced teachers
have often told us. First of all really *focus* the attention
on the new material, so that it goes in. Don't just give it
half your attention. And then a little later, test yourself,

repeating the learning to yourself, and doing that several times, to get those new circuits properly embedded. It also helps a great deal to consciously *tie in* the new bits of information with knowledge you already have, so that you establish a stable scaffolding for the new knowledge to slot onto.

What happens to our learning faculties as we get older?

The brain is a physical organ of course, so it ages as any other organ does. The research suggests that the normal developmental trajectory, barring mental illness, is for learning capability to increase markedly during our teens and early twenties and then to peak during our thirties, and then to decline very slowly as we get older. However there is a growing view among neuroscientists that there are several ways of slowing or even reversing losses in cognitive function. The most effective identified so far, as we discussed in greater detail in an earlier chapter, is regular physical exercise, which protects the brain by maintaining the health of the entire cardiovascular system. But as several research studies have shown, there seems to be no established *physiological* reason for cognitive function to diminish, as we've all been led to believe for so long;

> '*The good news is that there seems to be no physiological reason for the slowdown. Instead it seems to be a lot to do with the fact that we simply spend less time learning new stuff, and when we do, we don't do it with the same potent mix of enthusiasm and attention as the average child.*'[9]

The belief that older people can't learn so well has probably been very damaging; '*I can't learn because I'm past it,*' has become something of a self-fulfilling mantra for many older people. Whereas we know that lots of people go on producing excellent works of art and literature and music and science well on into their eighties. Indeed a significant case in point is one of the world's renowned experts on intelligence and its measurement, psychologist James Flynn. He is the scientist credited with establishing that the average IQ around the world seems to have increased by about 3 points every decade over the past hundred years or so,[10] largely because of the increased richness of people's experience. Or as he expresses it;

> *'Our ancestors were just as good as we are at practical intelligence, at dealing with everyday life. But we have developed the mental skills needed to deal with the demands of the modern world.'* [11]

This discovery has now officially taken his name, it's called the Flynn Effect. But he is now 82, and when he was asked in interview recently how he felt about his own cognitive abilities at that advanced age, his response was refreshingly robust;

> *'Oddly enough, I don't really feel I have fewer new ideas or am able to do less analysis than I could at 20! I find my working memory has slipped a bit. I've remained intensely active. I still run'* [12]

I love that opening phrase of his, *'oddly enough,'* as if this brain expert is genuinely surprised that his own brain is still lively! In fact he's still lecturing on two university courses. But that final comment is crucially important because it expresses the importance that James Flynn…a man very much in the know… attaches to continuing regular physical exercise to help maintain cognitive ability. I confess that particularly appeals to me since I still run as well! My golden retriever Gatsby takes me for a long run round Richmond Park every morning. And all the research suggests that remaining physically active carries an even more positive message for those who haven't made much use of their learning faculties for some time, and think they might just have curled up and died. The evidence suggests that they haven't;

> *'With a little exercise the brain can spring back to life. In one study, 40 minutes of exercise three times a week for a year, increased the size of the hippocampus...which is crucial for learning and memory. It also improved connectivity across the brain, making it easier for new things to stick.'*[13]

And just to drive that point home, another expert in the field, psychology Professor Douwe Draaisma, from Groningen University in The Netherlands puts forward a similar view in his recent book entitled *The Nostalgia Factory*. His research findings are very encouraging to anyone past the half-century mark; his advice briefly is that there is nothing to worry about, since any decline in memory function is slight and slow. He thinks that many older people have been *conditioned* into believing that their memories are failing, and the belief simply becomes self-fulfilling.[14]

So what have we learned from this chapter? Well I hope at least three things. One, that our ability to focus our attention is very much a finite resource rather than an infinite one, and that what we fondly call multi-tasking these days may turn out to be a somewhat inefficient behaviour. Two, that our brains can remain agile and flexible and adaptable for far longer into our adult and older lives than has hitherto been recognised. And finally, that in working hard to improve our focus or our attention, in the way we study and work, we are changing the way our brain works, and steadily developing an invaluable new skill, a skill moreover that can raise our game right across the spectrum of our lives.

CHAPTER SIXTEEN

I need at least 8 hours

Why do we sleep? It seems such an obvious and almost pointless question doesn't it? Because we're tired of course comes the answer. But in fact it turns out to be a far more complicated issue than we might expect. One that has challenged philosophers and scientists and doctors for centuries, and still does to this day. The fact is that although it has been deeply and seriously researched for so many years, much about the nature of sleep and it's primary function still lies in the realm of controversy rather than fact. As an example of the depth of that controversy we might perhaps cite a comment made recently by one very experienced researcher in the field, Robert Stickgold Professor of psychiatry at Harvard Medical School;

> *'I think this means,'* he observed,' *that we're still lost when it comes to understanding the role of different sleep stages in memory.'*[1]

To say that *'we're still lost'* is quite a tough admission for a senior scientist to make when he's talking about a field of inquiry in which he has been prominent for many years. In that report he was commenting on totally conflicting theories that had been put forward by highly experienced sleep researchers, one of them himself, on the role of the various stages of sleep we normally go through each night, in helping to process and 'fix' our memories. Helping to consolidate our memories is just one of many theories that have been proposed to explain the function of sleep in our lives. The current theories extend from regulating our emotions, to processing and sorting through all the information that has flooded into our brains during the day, to the relatively simple and straightforward one of saving energy. But even that explanation turns out to be not quite so straightforward as we might expect.

But while the fundamental reasons for sleep may remain something of a mystery, with lots of intriguing questions still seeking answers, there is absolutely no question about its profound and fundamental importance to our overall sense of well-being, which is essentially the reason for this chapter. The statements by all the leading researchers in the field are categorical.

'There is no tissue within the body and no process within the brain that is not enhanced by sleep, or demonstrably impaired when you don't get enough.'[2]

While another eminent neuroscientist declares without qualification,

'Sleep is the single most effective thing you can do to reset your brain and body for health.'[3]

That is a huge claim isn't it….the single most effective thing you can do …meanwhile widespread research has revealed that too little sleep not only messes with our emotions and our ability to make good decisions, but it severely reduces the effectiveness of our immune system.[4]

The primary stages of sleep

When we sleep it is well established that we pass through a regular series of stages until we reach the deepest sleep, and all the mainstream approaches to the study of sleep have focused on trying to define the function of these various stages. What precise role do they fulfil since the changing patterns of electrical activity in the sleeping brain can be very clearly identified. They reveal that we normally go through several cycles, with each complete cycle lasting roughly 90 minutes, and each one is made up of five distinct stages. We pass through four stages of steadily deepening sleep described as non-rapid-eye movement sleep, or non-REM sleep. The deepest of these stages, which is marked by long slow 'delta' brainwaves has been clearly shown to play a crucially important role in maintaining the on-going health of the brain. Then there is a period of what is known as rapid eye movement sleep, or REM sleep as it is normally described, because it is characterised by very rapid movement of the eyelids and very considerable brain activity, although we are totally asleep, which takes us back to the surface so to speak, and another cycle can begin. It seems that most people under normal circumstances might go through four or five either complete or partial 90 minute cycles each night.[5]

REM sleep

Much of the research has been focused on the stage of REM sleep because this seems to be the time when most activity is going on, in the brain that is. It's during this phase for example that most dreaming seems to occur, although we can actually experience dreams during any of the other stages. REM sleep is the time during which, paradoxically, the body is inert and virtually paralysed, but the brain waves show that the brain is highly active, almost as active in fact as it is in full wakefulness. It is this intense neural activity which has led to the dominant hypothesis that has held sway for so long, namely that sleep is really about giving the brain a chance to sort out and neatly file away all the stuff it has been conscious of during the day. According to this hypothesis, while we are lying physically inert in REM sleep, our brain is hard at work consolidating memories and extracting and laying down what have been described as *'themes and rules,'* from the mass of events and experiences and emotions that it has been exposed to during our waking hours.[6]

So what's the purpose of dreams?

It seems that all healthy people dream, and dreams have always been a puzzle. So vivid and so intense and yet so elusive. Little wonder then that attempts to interpret the purpose and the meaning of dreams have been a fascinating strand of exploration throughout human civilisation. Indeed at various periods those supposed interpretations have played an important part in shaping the very course of historic events. Witness the Pharoah's various plague dreams in the Old Testament that led to the release of the Israelites from slavery in Egypt. In more recent times of course, in the early 1900's, we've had Sigmund Freud, with his famous work *The Interpretation of Dreams*, in which he set out his firmly held belief that interpreting our dreams could unlock the messages they contained about our suppressed sexual desires. In proposing this theory so strongly it could well be argued that he completely re-shaped western society's views about human sexuality, although it's important to mention that those ideas seem now to have largely fallen by the wayside.[7]

Currently this key controversy revolves around the extent to which our dreams might be related to the consolidation of our daytime memories. Robert Stickgold from Harvard for example clings firmly to his view that there *is* a very strong connection;

> '*It's clear,*' he argues,' *that the brain does an immense amount of memory processing while we sleep, and it certainly isn't mere coincidence that while the brain is sorting out these memories and how they fit together... we're dreaming.*'[8]

So he's very much wedded to the view that dreams in a sense hold some kind of mirror up to the experiences we've had during our waking hours.

Professor Matthew Walker, from the influential Sleep and Neuroimaging Laboratory at the University of California at Berkeley, doesn't fundamentally disagree with this view, although he doesn't see this as their *main* purpose. He argues that the essential role of our dreams is to provide a sort of *rebalancing* of our emotions after a hard day's life,

> '*I think the evidence is mounting,*' he writes,' *in favour of dream sleep acting as an emotional homeostasis; basically rebalancing the emotional compass in a good way...,*'[9]

He cites as evidence for this view the experience that we've all had at various times, when even quite a short nap can transform a cantankerous child into a sweet tempered one, and even...as we all know... take much of the grumpiness out of an equally cantankerous adult. In this way, he argues, conjuring up an extremely powerful and evocative phrase, '*REM dreams act as a kind of balm for the brain.*'[10]

I have to say that I find that an extremely persuasive and attractive theory, and it certainly buttresses the idea that our periods of dream-sleep are essential to our general well-being and that we couldn't function normally without them. That has become an increasingly powerful argument in all the key centres of sleep research.

But what do they mean?

But when we come to the $64,000 question of what dreams *actually mean*, once again we find that there is no definitive hypothesis. One camp for example, represented by researchers such as Matthew Walker, argues, somewhat disappointingly, that the dreams themselves have *no intrinsic meaning*. The images or experiences within the dreams according to this view, are just the unimportant, more or less meaningless *side effect* or by-product of the underlying electrical activity in the brain, which is the important thing that is going on. Walker has even gone so far as to comment,

'I don't want to believe it, but I don't see large amounts of evidence to support the idea that the dreams themselves are significant.'[11]

The other camp, best represented perhaps by Robert Stickgold argues that the actual content of dreams is at least consistent with the idea that during the dreaming experience, the brain is filing away memories in a sort of coherent structure with other past experiences, to enable us to refer to them in the future. Although he too admits, he doesn't have much actual evidence to sustain that view,

'Dreams have to be connected in a meaningful functional way to improvements in memory...' But then he adds tellingly,' *I say this with fervent emotion, which is what I use when I don't have hard data!'*[12]

One can only admire the sheer honesty of the admission that he's prepared to replace the gaps in the data with fervent emotion! But the bottom line would seem to be that however much we personally may fantasise about our dreams, scientifically speaking, the jury is still out on the question of whether or not those dreams actually *mean* anything.

The secret chemical life of the brain

So where do we go from here? Well leaving aside those perennial issues we've been discussing of rest and dreams and memory consolidation, over the past handful of years a quite different line of exploration has now come to dominate much scientific thinking on the purposes of sleep. Essentially it has to do with clearing away the brain's waste products. Or as that idea is expressed in somewhat more scientific terms, it has to do with the need for the brain to cope with *'the biochemical consequences of metabolic activity during waking hours.'* That is to say, clearing away the free radicals and other waste products that are formed while the brain is hard at work like a furnace burning up so much energy during the day. Free radicals can do serious damage not only to the functioning of the brain, but more widely in the body's cells.[13]

It seems that scientists have now been able to build up a far more detailed picture of what might be called perhaps the *secret chemical life* of the brain, what it actually does when it's truly off line, when we're deeply asleep. And it turns out to be such a complex, but above all such a crucially important new understanding for all of us, that it has led to a raft of public health declarations designed to make us more aware of the dangers to our general health if we don't take sleep seriously enough. Medical scientists and institutions

are arguing that we now have a genuinely scientific explanation, as opposed to the personal and anecdotal one we
have always had, for the fact that an adequate amount of
sleep plays an overwhelming role in achieving greater well-
being, which after all is what this book is about. These
public bodies now argue that it is imperative that the new
information gets out into the wider public arena, to generate a major shift in people's understanding.

Taking sleep very seriously indeed

In the USA for example it is being given a much higher
national profile. No less an institution than the powerful
and authoritative Centre for Disease Control, is talking
about insufficient sleep having reached the stage of *a public
health epidemic,'* and about the need for a fundamental cultural shift, to establish a common understanding that adequate sleep is *'a non-negotiable priority.'[14]*

That is unquestionably strong language coming from a
major government organisation, and it would seem to be
based on figures given in the same article, that around 70
million people in the US, that's about one person in every
five of the population, suffer from inadequate sleep on a
regular basis. And they are not alone in sounding warning
bells that something is amiss. In the UK the prestigious
Sleep and Circadian Neuroscience Institute, (SCNI) based
at Oxford University, argues that on average adults are
sleeping fully two hours less a night than they were 50 years
ago, perhaps because we are living in an altogether more
highly pressured, no-time-to-stop society.

In a similar vein the American Academy of Pediatrics has
now thrown its considerable professional weight behind
the idea of all secondary schools starting at least one hour

later in the mornings, to enable sleep-hungry teenagers to fit in a bit more of it, on a regular basis. Why? Because all the research indicates that they are not just being lazy these teenagers, they do indeed *need* more than the average 7-8 hours. The latest reports indicate that over 1000 high schools have already adopted this idea, and that it does seem to be bearing fruit, with students being more attentive in class and showing improvements in exam grades.

Pilot studies in the UK that have tested a similar regime have produced promising results with students who have benefited from the later start showing improved grades in their first public examination at GCSE level. As a result those pilot studies are now being extended, and it would seem that the pressures for a change of this kind to be adopted more widely, can only grow, as more schools, and no doubt more parents, come to understand the findings of the new research.

And just to drive home the general point, we can go to one of the most prominent American researchers in the field, Mary Carskadon, a professor of Psychiatry and Human Behaviour at Brown University, who has focused much of her research on the sleep problems of young people. She argues that because sleep is such an everyday part of our existence, we haven't really grasped the seriousness of the change that has taken place in society over the past couple of decades, to drive down the amount of sleep young people are likely to have. The implications of those social changes, in Mary Carskadon's view, *'are scary, really scary!'[15]*

The heavyweight nature of those comments is likely to take most people by surprise. But if we put these expert views together they would seem to suggest that…at least in the western world…we might well be described as the most sleep-deprived generation in human history, without really being aware of it, or of its considerable adverse implications for our overall well-being.

The 24 hour society

It has become a truism to say that we have created for ourselves a genuine 24-hour culture, in the sense that the part of the 24 hour day that we previously allocated solely to sleep, is now widely allocated to a whole range of other activities. So we now have regular 24 hour city-centre life, 24 hour supermarkets, round-the-clock on-line shopping and entertainment and news channels, and all-night flights, and all-night trains and buses, not to mention 24/7 connectivity almost wherever you are in the world. None of that is going to go away of course. It can only grow and spread because it has brought so much that is valuable and life-enhancing. But what the neuroscientists and psychologists are telling us loud and clear, is that we're simply fooling ourselves if we believe that this non-stop activity isn't having its profound effects. There is no such thing as a free lunch they argue. In fact they are saying, there is a very substantial bill to pay for this growing trend to regard sleep as a kind of optional extra. In fact sleep has become so undervalued that it's not uncommon to hear people boasting about just how little sleep they can get by on, as if not giving in to sleep were a kind of special social achievement.

The professional research bodies, such as for example the wide-ranging sleep research institute in the UK, the SCNI we've quoted from earlier, puts the bill that has to be paid somewhat more formally when it declares,

'We know that this imposed social culture is in conflict with our basic biology and sub-optimal for our health.'[6]

That phrase, sub-optimal for our health, obviously covers a multitude of effects that the SCNI goes on to describe.

Decline in thinking skills, grumpy and irritable

It's quite clear that even quite small disruptions in the quality and the duration of our sleep, have an immediate knock-on effect on how we function, even if we're not immediately conscious of it. For example studies consistently show that people who regularly get less than around 8 hours sleep a night, commonly report that their efficiency and thinking skills haven't been affected in the slightest. They feel fine! However, when they're given a battery of standard memory and concentration tests, they simply don't perform well. When the sleep loss is more severe, the studies show just how rapidly that cognitive deterioration becomes apparent.

So after just one night without proper sleep for example, the researchers describe how we find it far more difficult to concentrate on an issue for any length of time in a meeting, or an across-the-table discussion, because our attention span is so much shorter. And we tend to be grumpy and irritable, a regular bear with a sore head, because being reasonably sociable in a stressful situation requires *energy and attention* we no longer have available. I suggest that we don't have to fly many long-distance night flights, or take part in many all-night shindigs, to have experience of what they describe academically as *cognitive deterioration*.

And it's clear that our cognitive abilities go steadily down-hill as we move into a second night with poor sleep. All the higher functions of the brain are powerfully affected. So anything to do with judgement or decision-making suffers, as does our ability to plan ahead or to concentrate on specific issues for any length of time. We may not be particularly drowsy, but we find it increasingly difficult if not impossible, to follow the thread of what's being said, and to respond coherently. We've all been there several times I'm sure, during the course of our business lives.

If we go on in this sleepless mode for any longer then for most of us... although admittedly not for all...there are some tough guys out there who can soldier on for longer and still deliver some sort of concentration...but for most of us, the brain practically shuts down, and refuses to function. Taking those effects together it is not difficult to see why major institutions at the national and international level are issuing this wake-up call, if you'll pardon the pun, to create a wider awareness of the fact that western societies have, in effect, become involved in a huge unplanned *experiment*, trading sleep-time for our brightly-lit, screen-obsessed 24 hour culture, with no sure knowledge of the outcome.

The new research: waste disposal

What the very latest research has done is to take us down to the level of the brain cell, so that we now have a much clearer picture of what is actually going on at the level of basic brain chemistry, when we don't get enough sleep. As you might expect much of the research at this level has been carried out with laboratory animals, for obvious reasons, you can't slice into a human brain after it has had too little sleep! But what the new studies reveal is that whether or not the brain is sorting and filing memories as we have been discussing, *biologically speaking*, deep sleep is an abso-lutely crucial *waste disposal time*.

> *'…until very recently, scientists couldn't even agree on the evolutionary reason why animals need sleep in the first place. But now they know that what happens during sleep, particularly in the brain, is critical to human well-being…not to mention a long life. That's why they also know that the cost of ignoring the latest science on sleep can be dear.'*[17]

So what does that mean exactly? Well all organs in the body need a constant supply of energy to keep functioning prop-erly, and as they burn it up they inevitably create various waste products that have to be cleared away. For most organs these waste products are largely broken down and carried away in the network of blood vessels that make up the lymph system, a key part of the body's waste disposal system. However the brain, which is by far the greatest consumer of energy of any organ in the body when it's on-line, is not gen-erously supplied with lymph vessels, so, we now know, other systems have evolved to carry away its substantial amounts of waste and potentially damaging free radicals.

But the catch as far as today's 24 hour culture is concerned, is that these waste disposal systems can *only* come into play when we reach the deepest stage of sleep as the 90 minute cycles we mentioned earlier, follow one another. And it's this repetitive cycle that really establishes the amount of sleep we need. There is no magic or correct number. As you would expect it varies from person to person. We only really know how much we need as individuals from how we feel when we wake up! Are we bright and breezy and ready to bounce out into the day, or are we tired and lethargic and have to drag ourselves to the station. We all have much experience of both of those feelings. But the *average sleep need* seems to fall out at a nice neat 8 hours, which gives us a kind of target to aim for.[18]

Cleaning up operations

During these essential periods of deepest sleep two vital cleaning up operations have now been identified. One is that the neurons that have been producing toxic free radicals when they were firing away all day, burning energy, turn to producing anti-oxidants to neutralise them. The second involves the huge army of support cells in the brain, which are known as glial cells. Unlike neurons these cells don't conduct electrical signals, essentially they provide support and structure and to some extent insulation. But it is now known that they have a vital additional role during deep sleep. They combine to create what the researchers describe as a sort of pump, flushing the metabolic debris and the harmful waste products out of the brain. The key point to hang onto is that this cleaning up operation takes *several cycles* of the deepest sleep, and we now know far more clearly what happens if we don't give it enough time.

We now know, says one leading researcher into the anti-oxidant process, that there is a lasting price to pay for even short periods of sleep loss;

> '...the cells are working hard but cannot make enough anti-oxidants, so they progressively build up free radicals and some of the neurons die off.'[19]

Neurons dying off in our brains is not what we want to hear is it?

So one crucial new understanding that comes out of this research is that sleep really only works well if we get *enough* of the deepest sleep. Of course there's a benefit for both mind and body coming from any form of rest including several hours of sleep. But it now seems clear that it is not enough for us just to go on snatching the few hours of sleep that we think we can spare from our work or our play. What this research seems to be saying is that only if we regularly give the brain *enough cycles* of deep sleep to enable the waste clearing operations to be completed, can we be sure of being at our most effective, at work and at play, and so avoiding those longer term problems.

So what can we do about it?

The obvious question that comes to mind is, can we catch up? If we have a tough sleep-deprived week can we pay back the debt by crashing out over the weekend, as indeed we often try to do? The answer so far would seem to be no better than a cautious maybe. There has been some research into precisely this scenario, involving healthy volunteers who arranged their lives so as to build up considerable sleep debt during the week, and then put in at least 10 hours a night over the weekend. The results of blood tests showed that there was some improvement, in particular in their insulin and blood sugar levels, which suggests that the strategy of trying to balance out the sleep account in this way can at least redress some of the effects. So it's a strategy that many of us will no doubt go on using, to try to maintain a more or less neutral sleep balance over a period of a week or so.

But what the scientists and doctors seem to be suggesting is that there are no easy remedies or short cuts to resolve the issue. The 24 hour culture and the demands it makes upon us are clearly not going to go away any time soon. What is needed they are saying, is a widespread social *re-branding* of sleep. So that instead of seeing sleep as sort of down time, something that in a sense takes us away from the pleasures and the stimulations of the 24 hour culture, we come to see it as an absolute necessity, part of our *evolutionary heritage* no less, and an essential precondition for living the full and active and healthy life we all seek.

That re-branding, or re-calibration can only happen at the individual level. And although it may seem strange to all of us, after so many decades if not centuries of research into the deep mysteries of sleep, the plain fact is that it is only in the past few years that this fuller *biological* understanding is emerging. It is now becoming clear just how powerful sleep is, more powerful than any drug, in *restoring and rejuvenating* both brain and body. As it was expressed in a recent science-based article on sleep;

> *'Getting the recommended seven to eight hours each night can improve concentration, sharpen planning and memory skills and maintain the fat-burning systems that regulate our weight.'*[20]

It goes without saying I think, that those are things we all want in our lives, and there's no doubt, it lies well within our capabilities to plan things in such a way that we achieve them. Once again I suggest, *awareness* is everything; it's the awareness and the deeper understanding of the situation that is the key to change in a positive, value-creating direction.

CHAPTER SEVENTEEN

It's the mouse that
does the moving

Read just about any Dickensian novel and before long you're bound to come across the faithful office clerk sitting on a high stool, poring over some heavy accounting ledger. Eventually he gets up, slams the ledger shut with a thud, and lugs it with considerable physical effort across the office to the bookshelves. And then staggers back to his desk with the next one. You had to be fit to be a Dickensian ledger clerk! The scene changed somewhat of course as the years went by, ledgers got lighter and the stools became chairs. But that basic scenario, record files of one kind or another being carried by someone from desk to filing cabinet, and back again, has been a very enduring one indeed, in workplaces of every kind all over the world.

But not any more of course. Nowadays it's only the mouse that does the moving. The admin-type person just sits. Sits and watches the screen, and moves the mouse backwards and forwards and clicks the forefinger, hundreds of times in a working day. And it's not just the admin guy is it? It's all of us. Managers and accountants, admen and analysts and scientists and writers, and engineers and lawyers and television producers... and the rest. We spend hours of each day sitting on our butts, and moving a mouse around to drive the screen that drives whatever endeavour we happen to be involved in. As indeed I am doing at this very moment.

It is in fact such a huge and universal transformation of the working environment, that has taken place only over the past 20 years or so, that it has led to whole new field of research; it's called... with only the most marginal application of imagination...inactivity research! And there's no doubt that it is something we should at least be aware off, partly because it affects so many of us, a huge swathe of the global working population, but also because once aware of it, we might well want to do what we can to adapt our lifestyle to avoid the worst effects of it. Because of course, such a huge daily programme of inactivity does indeed have effects. And I ought to add here perhaps that I have certainly modified the nature of my own working day to take this research into account, as indeed have the researchers themselves.

Basically studies across the world, from the US and Europe in the West to Australia in the East, all point very much in the same direction, they tell us that inactivity, particularly long periods of sitting inactivity in front of a TV screen or a computer screen or whatever, is bad news. It isn't doing anyone any good.

We've always had an inkling that prolonged inactivity of this nature can't be doing us a great deal of good. What has emerged in the part few years is a much clearer definition of the *no-good* that it is doing to us, that is to say the actual effects of just sitting for hours on end.

Some research studies

Let's look at a couple of the leading research studies to make that point stick. So there was a very large study carried out a few years ago by the American Cancer Society based in Atlanta Georgia. What they did was to re-analyse the data collected from studies over some 14 years, so a very long time period, and involving a very large body of subjects, no less than 123,000 people. Most of them middle aged. And they were careful to take into account other highly influential factors such as diet. When the results are expressed as bald percentages they are startling, hard to believe even, but they've been published in a very prestigious journal, *The American Journal of Epidemiology*[1] so we can have some confidence in their accuracy.

What they were trying to pin down was the overall effects on health of people who were inactive for long periods of the day, so they split the studies into two sub-groups. Those where people reported that they were *mildly inactive*, spending less than 3 hours a day sitting around, and those who described themselves as *highly inactive*, spending as much as 6 hours a day, pretty much sitting on their backsides. The results as I've said were nothing short of startling. They indicated that the people in the highly inactive, 6-hours-a-day group, had a substantially higher mortality rate over the period than the mildly inactive group. As high as 37% higher for the men, and 17% for the women. They haven't yet been able to explain this big difference between men and women, but their key point of course is clear; it is that long periods of inactivity like this are literally shortening people's lives.[2]

Another influential study reported in the same highly-rated journal comes from the University of Queensland in

Brisbane. This was also a very substantial study looking at the sedentary habits of nearly 9000 people, so again a very large sample. This time they concentrated on inactivity largely in front of a television screen, and again, the results are equally startling. They indicate that people who regularly watch around 6 hours TV a day are, on average, slicing as much as 5 years off their life expectancy.

And as the journal expresses it, these kinds of results, which are I suggest, pretty surprising for most of us, are supported by many similar studies in different environments, as the paper makes clear; *'There are many other studies reaching similar conclusions.'*[3]

So the key point emphasised by the researchers is that sitting still for hours at a time is a major health risk, *regardless* of what you do with the rest of the day. The analogy they draw is that just as you can't cancel out the effect of smoking 20 cigarettes a day, by eating a healthy diet, or by exercising aggressively at the weekend, so you can't cancel out the effects of sitting still for hours on end, by periodic bouts of high intensity exercise. The sitting still it seems, takes its toll regardless.[4]

So what does inactivity do to the body?

It probably helps to go into a bit more detail on the changes that have been identified in the body as a result of the sort of extended inactivity we've been talking about. Without being overly technical about it, let me just mention four changes that the researchers define, that I think are enough to make the point stick. Basically, they talk of *'a cascade of metabolic changes,'* that affect the way the body handles two key energy-producing substances, fats or lipids and carbohydrates or glucose, that need to be kept in balance in a healthy bloodstream.

- So one, because the muscles are given so little work to do they not only atrophy or lose mass, but they change from strength-type muscles that can burn fat, to what are known as 'fast-twitch' muscles that rely more strongly on sugars or carbohydrates.
- Two, the muscles actually begin to lose the crucial power packs or mitochondria in the cells, which also are there to produce their energy by burning fat.
- Three, so where does all that unburned fat go? It goes into the bloodstream, so that the blood becomes very fatty, which it's argued, could be the main reason why prolonged inactivity is linked closely to heart disease. And more fat is laid down in places where it's not supposed to be stored, such as the liver and the colon, where it can lead to several other complications.
- And four, a condition known as *insulin resistance* can occur; it's described by the researchers as being not dissimilar to diabetes in which unwanted and uncontrolled peaks or *spikes* as they are called, of glucose, build up in the bloodstream. We want to avoid those spikes.

How long before these changes begin to take place? Well, as one scientist has reported, Audrey Bergouignan, a human physiologist at the University of Colorado, the surprising fact is that they can begin to be seen in as little as *three days inactivity!*[5] Moreover, just to underline this point, these same forms of damaging changes were seen to occur even in normally fit and active people, when they were asked to change their life style for a few weeks, and spend their time sitting around on the couch, for the sake of the research.

But that I think is more than enough of the downside. Now that we're aware of the problem, what can we do about it?

So what can we do about it?

That's really the only question that concerns us isn't it? What can we do as individuals to reduce these damaging effects. And it is of course a question that has vastly different implications if the inactivity is a matter of choice, as opposed to being imposed on us by the working environment. If it's a matter of choice, someone who is retired say, and has time on his or her hands, and hasn't yet worked out what to do with it, then this new information might serve as a wake-up call, that it's time to start programming in regular bouts of activity to break up the sitting. And we're told that it doesn't have to be pumping heavy iron or taking up triathlons to make a real difference. Walking or jogging round the local park, playing golf, mowing the lawn, light gardening, or a walk along the river for half an hour can make a real difference. Anything that raises the pulse rate a little and gets the muscles working will bring huge benefits.

But if the inactivity is enforced in the sense of being part and parcel of the working environment, then it's obviously a much tougher nut to crack. For an increasing number of jobs right across the work spectrum, in every kind of setting, there is far greater in-built inactivity in front of a screen. One study for example involved hundreds of volunteers in different jobs, who were asked to wear inclinometers and accelerometers, to measure and record precisely how much activity they had during a typical day, and how much sitting time. It revealed up to a staggering 75% sitting down time. And all the evidence would suggest that that represents the growing trend. So what can we do?

Well the bad news... and it is bad news I'm sure for many of us...is that it doesn't look from the research as if we can compensate for all that inactivity, by having bouts of hyper-activity in the gym or on the tennis court at the weekend say. Periodic periods of high activity it seems, don't, as so many of us might hope or believe, *cancel out* the damaging effects of all those hours spent sitting most days.

That's quite a difficult finding to accept isn't it? I'm sure I'm not alone in believing that although I spend several hours a day sitting still at the computer stringing words together, that prolonged inactivity is in some measure *cancelled out* by my eagerness to get to the gym several evenings in the week, to burn off some of the frustrations and the lethargy that inevitably build up in front of a screen.

What the scientists are telling us is that although any exercise is good for us, and we shouldn't under any circumstances jettison it, it shouldn't be regarded as a *compensating* factor. Distinguished researchers in this field such as Dr. Alpa Patel[6] from the American Cancer Society and Professor David Dunstan from the Baker Heart and Diabetes Institute in Melbourne,[7] are very keen to re-affirm the immense value to our general physical and mental health of bouts of strenuous exercise. So that we know for sure that if we take the trouble to exercise for 40 to 60 minutes a day, we're going to have a significant health benefit. What we shouldn't do however, is to assume that such periodic exercise resolves the long-periods-of-inactivity problem. It doesn't. As David Dunstan has expressed it in interview,

> *'We shouldn't throw out the well-documented benefits of vigorous physical activity. Rather we should think of extensive sitting as another risk factor that should be addressed separately.'[8]*

So where do we go from here?

What the scientists involved in this research suggest is that we should seek out all the ways that we can to introduce brief *activity breaks* into our daily office routine, short bursts of what's described as low-intensity physical activity, so that we break up the periods of just sitting. Several of the scientists themselves have started to use treadmill desks, so that they can actually walk while they work. They don't have to walk at a particularly energetic pace, just strolling along at a regular pace seems to do the trick. Others make a point of choosing to handle their phone calls on the move, strolling round the office before they get back in front of the screen to deal with more of the emails.

The research suggests that these very short bursts of mild activity are enough to burn off some of the glucose that has built up in the bloodstream so that those unwanted spikes are reduced. One of the schedules that has been mentioned is getting up and walking around for perhaps 5 minutes in every hour. Getting up, walking to the water fountain and walking back say. It's also noted that a simple break from the computer screen of that nature, is likely to improve rather than reduce productivity.

Let me give the last word on this issue to Dr. Alpa Patel from the American Cancer Society,

> *'The nice take home message,'* she declares, *'is that anything is better than nothing. Just getting up and moving at all is taking a big step in the right direction.'*[9]

So there it is in plain language…anything is better than nothing.

Writing leads to better recall

We've been talking in this chapter about spending a long time in front of screens of one kind or another, and as you might expect, there's been some interesting research over the past couple of years to look at whether this rapid transformation from pen-on-paper to fingers-on-keyboard has had any effect on the way our brains function. There's no going back of course, we all know that screens are here to stay. But the research is interesting in that it does seem to reveal a profound change in *perception*. Some time ago University of Oxford neuroscientist Professor Susan Greenfield commented that a regular daily diet of several hours of screen time of various kinds cannot be regarded as a *neutral experience,* as far as brain function or brain wiring is concerned.

> *'It's hard to see,'* she has written, *'how living in this way on a daily basis will not result in brains, or rather minds, different from those of previous generations 10*

The interesting thing is that the new research would seem to bear out her prediction in some measure. It suggests that *typing* onto a screen rather than *handwriting* into a notebook actually does have an effect on the way we *think.*

One recent study for example at Princeton University in America, revealed a significant difference in the *recall performance* of students who took lecture notes manually so to speak, writing them down in longhand in a notebook, and those who typed notes onto a laptop. Although the screen workers recorded far more material, apparently their *recall* was far less. Were the neater, fuller typed notes better for revision however, as many of us might believe? Apparently not in this particular study. When the notes were used for revision study a week after the lecture, those students who had written out their notes by hand still had markedly better recall.

The explanation that has been proposed for the difference in recall is that because we generally write far more slowly than we can type, we are forced to work through and *comprehend* the ideas in the lecture as we receive them, so that we can select those that we wish to write down. That is to say, there is a clear, initial comprehension process going on in the case of the longhand note-takers, whereas that process would not appear to be there in the case of the typists.[11] That result would seem to be at the very least interesting for university students the world over.

But let me just bring this discussion to an end by mentioning an utterly fascinating glimpse of the brain going about its daily work that comes out of these studies. They've shown that when we are *reading* words, the same areas of the brain light up as when we are manually *writing* them. That would suggest that when we read words we are essentially *writing those words in our mind* as we read them. That's a fascinating insight into the way our higher faculties are profoundly interconnected. An acute reminder in a sense, of the complexity of the evolutionary journey homo sapiens has followed, achieving speech first, and then *re-using* and re-wiring those same networks as he went on to achieve writing and reading.

Chapter Eighteen

All you ever needed to know about the vagus nerve

Individual nerves are not often the subject of an entire chapter devoted solely to what they are and what they do. But…as nerves go… the vagus undoubtedly has a lot going for it. What's more, although most of us are likely to know little or nothing about it, recent research indicates that it plays an absolutely central role in several areas of our life, including above all, our general sense of well-being. And since that is the central theme of this book, and indeed the primary purpose of a Buddhist practice, it is I suggest, worth our knowing at least something about it, even if only as a sort of background knowledge to our daily experience. So let me try to establish its role with just two or three basic points.

We've known about this major nerve from way back since Roman times, largely because of the writings of a famous Greek anatomist called Galen, who was the personal physician to several Roman emperors. But of course it's the research that has been carried out over the past decade or so that has revealed just how deeply the vagus nerve seems to be connected with our overall sense of well-being. A whole host of researchers, coming from totally different directions and disciplines, although predominantly psychologists and neuroscientists as you might expect, have established that the vagus nerve plays an absolutely central role in our on-going life state from moment to moment; that is to say how we *feel* about our lives and what we happen to be doing at this moment.

The vagus nerve runs from the brain stem all the way down to the digestive system. It has many branches...vagus means wandering in Latin...that connect it to the lungs and the stomach for example, so it's deeply involved in the processes of getting vital oxygen and fuel into the body, and above all it's connected to the heart to control the heart rate and blood pressure. So it's constantly carrying a huge amount of information from those vital organs to the brain about what our body is doing, and the state that it's in, and a huge flow of instructions going the other way to keep things as close to being in balance as the situation allows.

And finally the vagus nerve might be called perhaps the calming nerve, since it is deeply involved in the process of calming us down and bringing us back to a settled and relaxed state, after we've been involved in a stressful situation. During our evolutionary journey that might well have been a genuine fight-or-flight, leopard-in-the-bushes survival event that set the heart racing and put all the body's systems on red alert. These days it might be anything from being late for our commuter train, to being involved in an argument perhaps, or a marital tiff of some kind, or receiving an unexpectedly stiff demand from the taxman. Any situations that unsettle us and throw us off balance, and perhaps even create a mild sense of panic. Whatever it might be we owe a great deal to the vagus nerve for getting us back to a more relaxed state, which is so much better for our mental well-being.

But its ability to achieve that invaluable stabilising, balancing, calming down process depends on something known as *vagal tone.*

So what is this vagal tone?

We can apparently think of 'vagal tone,' in very much the same way we think of muscle tone. Essentially it describes the strength of the activity of this nerve, or the efficiency with which it carries out it's work, and the speed with which it responds to the different situations and circumstances we encounter from moment to moment. It was commonly believed that this was almost entirely a question of inheritance, that it came so to say, with our DNA. More recently however it has been shown conclusively that we *can* take action to strengthen our vagal tone in various ways. And it's that development I suggest, that brings it into the range of our wider discussion. Having a high vagal tone as it's called plays a *crucial role* in our maintaining a stable and above all a *positive* life state in all those difficult and challenging circumstances that just keep on coming. We are back if you like to the very purpose of a Buddhist practice! So how might we go about achieving a stronger vagal tone?

That might raise the question in your head of just how vagal tone can be measured, so let's deal with that issue very briefly. It might seem strange to suggest that we can measure something as intangible and as tenuous as the tone in a single nerve, but it seems that there are several simple, well-established methods, all involve relating the breathing rate to the natural heart rate. They are not the same. Nor is our heart quite as regular as we might think; in fact it speeds up a little as we inhale, to push the freshly oxygenated blood around the body more rapidly, and then the heart rate slows down a little as we exhale, effectively to stop the heart from racing, as we breathe out the used air. This subtle variation is controlled completely automatically by the vagus nerve. The ratio varies considerably from one individual to another. but essentially the bigger the difference between your heart rate when you breath in, compared with when you breath out, the higher your vagal tone.[1]

So what are some of the benefits?

From almost any point of view, for people who are fortunate enough to have inherited high vagal tone, the kinds of benefits that the scientists talk about are considerable. In terms of basic physical health for example it would seem that the vagus nerve plays a key role in stimulating and controlling insulin production, so that these people are naturally better at regulating blood glucose and inflammation in the body, and as a result they are much less likely to experience various forms of heart disease or strokes or diabetes.[2]

In terms of mental or psychological benefits, we now know that the vagus nerve has a huge role to play in determining how well we can handle stressful and threatening situations. So people with higher vagal tone tend to be generally more emotionally stable and resilient, less prone to peaks of stress and anxiety, even in tough and challenging situations. So they are less likely to panic or fly off the handle when they encounter a crisis situation. And when they do fly off the handle, they get back down to their basic resting emotional state more rapidly.

And finally, people with high vagal tone have also been linked in the studies with high levels of acceptability and sociability. The research psychologists talk in terms of them being able to form stronger relationships and show more pleasure in social interaction, so that they are highly valued as friends. One researcher, Professor Stephen Porges at the University of North Carolina, a psychiatrist with a particular interest in understanding the neurobiology of social behaviour, argues that this is probably because the vagus nerve has connections to other nerves involved in eye contact and responsive facial muscles, and the ability to tune in to the frequency of the human voice, all of which would seem to be highly valuable qualities in terms of achieving strong interaction with other people.[3]

I would hazard a guess for example that someone like George Clooney has high vagal tone!

But taken together I don't think there can be any question that this remarkable combination of physical and mental and social benefits makes high vagal tone a highly desirable quality to have in one's life. So what practical steps can we take that might increase it's incidence and its effectiveness in our own lives?

So what can we do about it?
The American psychologist John Gottman, renowned for his work in parenting and relationship studies suggests that parents can play a major role in improving their children's vagal tone by coaching them in the way they handle their emotions;

> '…talking to children about their feelings and how to understand them, not being critical and judgmental, problem solving about emotional predicaments, coaching them on what to do, like alternatives to hitting or withdrawing when you're sad.'[4]

But the very good news for all of us ordinary mortals is that physical exercise immediately comes into the frame. It has been suggested that regular exercise, with the emphasis on the discipline of regularity, is one way in which we can improve not only our physical and muscular tone, but our vagal tone as well. Indeed it has been argued that this is one of *the* major underlying reasons why exercise is so good for you. That does reflect of course the research into the very considerable physical and mental benefits that we discussed at some length in an earlier chapter. Moreover it seems that the reverse is true, that people who are both overweight and who take little exercise tend to have low vagal tone. So however we look at it, there is a huge and accumulating amount of good, solid research evidence to suggest that building a routine of regular exercise into our lives is just sound common sense, a readily accessible gateway to a greater sense of well-being. Not just in terms of the immediate, short-term endorphin effect, but longer term, over the entire course of our lives.

But I think perhaps the most surprising recent findings, and the basic reason for wanting to write this chapter, have come from the series of studies carried out two years or so ago, by psychologist Barbara Fredrickson, and her research associate Nancy Havill, at the University of North Carolina at Chapel Hill. Fredrickson is a colleague of Martin Seligman in the sense that she is an early member of the positive psychology movement in the US. What Fredrickson would seem to be suggesting is that we can in some measure at least, *think* our way to stronger vagal tone, by consciously focusing on and therefore *cultivating* positive aspects of our character, such as gratitude and respect for others and social connectivity.

Some interesting research

Very briefly, Fredrickson became interested in the increasing number of studies which revealed a close link between high vagal tone and people experiencing a greater sense of emotional stability and general well-being in their lives. So she put together her own study. It involved a group of over 70 people. They all had their base level vagal tone measured at the outset, and then they were asked to do two things on a daily basis over a period of nine weeks. One was to actually make a note of all the positive emotions they experienced during the course of the day. So rather like maintaining a Gratitude Diary that we mentioned earlier. The other was to rate on a given scale the extent to which they felt engaged with and connected to the people they encountered during the day.

The results were remarkably positive in every sense. Those people who had been shown to have the highest vagal tone at the start of the 9 weeks reported the highest incidence of positive feelings during the study, so there was a clear link established between people with high vagal tone and the experience of positive feelings.

But a key result, and a quite extraordinary one in many ways, was that *all* the participants reported *an increase* in how positive they felt about their lives, and in their sense of social connectedness. That is to say they felt measurably more positive about their lives, and their relationships with others, just as a result of making a point of *recognising and recording* those two factors every day.

Moreover those individuals who had reported the greatest increase in their sense of well-being also showed the greatest increase in their vagal tone. That is to say making the *conscious effort to focus* on the positive aspects of their lives, even over so short a period as nine weeks, had served to strengthen and increase their vagal tone. That study was well received enough to be published in a professional peer-reviewed journal, the Journal of Biological Psychology.[5]

Creating a positive approach to life

Having achieved those results Fredrickson went on to carry out a somewhat deeper study which brought in a greater measure of what might be called *self-reflection* on the part of the study group. They were taught a simple form of meditation. They were then asked to record three elements each day over the course of the next nine weeks.

- How much time they spent meditating.
- What they felt were the strongest emotions they felt each day, either positive or negative this time.
- And how positive they felt about their relationships with the people they spent time with each day.

At the end of the period the results were again very revealing. Those people who started out with the highest levels of vagal tone recorded the greatest increase in positive experiences and in social connectedness. So once again there is this strong connection established between innate vagal tone and sense of well-being. Moreover those people who spent this regular and dedicated period of time each day in self-reflection, were shown to have a 'significant increase' in vagal tone.[6]

As a result of these studies Professor Fredrickson talks of the possibility of our creating for ourselves what she describes as a highly beneficial 'upward spiral,' a self-reinforcing cycle of positivity you might say. She argues that simply *encouraging ourselves*...which is essentially what her subjects were being asked to do...simply encouraging ourselves to reflect on the *positive events* in our everyday life, and the positive elements in our social relationships, serves to increase our vagal tone. That beneficial change *further increases* our sense of emotional well-being, which goes on to increase our vagal tone. Who wouldn't want to set such a virtuous circle going in one's own life?

So although this was of course a limited series of studies, I have to say that I find Professor Fredrickson's results not simply interesting, but immensely stimulating. Not least because they hold so much promise. Striving to respond positively and creatively to all the events we encounter in the course of the day, she suggests, markedly increases our actual *ability* to respond positively on a more regular basis. Moreover it is strongly in rhythm, if I may put it that way, with the promise that lies at the heart of a Buddhist practice.

The Buddhist perspective

As we discussed in an earlier chapter, at the heart of the Buddhist view of a healthy life lies the understanding that there is no fundamental distinction or separation between the physical aspects of our life and the spiritual. As we've seen, Buddhism uses the astounding clarity of the phrase 'two but not two,' to describe this relationship. That is to say the mind and the body may appear to be different entities, indeed in the West we are to some extent conditioned by a long history of medical and religious tradition to view them in that way. But the fundamental reality Buddhism has always argued, is that they are simply two different aspects of each individual life. So if you affect one you inevitably affect the other. They are wholly and inextricably interlinked.

Fredrickson's research is part of an increasing body of evidence to indicate that simply striving to *generate* an optimistic and positive approach to life powerfully strengthens our actual ability to *sustain* such a life-state on a regular basis, quite apart from all the other health benefits such as boosting the immune system and lowering blood pressure and leading to a more regulated heart rate. Thus if one looks at this growing body of medical and scientific research from a purely Buddhist standpoint, it would seem clear that a daily Buddhist practice, which involves a measure of meditation or chanting, can accurately be described as *life-changing*, since its primary purpose is to strengthen our ability to *choose* the positive option over the negative. Every day we are reminded that we can choose to challenge the negativity in our lives, which we now know can have such harmful effects on our physiological and mental health. Every day we can shift our lives towards the positive end of the spectrum, which we now know brings so many healthful benefits.

Good health has been well described as not simply the *absence* of sickness or anxiety at any particular point in time. It is rather the building in our lives of a sustained positive and optimistic outlook on life. And that essentially is what a Buddhist practice is about, offering us a mechanism, a method, for developing and sustaining a life state that is consistently hopeful and optimistic and resilient, so that we can establish that as the dominant perspective from which we will perceive and relate to our environment.

That does sound very much like the pathway to a strong vagal tone, don't you think?

CHAPTER NINETEEN

The secret history of altruism

You wouldn't think would you that altruism, that is to say being charitable and generous and giving and above all selfless towards other people would ever be a controversial and hotly disputed subject? But the surprising fact is that it has been so for decades, and indeed it still is to a large extent. As one recent scientific account puts it directly,

'Altruism has long been an evolutionary mystery.'[1]

It is primarily the 'selfless' bit that continues to trouble the evolutionary biologists, mainly because it is difficult to reconcile it with the fundamentally competitive dynamics of evolutionary theory. Meanwhile for the rest of us, we are slightly puzzled. Why? Because we believe that concern for the welfare of others is one of the outstanding and distinguishing characteristics of the sort of society we would all choose to live in. Some of the most celebrated studies into altruism for example have looked at the many hundreds of people who sheltered Jewish people during the Nazi occupation of Europe, and so actually risked their lives on a daily basis for others, whom they may have known only slightly as neighbours.[2] That represents perhaps the most powerful expression of altruism we are likely to encounter. But most of us are convinced that we could cite many cases of genuine altruism within the bounds of our own experience, everyday examples of people willingly sharing life-giving food and shelter and other resources with complete strangers in desperate need. The sort of selfless action that we take very much for granted in today's societies. The psychologist Martin Hoffman from New York University for example, argues that the roots of altruism lie in empathy, since it is the human ability to empathise with someone in distress or danger, and in a sense, actually *share* in some measure their suffering, that moves us to help them.[3] And it's noteworthy that Buddhism teaches that the richest and most meaningful life is one that enriches other lives.

Given this apparent disjunction between our personal experience, and the evolutionary biologists view, it is I suggest, not just interesting, but profoundly illuminating to look in a bit more detail at the nature of the continuing controversy. Partly because it enables us to look at altruism from a completely different perspective, so that we can see the actual roots from which it has arisen and so perhaps understand it more fully, and value it more highly. But also because it tells us something fundamental about human nature. It means we need to take our gaze away from the daily stuff that is all around us, just for a moment that is, and look at ourselves from a standpoint we very rarely take, if ever, namely the *evolutionary* one. Because of course, everything about us, all the attributes, all the qualities, are the result of this long journey of genetic and cultural evolution. At key points in our journey each of these attributes gave us some advantage big or small, that enabled us to survive and prosper against all the odds. That's the only reason that they have survived the long journey, otherwise they would have been jettisoned along the way. We are today if you like, very much the product of where we've come from. The outcome of all our long yesterdays. As Robert Winston expresses it in his fascinating book *Human Instinct*,

> 'Our minds are firmly rooted in our evolutionary past. Our reason is bound up in layers of instinct....Not only do we have a Stone Age body with many vestiges of our past, we also have a Stone Age mind.'[4]

Darwin's problem

That's certainly presents us with a somewhat divergent view of who we are doesn't it? But you can see that from that perspective, the overwhelming question about altruism is why? Since altruism clearly exists as part of human nature…we may not practice altruism always, but we do practice it often enough to be able to claim that it's very much part of being human… then we have to search around to define the evolutionary advantage that it gave us. And that it seems, has been immensely difficult to nail down. The key argument being that doing things for other people that are completely selfless, and that may even *disadvantage us* in many cases, might even get us killed, isn't, on the face of it, the greatest way of surviving and getting our genes passed on, which is what evolution is all about. Indeed this question of how altruism evolved in human behaviour has actually been called 'Darwin's problem.'[5]

Seeking an alternative explanation

As a direct result of this unresolved dilemma, for much of recent scientific history the quest among anthropologists and evolutionary biologists has been to search for the early roots of altruism among those few remaining hunter-gatherer societies who continue live today in a way that's very close indeed to the way our own *direct* ancestors lived all those years ago, on the savannahs of East Africa. Among these tribes, such as those living in the Kalahari Desert in south western Africa, they find very clear evidence of a form of altruism that has evolved essentially as a result of the extreme closeness of the relationships in such a tribal culture. In these tribes for example any one individual is directly related to a very high proportion of his fellow tribesmen through many generations of intermarriage. The crucial effect of this is that the vast majority of the people in the tribe carry very much the same genes to a greater or lesser extent. So that individuals who are generous or giving or altruistic to their fellow tribesmen are almost certainly assisting in the survival and passing on of their own genes, whether or not they are aware of the precise nature of the shared kinship.

And even if they aren't related in some way, every individual in these tribal societies is highly dependent upon everyone else in all kinds of ways, throughout their entire lives. Everyone depends upon their fellow tribesmen and women for help and support and mutual defence. In such a culture it's clear to both parties that any overt act of generosity or support towards a fellow tribesman will not go unremembered. Many people will know about who owes a favour to whom so to speak. And so at some stage, over a shorter or a longer period that favour is available to be called in.

Indeed in these close-knit human communities, immensely similar to those in which our own neural networks evolved, something as apparently inconsequential as *gossip* has always been a big deal, a really fundamental part of social communication. In this sort of environment any notably generous and helpful 'altruistic' acts towards others is gossiped about and becomes widely known throughout the community. So, the argument goes, individuals who typically carry out such acts of altruism tend to become popular and well-liked among their fellow tribesmen, as being generous and giving and generally supportive; *the* man or woman to go to when you need a helping hand. And almost as a direct result, they become more attractive as a highly desirable partner. So the persistent habit of altruism, does if you like, substantially boost their chances of finding a good partner and passing on their genes.

Indeed one renowned evolutionary biologist, Christopher Boehm from the University of Southern California, who has made this his special field of study among several primitive peoples in the Amazon basin for example, argues that over the course of our evolution, the beneficial effects of *tribal gossip* and hearsay of this kind, could have been a major driver in the emergence of altruism as a significant aspect of the modern human character. And he is by no means alone. Gossip it seems has played a key and indeed central role in our evolutionary journey. As Yuval Harari notes;

> *'The new linguistic skills that modern Sapiens acquired...
> enabled them to gossip for hours on end. Reliable information about who could be trusted meant that small bands could expand into larger bands and Sapiens could develop tighter and more sophisticated types of cooperation. The gossip theory might sound like a joke but numerous studies support it. Even today the vast majority of human communication...whether in the form of emails, phone calls or newspaper columns...is gossip.'*[6]

A living testament to altruism

Thus despite the uncertainty in the arguments of the evolutionary biologists, we all know from our own life experience that people, many people indeed, do carry out utterly selfless and generous acts that have *nothing whatsoever* to do with blood relationship or the possibility of the favour being returned. I've mentioned already the many people who selflessly risked their lives to protect Jewish people in Nazi occupied Europe. At the Holocaust Memorial Museum in Jerusalem over 6000 trees have been planted to honour their memory. These trees grow there today as a beautiful living testament to the strength and the courage and the true selflessness, the *pure altruism* of many thousands of ordinary people. As Robert Winston puts it directly,

> *'The bottom line is we seem to be much nicer to other people than would be expected if this were simply to benefit our selfish genes.'[7]*

Meanwhile there is another interesting interpretation of the evolutionary roots of altruistic behaviour that is now widely supported among evolutionary biologists and psychologists, which has come to be known as *'group selection.'*

Altruism for the benefit of society

In fact it was the proposition first put forward by Darwin himself, but it's only relatively recently that it has come to establish *'a new consensus,'* among scientists.[8] Basically it argues that individuals are prepared to put themselves at a personal evolutionary disadvantage, simply to create a wider benefit for the whole family or community or society of which they are a part. The overwhelming thrust of this argument is that any group in which people were prepared to cooperate in this generous, supportive, self-sacrificing way, would strongly out-compete tribal groups who had not adapted to cooperate in the same way. Thus the genes of *everybody* in the more cooperative, more altruistic group would have a greater chance of being passed on to their successors,…and so on down the many intervening generations to us…to arrive as a clearly identifiable part of our make-up today. And find its testament in those 6000 beautiful trees.

To go back to Darwin, in *The Descent of Man*;

> *'…an advancement in the standard of morality* (as expressed for example in strongly altruistic behaviour) *will certainly give an immense advantage to one tribe over another. A tribe including many members who… were always ready to aid one another, and to sacrifice themselves for the common good, would be victorious over most other tribes; and this would be natural selection.'*[9]

Notice that Darwin chooses to use there the words, *'immense advantage.'* That is the scale of the evolutionary advantage that, he argued, is brought by the individual's willingness to subdue their personal and often selfish interests, to create a greater value at the level of their group or community. And it is that generous and selfless behaviour which has led, over the manifold generations, to this remarkable quality of altruism, which is so important and so rewarding a quality in human nature today.

David Sloan Wilson concludes a recent essay with the words,

> *'Group selection has been an exceptionally strong force in human genetic and cultural evolution.'*[10]

Philosopher and neuroscientist Sam Harris in his book on social behaviour, *The Moral Landscape*, goes even further;

> *'There may be nothing more important'* he writes, *'than human cooperation...Cooperation is the stuff of which meaningful human lives and viable societies are made.'*[11]

Altruism he is saying, is part and parcel of a truly meaningful human life.

Altruism has become instinctive

On a purely subjective level we all know that acting generously and altruistically towards others hugely strengthens our own sense of self-worth, and our belief that we are making a contribution to the well-being of the society we inhabit. And this deeply-felt personal experience is now being directly verified by an increasing amount of research among neuroscientists. It even shows up in MRI brain scans for example, which confirm that this subjective sense of well-being that we feel through acts of altruism and generosity is actually reflected in much higher activity in the brain's reward systems.[12]

Evolutionary anthropologist Michael Tomasello, a long-term researcher on the evolution of cooperation in human society, pulls all the threads together and argues that so many areas of evidence now establish the way in which human intelligence has evolved essentially on the basis of *trust and selflessness* among members of a tribal group, which has given us the huge advantage of shared awareness and cooperation and coordination, in coping with challenges and crises. This has prevailed for so many generations he argues, that this essentially altruistic way of living has become *'instinctive in our species.'*[13]

That definitive phrase that Tomasello chooses to use there, *'… instinctive in our species'* represents in a sense the final link in the evolutionary chain. Tomasello describes for example how in experiments with young children that he himself has designed, they are naturally and instinctively cooperative.[14] He notes that if you drop something in front of a two year old he or she is very likely to bend down and pick it up for you. This is not a learned behaviour, he explains, but a totally *instinctive* one. He argues that this research helps to explain why acts of selfless altruism and compassion and generosity have come to carry such a powerful moral significance in society; they are universally praised as being positive and value-creating. Whereas the reverse, overt selfishness and rejection or neglect of others who are in need, is universally perceived as being antisocial and negative and destructive.

Deeply embedded in the human psyche

And this instinctive nature of altruism is borne out in the many everyday street-level studies that reveal for us that quite small and seemingly inconsequential altruistic gestures, such as offering a smile for example to a worried-looking stranger, or a word of encouragement to someone, or a helping hand on the spur of the moment; they all bring an elevation of the spirit that lasts way beyond the fleeting moment of the event itself. And when we give freely of our time and energy in concerning ourselves more deeply with the needs and anxieties of others, rather than concentrating, as we so easily tend to do, on our own current crop of problems, it has been shown that this level of altruism can change fundamentally the way we feel about *our own* lives.

It can deliver a huge boost to our own sense of self-worth and the ultimate value of our own lives. As the American psychologist Sonja Lyubomirski, who has spent much of her career working in this area, explains;

> 'What scientific research has contributed to this age-long principle is evidence that practising acts of kindness is not only good for the recipient, but also good for the doer. …This is because being generous and willing to share makes people feel happier.'[15]

And again, in describing a particular case study in which five women, despite suffering quite severely themselves from multiple sclerosis, volunteered to help and support a large group of other multiple sclerosis patients;

> 'Their role as peer supporters appeared to shift their focus away from themselves and their problems and towards others. They recounted acquiring improved non-judge-mental listening skills and becoming more open and tolerant of other people. They also reported a stronger sense of self-esteem and self-acceptance for example, and confidence in their ability to cope with life's ups and downs and managing their own disease.[16]

The controversy and the debate that have gone over the past decade have led to a much greater understanding and appreciation of just how deeply embedded altruism has become in the human psyche. No one would say that there aren't abundant reserves of selfishness inherent in the human psyche as well of course. But there is clear evidence, right across the spectrum of sociology and psychology and neuroscience, that *giving*, giving rather than taking, simply makes us feel good; that there is a powerful happiness-effect within our own lives that comes from developing a compassionate and altruistic approach to others.

The neighbourhood effect

Moreover is has now been clearly shown that there it a far wider social benefit. A number of sociologists including for example Robert Sampson from Harvard, have demonstrated in some of their latest research that the strength of our social connections, the levels of altruism and compassion and willingness to support others, are absolutely decisive factors in how effectively whole communities function and cope with challenges. They have gone so far as to attach a label to it. They have identified a quality that they call '*the enduring neighbourhood effect*.' Sampson describes how this wider social awareness and concern for others determines how whole communities are able to bond and pull together, not simply to deal with what he calls '*everyday challenges*,' such as anti-social behaviour, but far more than that, to surmount and recover from major life-threatening crises such as the Japanese earthquake and tsunami of 2011, and the perfect storm that struck New York in 2012.[17]

A Buddhist footnote

Since we've been talking about the role of altruism in our lives perhaps it's fitting to give the last word to Buddhism, since Buddhism has always taught that nurturing a compassionate and altruistic approach in our lives, focusing outwards rather than inwards, giving rather than taking, is a powerfully enriching, value-creating way of life. It's an approach to daily life that leads to the most rapid growth in the resilience and resourcefulness and sense of well-being in our own lives, as well as enabling us to create the greatest value in the lives of others.

But I think it's important to underline what we have witnessed in this discussion. We have seen a group of eminent and relatively hard-headed social scientists, defining in some detail, how such an outward-looking, and contributing approach to life, not only gives expression to one of the deepest impulses in our nature, but it triggers a whole cascade of positive effects, and enables people and societies to live more creatively and harmoniously together. And that's what we all want isn't it, when it comes down to it? We all want to live in peaceful, and above all cooperative and supportive societies in which people genuinely care about what happens to their neighbour, and fully respect the lives of others. We know full well that we all benefit if we cooperate. We all lose out if we don't.

What is particularly interesting I suggest, is the sheer extent of the overlap, the similarities and the echoes between what Buddhism has been telling us for so long, and the findings of these modern sociologists and psychologists. It's important of course not to put it any stronger than that, not to draw too many parallels or inferences. Certainly we shouldn't seek to present the research findings as a sort of intellectual scaffolding around any particular Buddhist perception, because it patently isn't.

But it is undeniably interesting isn't it, that classical Buddhist teachings coming from profound reflection on human nature should be so powerfully borne out by wholly modern sociological studies?

CHAPTER TWENTY

The evolutionary roots
of friendship

Friendship undoubtedly falls into that category of circum-stance famously occupied by mother love and apple pie, we all want it in our lives. We instinctively understand just how profoundly friendships enhance and enrich our lives in countless ways. We are in our deepest nature a gregarious animal. We earnestly seek fulfilling and harmonious and above all lasting friendships and relationships at all levels in our lives. When we achieve them, at work and at play for example, they buttress and reinforce our creative energies. We become energised so to speak to pursue many other outward objectives in our lives. When those relationships break down for whatever reason, it can have a devastating effect in many areas of our life, not simply those associated with the relationship that has gone wrong. We all know that, and almost without thinking about it, almost as a matter of course, we expend a very considerable share of our time and energies supporting and maintaining and nur-turing our friendships at various levels.

What is intriguing is the extent to which ordinary everyday friendships of the sort that we all take pretty much for granted, and which bind us all together in overlapping networks, have become a keen focus of sociological and psychological research in recent years. What that research has done, like so much of the research we have discussed in these chapters, is to peel away some of those layers of familiarity. In doing so it inevitably raises our level of awareness and understanding, which is I suggest, of considerable value in itself. And perhaps the most surprising truth it has revealed is the extent to which this friendship thing is a deeply embedded part of our evolutionary nature. To the extent in fact that the existence of a network of friends and contacts has emerged as a significant factor in our overall health and well-being. Lauren Brent for example, a research biologist at Exeter University in the UK, is one among many whose work focuses on the way in which our friendships and our relationships with others, impact profoundly upon our mental and physiological well-being. She writes;

> *'We need friends. They have a positive impact on our health and mental well-being... In fact our bodies react to a lack of friends as if a crucial biological need is going unfulfilled. This is not surprising. For us humans, friends are not an optional extra, we have evolved to rely on them.*[1]

That is a powerfully revealing statement isn't it? Not an optional extra, she argues, but an important part of our evolutionary make-up. American psychologist Barbara Fredrickson goes even further on the basis of her own wide ranging research into social connectedness, describing friendship as a potent *'wellness behaviour,'* and defining the absence of meaningful relationships and friendships as being comparable, in its effects on bodily health, to the damaging behaviours we are so frequently warned about such as smoking, drinking too much alcohol and obesity.[2]

So clearly the roots of friendship and connectedness go far deeper into our emotional and psychological make-up than perhaps we realise.

Back to the beginning

You can't travel very far in friendship research without bumping into Robin Dunbar. He is the acclaimed evolutionary psychologist from Oxford University who has explored more than most just how deep, just how far back those roots go. He has been able to provide us with some intriguing insights by going right back in a sense to *before* the beginning...before the beginning of us as homo sapiens that is. He's carried out a whole series of ground-breaking studies looking closely at the role of friendship behaviour in the lives of our closest pre-human evolutionary cousins, the higher primates, and then tracing the evolution of that behaviour on into our own lives in modern human society.

His key findings substantially reshape our frame of reference, in the sense that they reveal the extent to which friendship and relationship behaviour has come to *dominate* the lives of these primates, both in terms of the amount of time and energy that is taken up in maintaining close relationships through various grooming rituals, and in the scale of the physiological response. The grooming rituals for example actually trigger the release of endorphins, the so-called feel-good hormones, in the brain of the animal that is being groomed. It's this deeper, physiological response, Dunbar argues, that creates the deep bond of trust that nurtures and maintains the network of friendships that is so essential to the animal's survival.

One of the key principles that his research has revealed at work in shaping friendship networks among primates, and that has played a key role in our own evolutionary development, has led him to come up with his famous number, now universally called, 'Dunbar's number,' to describe the circle of meaningful friends our brains have *evolved* to cope with.

On the basis of his extensive research he argues that the average individual has evolved to maintain a core group of around 15 close friends, and a total extended social network of around 150. Moreover, as he makes clear, his research into social groupings in modern societies has broadly supported this finding;

'I have calculated that our social group size should be around 150... This turns out to be both a common community size in human social organisation and the typical size of personal social networks.'[3]

As you would expect there's been a great deal of debate and argument around Dunbar's famous number since it is a wholly new insight. But it has been generally welcomed as a genuine addition to our understanding of a key aspect of modern human behaviour; the evolutionary roots you might say of the way in which we maintain stable networks of friends today. When I carried out a swift and, I hasten to add, a totally unscientific survey amongst a sample of friends and acquaintances, this figure of 150 seemed to be in the right ballpark, when people took into account their extended family groupings and work colleagues and sports partners and so on. But we are of course talking about an average figure, so there will be a wider range of individual social groupings both below and above that figure of 150.

Facebook has thrown something of a spanner in the works of course by choosing to use the same word 'friend,' to describe a wholly different kind of relationship, a largely virtual on-line relationship which can extend virtual networks to several hundreds or more. But we'll come to that in a minute or two. Meanwhile Dunbar's Number of 150 is standing up remarkably well to further scrutiny.

But what about the essential investment of time?

That's the crucial question that Dunbar goes on to pose. He makes it clear that in this respect we humans are fundamentally in the same boat as our primate cousins. That is to say some measure of *paying-attention-to* time, some real investment of time and energy, is an essential aspect of establishing an initial bond between individuals, and then investing further energy to maintain that bond in a strong enough form to hold people within a coherent social group. It's this attention remember that releases the feel-good endorphins and the sense of trust, both of which are essential to keeping that bond alive and functional. Trust is essential for people to act with sustained commitment towards others.

So how he asks, did our immediate ancestors devise ways of binding together a group as large as 150? Dunbar argues that with hunting and tracking and water and log-carrying and so on to get done, there simply wasn't enough time in our immediate evolutionary past for a constant series of one-to-one contacts in any individual's day, so crucial to maintaining that friendship bond. In answer to that tricky problem Dunbar intriguingly identifies three *cultural adaptations* that, he argues, were developed by our immediate ancestors to enable them to maintain those bonds of friendship and cooperation that played such an essential role in sustaining their daily lives. As he explains,

'It seems we have exploited three additional behaviours that are very good at triggering the release of endorphins but can be done in groups, allowing several individuals to be 'groomed' at the same time.'[4]

It's more than a little surprising isn't it, to see that word 'groomed,' which is used so often of course in describing primate behaviour, to be used to describe human behaviour? Behaviour moreover that has continued to evolve, to play an even more powerful role in our own social interaction today.

What are these behaviours? Well first he argues came laughter, and as we all know so well today, laughter amongst a group of people in the pub or over the supper table, sharing in a joke or a story, is an immensely powerful bonding mechanism for bringing people closer together and establishing a greater degree of intimacy.

Next he argues came singing or chanting. We only have to think about the widespread pleasure in community choral groups, and the singing of songs such as *Abide with me* or *You'll never walk alone* on the football terraces, or indeed the chanting taken up by a group of people joined together in a movement of some sort, to recognise just how powerfully today, singing or chanting in unison can bind groups of people together.

And finally Dunbar talks of the crucial importance of the advent of language as the most powerful and creative mechanism of all for enabling long-term communication and bonding of individuals and groups of people together. The actual emergence of language in human evolution still remains shrouded in mystery. Nobody knows quite when and how it emerged, but the historian Tom Wolfe goes even further in his book *The Kingdom of Speech* to describe language as without question, mankind's greatest artefact, the ultimate *'tool crafted by humans'* that has allowed us to become not simply overwhelmingly more powerful than any other species on Earth but virtually masters of the universe we inhabit.[5]

Our personal social networks

Dunbar emphasises the point that we can of course feel some sort of an underlying bond with much larger groups or 'super-groups,' as he calls them, which we can recognise most readily perhaps in religious institutions, or in schools and colleges and groups of sports fans. But that doesn't in any way replace this average figure of about 150 people, for our *personal friendship networks*. About half of that figure he estimates is likely to be extended familial relationships at one level of remove or another, which tend to remain fairly stable over an entire lifetime. The remainder are non-kin relationships of friends and colleagues and sports partners and so on, which, as we have all experienced, are very likely to change over the course of our lives.

It's these non-kin relationships that are very susceptible to weakening and decay unless we invest that precious time and energy in maintaining them. The remarkable thing is that, if we listen to the biologists, maintaining this network of friendships would seem to be so important to our overall physiological well-being, that evolution has shaped us to do just that, to invest that time and energy in friendship activity rather than in other ways.

The biology of friendship

It's the biologists who strip away the film of familiarity to get beneath the skin of friendship so to speak, to reveal not only how important this network of relationships is to our general well-being, but the essential reward systems that we have evolved to induce us to maintain it. Lauren Brett from whom we quoted earlier, is one of those biologists. As she explains,

> 'That's why evolution has equipped us with the desire to make friends and spend time with them. Like sex, eating, or anything a species needs to survive, friendship is driven by a system of reinforcement and reward. In other words, being friendly is linked with the release of various neurotransmitters in the brain and bio-chemicals in the body that make us feel good.'[6]

One of the most important of those evolutionary bio-chemicals that we mentioned earlier, in relation to primate grooming, namely endorphins, is also released by exercise, which is why we so often get that buzz of good feeling after a bout of vigorous exercise. In one notable series of experiments Robin Dunbar combined both. He asked a group of volunteers to row for him, either singly or in pairs, and he measured the levels of endorphins in their bloodstream both before the event and after. The result of the measurement after the event was striking. All the people involved exerted very much the same amount of *physical* effort of course, whether they were on their own or with a partner. But those who rowed in pairs, and therefore had to really focus their attention on synchronising their physical efforts with another person, released far more endorphins than those who rowed alone. That is to say, the simple fact of having to establish some sort of *relationship*, in matching their physical effort to another human being became an important bonding factor, and so led to the release of a greater amount of the reward hormone.

The similarity factor

That word 'relationship' is crucial in that statement, in that it implies something of substance, some deeper sharing, of views or tastes or activities. Indeed in answer to the direct question, *'of the many people we encounter in modern life, how is it that we select so few as close friends?'* the research seems to offer a remarkably simple answer. It turns out that we tend to make friends with people who actually *represent* some recognisable aspect of ourselves in some significant way.

In fact the science goes much further. Some studies indicate that our closest friends are likely to be more *genetically* similar to ourselves than would be expected by pure chance. A study by Nicolas Christakis from Harvard for example, came up with the astounding result that close friends can be as similar to ourselves genetically as fourth cousins. It's important to point out that no one has the slightest idea of the mechanism involved. How could we possibly, with our ordinary senses, recognise and single out people who in some way are genetically similar to ourselves? It remains very much an intriguing mystery. Although it is of course true that our personality is shaped in part at least by our genes, and if we like to be around people whom we perceive as having a similar personality to ourselves, then they could well have similar genes.[7]

A footnote on virtual friends

This is no place for an in-depth discussion of the impact of social media on friendship, but since we live in an ever more connected society, we ought perhaps to look briefly at the wholly new modes of friendship at a distance. Friendships, acquaintances, connections, call them what you will, formed and sustained solely on the internet. In many ways of course this could be seen as a largely linguistic issue. The fact that Facebook for example, chooses to use the same word, 'friends,' to describe complete strangers whom we may encounter solely on the web, bears no meaningful relationship to what Robin Dunbar is talking about, when he describes the kinds of social network of friends that we create as part of our long evolutionary development. They are poles apart. That having been said, since we are all caught up in the interlinked internet phenomenon in one way or another, scientists have begun to examine its effects.

The most conspicuous change of course has been the huge increase in the number of people with whom we are likely to have some kind of connection, either sporadic or enduring. However, as one researcher has expressed it, the dynamics may have changed radically, but fundamentally what we are seeking, the personal *incentives* so to speak, have remained the same. That is to say, the so-called 'friendship network' may seem to be cast far more widely, but within it we set out to find that core group of people who will support us emotionally, gossip with us, be there for us. The emotional dimension therefore is very much the same,

> *'we still have our core group of friends, the ones we hang out with the most, whether that is online or offline.'[8]*

However these researchers also describe the wider network as fulfilling a different role, enabling us to sustain a network of what they describe as 'weak ties,' or peripheral friends; relationships maintained through very occasional posts or messages, where previously they simply would not have existed, or would have been allowed to fade away. At the very least this medium enables us to support or encourage people we might never or rarely encounter face to face, but who share some common interest. Everybody benefits from support, however infrequent; the receiver certainly does but so too does the giver of the encouragement, or the praise or the congratulations.

That interpretation is strongly endorsed by another friendship scientist, professor Nicole Ellison from Michigan State University, whose work explores the social dynamic of the new media. In fact she creates a striking if somewhat unexpected analogy for us. She suggests that engaging with other people online, in all sorts of seemingly casual and inconsequential ways, such as responding to a brief question, or wishing someone a happy birthday, or simply 'liking' a comment or a photograph, fulfils very much the same role, she argues, as the care and the attention that is displayed by our primate cousins in their crucially important rituals of nit-picking social grooming![9] I haven't been able to look at Facebook messages in quite the same way since reading that comment. But what is undoubtedly true is that in carrying out these simple acts of communication, we are sending a clear signal that we are prepared to devote some time specifically to *pay attention* to another person's life, and in some measure, present an opportunity for reciprocal attention.

So it's not so much I suggest, that 'Dunbar's number' with its deep evolutionary roots, is being challenged, as that it is being *added to*. Technical evolution you might say, has driven the evolution of another sphere of friendship in our lives, *the peripheral sphere*, the so-called weak ties, sustained by a lesser flow of occasional messages of support and congratulation, but undoubtedly creating substantial social value.

However it would seem clear that the *emotional* bonds that characterise our most important relationships, and our closest personal networks can only be established by periodic face to face contact. We very much need that close physical contact to maintain the deep bonds of trust and support, that, as the psychologists tell us, have such a *'positive impact on our health and mental well-being.'*

The bottom line… friendships we now know are not in any way a marginal or inconsequential aspect of our lives. They play, we now understand, a key role in our daily experience of well-being.

CHAPTER TWENTY ONE

Just beneath the surface
of everyday

We started out on the journey taken by this book… in the world of science. And the fundamental story of modern science is that of the surprising and the unexpected. Things are rarely if ever what they seem. What we experience with our senses, what we *know* to be the hard and fast nature of reality turns out very often not to be the case. That is unquestionably very hard for most of us to take on board, but time and time again we come across a sense almost of wonder expressed by scientists, as they come to perceive more and more of the disparity between our intuitive understanding of the world about us, and the true nature of that reality. The Italian physicist Carlo Rovelli for example in one of his brilliant lectures;

> *'Ever since we discovered that the Earth is round and turns like a mad spinning top we have understood that reality is not as it appears to us: every time we glimpse a new aspect of it, it is a deeply emotional experience. Another veil has fallen.'[1]*

Or as the theoretical physicist Brian Greene has expressed it in *The Fabric of the Cosmos*,

'The overarching lesson that has emerged from scientific inquiry over the last century is that human experience is often a misleading guide to the true nature of reality. Lying just beneath the surface of everyday, is a world we'd hardly recognise.'[2]

Lying just beneath the surface of everyday he says, so it's not by any means a rare and esoteric issue. The *surprising* nature of reality is commonplace and everyday and all around us.

You could say that it started indeed way back with Copernicus in 1543 when he took on the immensely challenging task of convincing his peers that what they took to be their firm grasp of reality was just plain wrong. The Sun *didn't* revolve around the earth every day. It took his painstaking mathematical observations to prove that what they saw, what *we* see every day, the sun travelling smoothly across our skies from East to West, is just an illusion. Nowadays of course we no longer need convincing, we have simply become accustomed to the fact that human experience is often a misleading guide to the true nature of reality, and we accept what the scientists tell us from their observations. None of us has actually *seen* the Earth revolving round the Sun.

And that process has gone on continuously since then. As the scientists over the years, have peeled away layer after layer of our ignorance and our illusions, to reveal more and more of the way the world really works, so they have revealed a reality that is not just mildly different from our everyday sensory perception, but one that often runs directly counter to what we feel to be plain common sense.

If we look at the view of the world we get from our most important senses, which are the very basis of our perception, we now know that our hearing for example has evolved to detect quite a small fraction of the huge spectrum of frequencies that are created in the world around us. We just can't hear the rest. They simply don't exist for us, since they are beyond our perception. In very much the same way, we now know that our eyes have evolved over the millennia to detect quite a small section of the entire spectrum of electro-magnetic waves, and we can therefore only see what lies within our range. What lies outside that narrow range once again simply doesn't exist for us, since it is invisible. Similarly, we now know that even in the everyday world of objects that furnish our homes and offices, the solid table and the solid chair that we sit on, far from being solid, are in fact composed of quadrillions of atoms and molecules that are very largely *empty space*; tiny central nuclei surrounded by vibrating shells of electrons.

I use that phrase 'we now know,' in those sentences fully realising that it is at best only partially satisfactory; *knowing* these things in our heads isn't at all the same thing as grasping the essential truth of them. But the point I really want to make is that that Brian Greene's key phrase about the physical world, '...*experience is often a misleading guide to the true nature of reality,*'[3] could equally be applied, I would argue, to much Buddhist thought,

Thus much of Buddhist teaching is really about getting us to look again at some of the ordinary everyday, seemingly common-sense assumptions that we carry around with us, brushing away the film of familiarity, sharpening up the lens through which we see the world, so that we get to see it slightly differently. It remains the same old world, it's just that our perception of it is somewhat different, and the changed perception can change fundamentally the way we behave towards ourselves and towards others, and in that sense, gradually *reshape* our lives. Gradually but oh so profoundly. As the modern philosopher Robert Solomon reminds us, how we *think* about ourselves... really changes *who* we actually are.

What does Buddhism have to say about relationships?

As we saw in the previous chapters, evolutionary psychology and biological chemistry in their different ways, strip away that film of familiarity to make it clear that relationships are not in any way a marginal aspect of our lives; they lie we now learn, at the very centre of human growth and development. But they don't tell us much about the 'how.' About how we can go about building these strong and enduring relationships that we clearly need as the very basis of our well-being.

Buddhism seeks to do just that.

It is as we've seen, a profoundly *humanist* religion, firmly grounded from first to last in human values and qualities, and it also seeks to peel away those layers of familiarity, albeit in a wholly different way. In doing so it takes us to the heart of what friendships and relationships are really about. Thus although a regular Buddhist practice is aimed in every way at enabling *individuals* to build a strong, creative, resilient inner self, it is fundamentally an *outgoing* activity. It cannot be expressed in isolation, inside our heads as it were. It only becomes meaningful as something that is lived outwards, in society, in and through friendships and relationships.

So the daily intention to *live* as a Buddhist, rather than simply to *know* and understand Buddhist principles, becomes apparent above all, in the way we approach the relationships that occur at every level in our lives throughout each day. And here I am using that word relationships in the very broadest sense, embracing all the encounters, all the people we bump into so to speak, as we move through each day, from our partners, to other parents as we put the kids into school perhaps, to ticket sellers and travelling companions and work colleagues and clients and strangers, and on and on throughout the day. People we know well or hardly at all. People we like, and people we may not have any particular feelings for.

Basically Buddhism teaches that the way we handle each of those encounters has far wider and deeper implications for our underlying sense of well-being, and indeed for theirs, than we might commonly believe. So what specifically does Buddhism have to tell us about creating the greatest value out of all these encounters?

What do we mean by respect?

Right at the top of the list comes the idea of respect. It is a central pillar of Buddhist thought. What it comes down to is that if we wish to live in a society that is based fundamentally on respecting the dignity and the humanity of other people, as undoubtedly the vast majority of us do, then *we* have to demonstrate that respect as a core quality in all those relationships and encounters we've talked about. We're not required to like people, we're only human, we can't like everybody. Still less are we required to admire them. Buddhism however does ask us to nurture within ourselves the ability, whatever the circumstances, to focus not on their differences from ourselves, but on their profound underlying similarity, their common *humanity*. So in that sense Buddhism might be said to have a profoundly revolutionary vision of the way in which societies should work, based on each person learning how to respect every other person with whom they come in contact. It was revolutionary when it was first propounded by Shakyamuni, all those years ago. When it is expressed in these stark terms it's clear that it is still revolutionary today. Because it doesn't come easily, we don't do it naturally. We have to school ourselves to overcome the impulsive pull of our own ego... more frequently.

The heart of the matter

But unquestionably it is very much the heart of the matter. Buddhism is based upon the idea of individuals having freedom of choice. Thus it argues, the way we experience a relationship is also a matter of choice. We have the power that is, to choose whether we experience any particular relationship in a negative or a positive way. It is of course all too easy for us to fasten onto what we feel to be the errors, or inconsistencies and irrationalities of other people's behaviour that make relationships difficult or inconvenient for *us*. All those things that make them seemingly unattractive or objectionable to us. Different from us. Other. Not part of the way we want our world to be.

Indeed, if we leave aside the wider world for a moment, I am very much aware from my own experience that it is all too easy to slip into patterns of behaviour that are basically disrespectful, even with people who are very close to us, even with people we love and seek to protect. We can find ourselves disrespecting them in the sense of using them to achieve our own goals, or disregarding their views. The tendency to use other people for what we see as our own vitally important ends, seems to be very strongly embedded in human nature.

So the battle, Buddhism reminds us, starts *within our own lives*, within our very close environment. And Buddhism makes it clear that it *is* a battle, essentially a struggle to accept complete responsibility for our own lives.

The reality of responsibility

And that very idea, of accepting total responsibility for our own lives, is absolutely central to the Buddhist view of building the strong and enduring relationships at every level in our lives, that we seek and need. It's a nicely rounded phrase, 'accepting responsibility for our own lives,' and it rolls smoothly off the tongue. We all know instinctively what it means don't we? But it's very smoothness and familiarity can, I suggest, make it deceptive. When relationships don't work out as we would like for example, for whatever reason, we all too often, and quite instinctively, locate the *root cause* for the breakdown outside ourselves. It doesn't work we commonly say, because of something *they* have done, or because of something in *their nature* that is illogical or careless or awkward or simply annoying. Professor Martin Seligman has called this sort of situation '*the dishwasher fight*,' to indicate just how commonly this sort of thing occurs even in very close relationships, or perhaps *most often* in very close relationships![4]

In my experience it is uncommonly difficult to learn to live with the Buddhist dictum that relationship problems, small or large, can't be resolved by looking for the *other person* to change, until they meet our specification so to speak. However much that might seem to *us* to be the obvious way forward, Buddhism awkwardly tells us that the reverse is true. Taking responsibility for our lives means that when *we* are suffering in whatever way, then it's *our* problem to solve, and the solution can only lie within us, not with someone else. If that were the case we would be handing over responsibility for our pain to someone else. Again that's childhood isn't it, rather than adulthood? Weakness rather than strength.

We have all been through this sort of circumstance many times over. We are hurt or offended or in some way put out by a friend at work or at home for example. It is perfectly natural for us to withdraw behind our defences to protect ourselves. That's what defences are for, to withdraw behind. And then we begin to list all the faults in the other person that have clearly led to the hurt or offence. From then on the solution seems simple. We just have to get the other person to change in this way or that, and then everything will be fine. Simple. We might even go so far as to work out strategies for ensuring that the changes in the other person take place. We know that people do go to extraordinary lengths to mould and change the behaviour of others to make relationships work. We might even persuade ourselves that the changes have taken place so that just about everything in the other person is now fixed to our satisfaction. And when the original behaviour re-asserts itself, it can lead to even greater frustration or hurt. What went wrong? Why has the other person let us down yet again, in this thoughtless or selfish way!

Moreover, as we know to our cost, it doesn't stop at one relationship. Experience shows that the pattern often repeats itself. It is very often the case that people move off to a new place, or a new job, or a new relationship, and a very similar sequence of events take place. Why? It is undoubtedly one of the most difficult life lessons to learn, that we have to deal effectively with the causes *within us*. We can't somehow run away from them by changing location or partner, any more than we can run away from our physical appearance.

From Buddhism therefore one of the most valuable understandings that we get about building and maintaining strong relationships at whatever level, about *life* indeed, is that the *effort* to make things work out, the *action* to change things about the relationship that cause pain or suffering or recurring difficulty, have to come from within ourselves, since the only person whose patterns of thought and behaviour we can control is ourselves. If we are seeking to change others, then we may have a long time to wait.

Independence works

Then there's the key issue of dependency. Putting it at its simplest, Buddhism argues that our ability to be happy and fulfilled in our lives is a matter of choice. Our choice. No one else's. As it has been expressed by one of the greatest modern writers on Buddhist values, Daisaku Ikeda,

> '*Happiness is not something that someone else, like a lover, can give to us. We have to achieve it for ourselves.*'[5]

It is, he is telling us, always our deal. It has solely to do with how we *choose* to perceive and respond to the daily circumstances and vicissitudes of our life, the ups and downs, the bumps and knocks, the highs and the lows that we all experience. When things are going swimmingly there is generally no problem of course. When things become troublesome we have the choice, either to use these problematic circumstances as a kind of justification for our sense of failure or our sadness, or alternatively to see them as something that by challenging and overcoming, we can strengthen our sense of capability. The nature of the choice we make has a powerful effect on how we feel during the episode itself, and in its aftermath. Is it positive or negative? Is it happy or sad? The key point is that no one does it to us. We do it to ourselves. The *choice* is always ours.

If we now transfer that thought to the arena of our close and personal relationships, it has a profound effect upon how we perceive them, and on how we might work to make the very most of them. If for example we see our happiness or our fulfilment as an individual, *strongly dependent* upon our partner, that may seem on the face of it, to make us feel closer and more intimately bonded together. But if we dig a little deeper we can see that potentially it is a recipe for instability and even considerable unhappiness, even if that person happens to love us dearly. It makes our life state at any moment or, more seriously our sense of self-worth, basically dependent upon the shifting high and lows of someone else's life. We come to see our happiness as largely dependent upon the existence or the behaviour of our partner.

If we reverse the roles, it helps us to see the nature of the problem. If our partner's happiness and sense of self-worth is largely dependent upon us, it might temporarily make us feel good to be *in control* so to speak. But it can only be unstable and unsettling in a long-term relationship, if only because it can become such an immense burden to be responsible for another person's happiness. It can eventually undermine even the strongest loving relationship. That is perhaps one of the reasons why such a high proportion of modern marriages end in divorce after a few years, because of the sheer strain imposed upon such relationships by wholly unrealistic expectations. *'We've found them at last, and now they will make us completely happy!'*

The power of gratitude

And finally, let me just mention en passant another quality that is prominent in the Buddhist, as indeed in several other traditions, that advances and enriches lives in constantly surprising ways. And it's this quality of gratitude. We've all experienced how just a few words of appreciation, however short, however simple, can bring an extraordinary warmth and sense of shared humanity into any situation, even the most casual and superficial. Over a shop counter for example, or at the check-out, or on a bus, or on the phone indeed where we spend so much more of our time these days. Multiply that simple exchange dozens or even hundreds of times a day, in relation to all the encounters we have with other people, at every level of intimacy, and you can see that almost without our being aware of it, it can transform the nature of our whole day, and over time, the nature of our life. That's how fundamental it is. That's how *transforming* the quality of gratitude is. Everybody benefits, the giver of the gratitude, the receiver, and everybody within earshot. We all experience a strengthening of our sense of the value of just being alive.

Thus the Buddhist view of successful relationships, at every level, close to and further removed, is absolutely practical and down-to-earth. There's nothing even vaguely mystical about it. It goes back to that underlying principle that we discussed a moment ago, that runs like a thread of steel through Buddhist teachings, we alone are responsible for our lives and the choices that we make. Essentially it argues that in any field of life, in relationships with a partner or with family and friends and work colleagues, throughout Robin Dunbar's personal network indeed, the most resilient and satisfying and value-creating relationships, cannot be sustained on the basis of mutual dependence, even if that's how they start out. To be long-lasting they have to mature. They need a clear sense of independence, and the awareness of individual responsibility. Allied of course to a profound respect for the wholeness of the other person's life.

And it rounds off this exploration of the value of a dual perspective. It goes without saying I think, that we can only get the most rounded picture of friendships and relationships, of life itself indeed, if we put the two together, the science and the Buddhist philosophy. One without the other leaves us with an incomplete and partial view. So the science tells us where it came from, this prominent dimension in our lives, and how crucially important it is to our balance and well-being. And the Buddhist philosophy explains for us just as clearly, the values and the behaviours that enable us to build our relationships into a strong and stable platform… for our entire lives.

THE END

List of References

Chapter One
A personal journey

1. Martin Seligman Flourish p 63
2. Sonja Lyubomirski The How of Happiness p 2
3. New Scientist (NS) 04.10.14. p 37
4. Sam Harris The Moral Landscape p 2
5. Robert Solomon Spirituality for the Skeptic p 140
6. ibid p xi
7. ibid p 4
8. ibid p 6
9. ibid p xiii
10. ibid p 21
11. Time Feature 01.12.14 p 18

Chapter Two
A brief excursion into Buddhist humanism

1. Mark Williams, John Teasdale, Zindal Segal, Jon Kabat-Zinn The Mindful Way through Depression
2. Arnold Toynbee Choose Life p 27
3. Daisaku Ikeda. The Living Buddha p 4
4. Dalai Lama, The Universe in a Single Atom, How Science and Spirituality can serve our world p 24
5. Edward Conze Buddhism A Brief History p 3

6. Thich Nhat Hahn The Heart of the Buddha's Teaching p 3

7. Nicholas Christakis, Prof. Of Medical Sociology, Harvard. Article in NS 03.01.09

8. Daisaku Ikeda World of The Gosho Vol 1.

Chapter Three
So what is the value of a dual perspective?

1. Robert Solomon Spirituality for the Skeptic p 25

2. The Dalai Lama The Universe in a Single Atom. How Science and Spirituality can Serve our World p 24

3. Albert Einstein. 1954 p49. This interesting quotation is discussed at some length by Sam Harris in the notes to The Moral Landscape p202

4. Dalai Lama ibid p 62

5. Ibid p 13

6. ibid p 5

7. Arnold Toynbee Choose Life p 36

8. Robert Solomon Spirituality for the Skeptic p ix

9. Robert Solomon ibid p 66

10. Alister McGrath 2015 The Big Question: why we can't stop talking about Science, Faith and God

11. Tsunesaburo Makiguchi quoted in Daibyaku Renge Oct 2010

Chapter Four
Oneness of self and environment

1. A.C. Grayling. Prof of Philosophy, Birkbeck College. London. Article in New Scientist, 04.08.10.

2. Thich Nhat Hahn The Heart of the Buddha's Teaching.

3. NS 14.02.15 p 28

4.   Daniel Dennet Kinds of Minds p 29
5.   William Woollard The Case for Buddhism p 49
6.   NS 06. 12.14 p 34
7.   Lisa Grossman NS 14.11.15 p 31
8.   Kristoff Koch NS The Human Brain p 85
9.   R Feynman The Characteristics of Physical Life p 149
10. Wangerie Maathai BBC R4 Documentary May 2010
11.   Sam Harris The Moral Landscape p 114
12. Daisaku Ikeda The Wisdom of the Lotus Sutra Vol 1 p149
13.   Robert Solomon. Spirituality for the Skeptic. P 139
14. Robert Winston Human Instinct p 93

Chapter Five
The brain that evolution gave us

1.   Kristoff Koch NS Collection The Human Brain p 10
2.   Tony Prescott. Prof. Cognitive Neuroscience University of Sheffield. NS 21.03.15 p 36
3.   Rita Carter Mapping the Mind p 6
4.   Max Tegmark NS The Human Brain p 95
5.   Patricia Churchland Touching a Nerve: The Self as Brain
6.   Yuval Noah Harari Sapiens 2011 p 9
7.   NS 04.10.14 p 38
8.   Daniel Goleman Emotional Intelligence p 89
9.   Martin Seligman What You Can Change…and What You Can't p 57
10. Cerebral Cortex vol 10 p 295. Daniel Goleman Emotional Intelligence p 25
11.   Michael O'Shea NS The Human Brain p 9
12. Ian Morris NS 18.04.15 p 30
13. Yuval Harami 2015 Sapiens p 31
14. Ibid p 10

Chapter Six
The emotional dimension

1. Daniel Goleman Emotional Intelligence p 4
2. Jill Bolte taylor My Stroke of Insight p 19
3. Daniel Goleman ibid p 4
4. Rita Carter Mapping the Mind p 98
5. ibid p 17
6. Robert Winston Human Instinct p 31
7. Jill Bolte Taylor My Stroke of Insight p 18
8. Daniel Goleman Emotional Intelligence p 59
9. NS 12.11.11 p 39
10. Antonio Damasio quoted in Emotional Intelligence p 28
11. Robert Solomon Spirituality for the Skeptic p 73
12. ibid pp 61/62
13. Daniel Goleman Emotional Intelligence p 29
14. William Woollard The Reluctant Buddhist p107

Chapter Seven
Changing the wiring diagram

1. Pascual-Leone's research is aimed at understanding the mechanisms that control brain plasticity across an individual's lifespan and how it may be modified to create the optimal behavioural outcomes. Wikipedia profile
2. NS 21.02.15 p 33
3. ibid p 33
4. NS 21.02.2015 p 31
5. ibid p 31
6. Nature Neuroscience vol 12 p 1379 NS 21,02. 15 p 32
7. ibid p 32
8. Daniel Goleman Emotional Intelligence p 43

9.   Interview James Flynn NS The Human Brain p 45
10. Science vol 250 p 225
11. Plomin Nature Nurture and the Transition to Early Adolescence p 203
12. Howard Gardner quoted in Emotional Intelligence p 37
13. Daniel Goleman Emotional Intelligence p 87
14. ibid p 88
15. Martin Seligman quoted in Emotional Intelligence p 88
16. Martin Seligman What You Can Change...And What You Can't p 5
17. ibid p 5

Chapter Eight
Effort and grit and the marshmallow test

1.   Walter Mischel 2015 The Marshmalow Test: Mastering Self Control
2.   Interview Walter Mischel NS 27.09.14 p 28
3.   ibid p 28
4.   Martin Seligman Flourish p 116
5.   ibid p 116
6.   Daniel Goleman Emotional Intelligence p 68
7.   Angela Duckworth NS 08.03.14 p 32
8.   PNAS vol 108 p 2693
9.   Martin Seligman Flourish p 118
10. NS 28.01.12 p 3
11. D. Jones. NS 12.03.16. pp 29-31
12. NS 08.03.14 p 34

Chapter Nine
Get me to the gym in time

1. John Ratey 2015 Harvard Medical School
2. NS 09.11.13 p 45 and NS 22.08.15 p 33
3. ibid p 45
4. Teal Burrell NS 22.08.15 p 34
5. Yuval Noah Harari Sapiens p 9
6. Neurotransmitters are chemicals in the brain that enable nerve impulses to be passed from one neuron to another. Very briefly, neurons in the brain form elaborate networks through which these nerve impulses or action potentials pass. Each neuron may have 15000 connections with neighbouring neurons. However these connections are not hard wired. The neurons do not actually touch one another. Between the end or the terminal of one neuron and the reception point on the next there is a minute gap. This is the synapse. When an action potential travelling along a neuron reaches this synapse it triggers the release of chemicals into the synaptic gap that travel across it and bind to specialised receptors on the other side, and thus pass on the signal. Thus neurotransmitters play an immense role in shaping our everyday life and behaviour and our life state at any particular time. There are many different kinds of neurotransmitter. The exact number is still unknown, but over 100 have been identified.
7. Prof. David Raichley NS 09.11.13 p 47
8. ibid p 47
9. Edward Archer NS 28.02.15 p 35
10. Prof. David Raichley NS 09.11.13. p 47
11. John Ratey NS 09.11.13 p 47
12. Arthur Kramer NS 09.11.13 p 47

Chapter Ten
The universal pursuit of happiness

1. Thomas Jefferson American Declaration of Independence
2. Gary Mills Inventing America
3. Robert Solomon Spirituality for the Skeptic p 6
4. Pascal Bruckner quoted in NS 16.04.11 p 51
5. Martin Seligman Flourish p 9
6. Sam Harris The Moral Landscape p 183
7. NS 25.09.10 p 46
8. Daniel Goleman Working with Emotional Intelligence p 12
9. Tal Ben Shahar Pursuit of the Perfect 2009
10. Mark Williams, John Teasdale, Zindal Segal, Jon Kabat-Zinn The Mindful Way Through Depression.
11. Dr. Steven Southwick, Prof. Of Psychiatry Yale School of Medicine. Feature Time 01.06.15. Resilience: The Science of Mastering Life's Greatest Challenges.
12. Martin Seligman Flourish p 20
13. Barbara Fredrickson quoted in NS 13.07. 12 p 49
14. Sonja Lyubomirski The How of Happiness p 15
15. ibid p 14
16. Barbara Fredrickson Review of General Psychology vol 2 p 300
17. Barbara Fredrickson Journal of Personality and Social Psychology vol 84 p 365

Chapter Eleven
The how and where of well-being

1. Richard Layard quoted in NS 15.04. 11 p 49
2. Sonja Lyubomirski The How of Happiness p 41
3. ibid p 41
4. Richard Layard Happinesss p 188

5.   Sonja Lyubomirski The How of Happiness p 66
6.   Eckhart Tolle A New Earth: Creation of a Better Life
7.   Teal Burrell. New Scientist. 28.01.17 pp30, 33
8.   Martin Seligman Flourish p 110/111
9.   Sonja Lyubomirski The How of Happiness p 125
10.   Sam Harris The Moral Landscape p 55
11.   Sonja Lyubomirski The How of Happiness p 26

Chapter Twelve
The oneness of mind and body

1.   Arnold Toynbee Choose Life p 27
2.   James Shreeve The Neandertal Enigma
3.   NS 08.06.12 p 35
4.   Robin Dunbar quoted in NS 24.05.14 p 35
5.   Robin Dunbar quoted in 08.06.13 p 35
6.   NS 27.08.11 p 33
7.   ibid p 33
8.   ibid p 33
9.   ibid p 33
10.   Steven Cole quoted in NS 24. 01.15 p 10
11.   NS 27.08.11 p 34

Chapter Thirteen
Getting a handle on anxiety

1.   Daniel Goleman Emotional Intelligence p xiii
2.   Martin Seligman What You Can Change…and What You Can't p 49
3.   ibid p 49/50
4.   Sally Winston quoted in Time Feature Article on Anxiety 05.12.11 p 40
5.   Cortisol is a steroid hormone produced by the adrenal gland which sits on top of the kidneys. There is normal

diurnal variation of cortisol in the bloodstream that reaches a peak around 8am and a low point between 12 midnight and 4am. However several circumstances can produce elevated levels of the hormone for prolonged periods, notably events that lead to anxiety and depression and above all stress. The effects of these prolonged elevated levels can include among other things, a reduction in the effectiveness of the immune system, reduced bone formation and muscle wastage. It has been shown that Cortisol levels can also be increased by activities such as excessive caffeine consumption and too little sleep. Levels can be reduced by for example music therapy, massage, meditation and laughter. Wikipedia.

6. Time Feature Article Anxiety 05.12.11 p 39.
7. ibid p 39
8. Martin Seligman Flourish p 66. The Journal of Applied Behavioural Science Aug 16th. 2015:0. Academy of Management Review July 1st 2015:40. 370-398
9. Wikipedia on John Gottman
10. Martin Seligman Flourish p 67
11. Daniel Goleman Emotional Intelligence p 11
12. Time Feature Article on Anxiety p 40
13. Diego Pizzagalli quoted in Time 05.12.11 p 40

Chapter Fourteen
A change of attitude

1. Nichiren Daishonin Writings of Nichiren Daishonin vol 1 p 302
2. Martin Seligman What You Can Change...and What You Can't p 115
3. ibid p 115
4. Sonja Lyubomirski The How of Happiness p 154

5.   ibid p 155
6.   ibid p 158
7.   ibid p 163
8.   Daniel Goleman Emotional Intelligence p 57
9.   Daisaku Ikeda Buddhism Day by Day p 249
10. Martin Seligman What You Can Change...and What You Can't p 115

Chapter Fifteen
The attention imperative

1.   NS 04.10.14 p 35
2.   Sam Harris The Moral Landscape p 103
3.   Adam Alter. 2016. Irresistable, why we can't stop checking, scrolling, clicking and watching.
4.   NS 16.08.14 p 26
5.   Daniel Goleman Emotional Intelligence p 227
6.   NS Caroline Williams The Human Brain p 119
7.   Web site American Psychological Association. Oct 2011. Vol 42 No 9. p 44
8.   Mark Williams, John Teasdale, Zindel Segal, Jon Kabat-Zinn 2007 The Mindful Way through Depression
9.   NS 04.10.14 p 38
10. Alun Anderson NS 30.07.16 p 44
11. Interview James Flynn NS The Human Brain p 46
12. ibid p 47
13. PNAS vol 108 p 3017 NS 04.10.14 p 38
14. Douwe Draaisma 2015 The Nostalgia Factory: Memory, Time and Ageing

Chapter Sixteen
I need at least 8 hours

1.   Robert Stickgold professor of psychiatry Harvard medical School. NS The Human Brain p 125

2. Matthew Walker, Prof. Of neuroscience and psychology, Sleep and Neuro-Imaging Lab. UCLA Berkeley. NS 28.05.16 p 32
3. Matthew Walker Time Feature. 27.02.17. p 56
4. Matthew Walker. NS 28.05.16 p 32
5. Mathew Walker NS 14.10.17. p 32
6. NS 15.03.08 p 31
7. Emma Young NS The Human Brain p 125
8. Robert Stickgold NS The Human Brain p 125
9. Matthew Walker NS The Human Brain p 126
10. ibid p 126
11. ibid p 126
12. Robert Stickgold NS The Human Brain p 128
13. NS 15.03.08 p 32
14. Time Feature 27. 10.14 p 36 and web site, Sleep and Circadian Neuroscience Institute, Oxford
15. Mary Carskadon quoted in Time 27 10.14 p 35
16. Sleep Research Institute SCNI web site and BBC web site Science, Human Body and Mind. The Science of Sleep
17. Alice Park. Time Feature. 27.02.17 p 56
18. Sigrid Veasey quoted in Time Feature. 27.10.14 p 37
19. Maiken Nedergaard, co-director of Center for Translational Neuromedicine quoted in Time Feature. 27.10.14 p 38
20. Time Feature. 27.10.14 p 36

Chapter Seventeen
It's the mouse that does the moving

1. Alpa Patel American Cancer Society Journal of Epidemiology vol 172 p 419
2. NS 29.06. 13 p 45
3. ibid p 45

4. ibid p 45
5. Audrey Bergouignan quoted in NS 29.06.13 p 47
6. Dr. Alpa Patel is a cancer epidemiologist. She was the principal investigator on one of the largest contemporary population studies in the USA, focusing on the role of physical inactivity, sedentary behaviour and obesity in relation to cancer and overall longevity.
7. Prof David Dunstan, head of the Physical Activity Laboratory at the Baker Heart and Diabetes Inst. Melbourne. Research focuses on the health consequences of physical inactivity of all kinds, TV watching, sitting in cars, desk and screen-bound work.
8. Prof. David Dunstan quoted in NS 29.06.13 p 45
9. Dr. Alpa Patel quoted in NS 29.06.13 p 47
10. Susan Greenfield Speech House of Lords Feb 2009
11. P. Mueller Princeton University quoted in NS 01.11,14 p 43

Chapter Eighteen
All you ever needed to know about the vagus nerve

1. NS 13.07.13 p 48
2. ibid p 48
3. ibid p 48
4. John Gottman. Quoted in Emotional Intelligence p 227
5. Barbara Fredrickson Biological Psychology vol 85 p 432
6. Barbara Fredrickson Psychological Science doi.org/ m3x NS 13.07.13 p 49

Chapter Nineteen
The secret history of altruism

1. NS 24.01.15 p 37
2. ibid p 37

3. John Hoffman quoted in Emotional Intelligence p 105
4. Robert Winston Human Instinct p 2/3
5. Charles Darwin. The Descent of Man quoted in NS 06.08.11 p iii
6. Yuval Harari Sapiens p 26
7. Robert Winston ibid p 164
8. David Sloan Wilson quoted in NS 06.08.11 p viii
9. Charles Darwin The Descent of Man quoted in NS 06.08.11 p ii
10. David Sloan Wilson quoted in NS 16.08.11 p viii
11. Sam Harris The Moral Landscape p 55
12. Paul Zak quoted in NS 10.11.12 p 44
13. Michael Tomasello quoted in NS 10.11.12. p 44
14. Michael Tomasello Max Planck Institute web site
15. Sonja Lyubomirski The How of Happiness p 126
16. ibid p 131
17. Robert Sampson quoted in NS 11.05.13 p 28

Chapter Twenty
The evolutionary roots of friendship

1. Lauren Brent quoted in NS 24.05.14 p 37
2. Barbara Fredrickson quoted in NS 13.07.13 p 49
3. Robin Dunbar quoted in NS 24.05.14 p 36
4. ibid p 36
5. Tom Wolfe. The Kingdom of Speech. Quoted in Time Mag feature 05.09.16. p 44
6. Lauren Brent quoted in NS 24.05.14 p 37
7. Nicholas Christakis and James Fowler quoted in NS 24.05.14 p 39
8. Danah Boyd quoted in NS 24.05.14 p 40. Dr Danah Boyd has been described as one of the most influential women in technology (Wikipedia). She is currently working at Harvard University, New York State

University and with Microsoft. Her research has focused on the use of large scale social networking such as Facebook and My Space by US teenagers.

9. Nicole Ellison quoted in NS 24.05.14 p 40

Chapter Twenty One
Just beneath the surface of everyday

1. Carlo Rovelli Seven Brief Lessons on Physics p4
2. Brian Greene The Fabric of the Cosmos p 5
3. ibid p 5
4. Martin Seligman What You Can Change…and What You Can't p 117
5. Daisaku Ikeda Faith Into Action p 36

Buddhism   p 19-23
- a daily lifetime training program
- aimed to shift our life towards positive end
- develop mental toughness & resilience
- change our attitude/response to challenges
- build an inner core of optimism, resilience and confidence
- Is not to remove anxieties, but they don't take over.
- develop an ability to see all things from a positive constructive point of view
- learn to turn "the grey" around & create value out of it
- As we change, we are changing the environment we inhabit

- Is essentially about empowering people.
- We need the conviction that we have the potential to achieve change towards a positive end
- Buddhism is a <u>method</u> for achieving a consistent sense of optimism in our daily lives, and the positive influences on our environment.
- It is a compassionate discipline of daily practice
- It is fundamentally about social change, about creating a society based essentially on respect for the dignity of all life.

Buddhism is strongly focused on the attainment of happiness as <u>the</u> fundamental objective of human life.
It has the essential belief in the power of the human spirit
It teaches achieving happiness for ourselves + others is essentially what life is about.
- We have to <u>learn</u> how to achieve it.
How to <u>create</u> it for ourselves.

CPSIA information can be obtained
at www.ICGtesting.com
Printed in the USA
BVHW030812091121
621172BV00003B/18

9 781786 230973

Ikigai
The Japanese Art of Living

Keira Miki

DIAMOND BOOKS

www.diamondbook.in

© Author

Publisher : **Diamond Pocket Books (P) Ltd.**
X-30, Okhla Industrial Area, Phase-II
New Delhi-110020
Phone : 011-40712200
E-mail : sales@dpb.in
Website : www.diamondbook.in
Edition : 2021

Ikigai (The Japanese Art of Living)
Author - *Keira Miki*
Translator - *Nidhi Verma*